KU-595-584

Finding and Using Health and Medical Information on the Internet

Sue Welsh, Betsy Anagnostelis and Alison Cooke

About the authors

Sue Welsh is a freelance webmaster who has contributed to the Resource Discovery Network (RDN) Web site and is now working on the RDN's Virtual Training Suite. She also works as a money advisor for the National Association of Citizens Advice Bureau. Sue has previously worked in several medical libraries and was a project worker for OMNI (Organising Medical Networked Information) for three years.

Betsy Anagnostelis is Librarian at the Royal Free Hospital Medical Library, Royal Free & University College Medical School of UCL. Betsy has delivered training in using the Internet for health and medical information since the mid-1990s, and has worked with OMNI in developing guidelines for resource evaluation. She is a member of the editorial board of the newsletter *He@lth Information on the Internet* and edits the Innovations Online series for the journal *Health Information and Libraries Journal*.

Alison Cooke is also based at the Royal Free Hospital Medical Library where she is currently Information Skills Trainer. Prior to joining the Royal Free, Alison worked as a researcher and has completed a PhD on information quality issues associated with health and medical information available via the Internet, the findings of which have been published by Library Association Publishing in, 'A guide to finding quality information on the Internet: selection and evaluation strategies'. Alison has also been involved in training in the use of the Internet and other electronic sources of information for a number of years, and is involved in the OMNI and BIOME projects, including working on the development of the resource evaluation guidelines. She contributes regularly to the newsletter *He@lth Information on the Internet* and writes the 'Internet news and reviews' section of the *British Journal of Clinical Governance*.

Contents

Chapter 4
Diseases, rare diseases and outbreaks 37

Chapter 5
Consumer health information 41

Chapter 6
Data to support biomedical research 48

Chapter 7
Finding out about research funding and research projects 58

Chapter 8
Finding a job 66

Chapter 9
Keeping up-to-date 72

Section 2 - Finding information on the Internet 78

Chapter 10
Search engines 82

Chapter 11
Metasearch engines 104

Chapter 12
Web directories 112

Chapter 13
Health and medical Web search engines 121

Introduction

An increasing number of healthcare professionals, health consumers and patients are turning to the Internet both to find information and to use it as a communication medium. The rapidity with which access to the Internet is flourishing is now well-documented[1] and commentators have described it as 'a wonderful new technology', which, 'if used properly ... can benefit people greatly'.[2]

The possibilities of the Internet have been outlined in a number of reports. Key benefits include its potential to relay information, to enable informed decision making, to enable more active participation in healthcare decisions with potentially better psychological outcomes, to promote healthful behaviours, to promote peer information exchange and emotional support, to improve consumers' skills for self-help, and to reduce the financial burden of care and managing demand for health services.[3, 4]

According to a 1998 survey by P\S\L Consulting Group,[1] the majority (80%) of physicians across all countries surveyed had access to or owned a computer. Almost half of all physicians had accessed the Internet irrespective of computer ownership. The top reasons for which respondents believed physicians would want to use the Internet were:

- to obtain general information / education (43%),
- to obtain medical information (27%),
- for email / communication (22%), and
- to access the medical literature / journals (22%).

Fifteen percent of all physicians (Internet users and non-users) across all surveyed countries had recommended to patients that they should use the Internet to find health information.

In a separate survey, Confirmed Internet User (CIU) physician respondents said they use the Internet:

- to access disease information (95%),
- to read medical journals (88%),
- to obtain drug information (86%), and
- to visit physician association sites (80%).

While a majority of CIU physicians (72%) reported that they received medical newsletters via email, a minority (28%) said that they subscribed to medical/healthcare discussion lists.

Away from the clinical environment, these technologies have long been exploited to the full by medical researchers and a 1998 UK survey estimated that over 24% of General Practitioners already had access to the Internet.[5]

Consumers and patients can also find valuable sources of information, including references to state of the art treatments and ongoing clinical trials,[6] as well as the electronic equivalents of patient support groups. Studies indicate that consumers may indeed prefer to use this medium:

> Internet users thought online information and support groups were more convenient to use, offered better emotional support, were more cost-effective, and provided better medical referrals than doctors. By a narrow margin, they also believe that the online groups are a better source of medical information than doctors.[7]

Access to the Internet is fast increasing among UK households, and health and medical practitioners are increasingly reporting instances of informed patients bringing information gleaned from the Internet with them to the consultation.[8] The Internet also provides a means by which health services and practices can promote information to their own patient base, from advertising opening hours and specialist services, to providing in-practice or remotely-accessible patient information targeted to the needs of a specific local community.[9] Indeed, increased access to health and medical information provided by the Internet has begun to influence the manner in which patients communicate with healthcare professionals.[1, 8]

The question soon will not be 'why should I acquire access to the Internet?' but rather 'how much longer can I afford not to have access to the Internet?'. An important challenge for the future for healthcare professionals will be, not only their own discriminating use of the Internet, but also the ability to help patients navigate through the maze of available information, and proactively to offer advice, support and information through the new communication medium.[9, 10] This book provides a starting point for those relatively new to the Internet in acquiring the skills of finding, evaluating and using health and medical information in a discriminating manner.

Overview of the book

The book has been divided into five sections as follows.

The 'Internet Quick Tour' takes the reader on a journey through the wide variety of information resources that are currently accessible through this medium. These are: tools for reference, material to support teaching and continuing medical education, resources to support evidence-based practice, consumer information, materials for keeping up-to-date, information for job seekers, biomedical research data, and information about research projects and sources of funding.

An essential aspect of effective Internet use is knowledge of the wide range of tools for finding information. The second section of this book, 'Searching for information', examines in detail the different types of search tools that are currently available and how they can be used to best effect. These tools include generic search engines, metasearch engines, subject directories, gateways to high quality resources, as well as a range of other tools focusing on health and medical information. Aspects of searching bibliographic databases available via the Internet and finding electronic journals are also discussed.

'Communication' looks at tools for communicating via the Internet, focusing on email, mailing lists and newsgroups, and considers some of the issues associated with their use for disseminating healthcare and medical information.

The ease with which information can be published via the Internet and its dissemination potential has engendered a number of concerns. These are discussed in detail in the 'Evaluation' section. Ways in which to seek and select high quality information resources are also suggested.

Lastly, 'Taking control' looks at using your Internet browser to best effect, and includes suggestions for organising your view of the Internet and creating your own Web pages.

This book aims to provide a starting point for those relatively new to using the Internet. Although little experience is assumed, it is hoped that even seasoned users may find a number of helpful hints. It is not meant to be used as a directory of resources – many other printed and online sources exist that attempt to achieve this. Rather, its emphasis is on offering advice in the development of skills in finding and using health and medical information.

The authors are keen to receive feedback from readers. An email address is provided for that purpose by the publishers at: pubs@aslib.com, subject: Health and Medical. Subsequent editions will aim to build on the current first edition in ways that our readers recommend.

Note on Internet addresses

In order to facilitate the reading of this book, Internet addresses have not been included in the main body of the text. Instead, they are grouped together in alphabetical order, at regular intervals, close to where they are first mentioned in the text. There is also an alphabetical listing of all sites that are mentioned, towards the end of the book. All sites were checked in February 2000.

References

1. P\S\L Global survey points to increasing use of Internet by physicians [press release], 1998. Available from: http://www.pslgroup.com/PSL_whatsnew.htm

2. US Food and Drug Administration. FDA and the Internet: advertising and promotion of medical products; 1996. Available from: http://www.fda.gov/opacom/morechoices/transcript1096/fdainet7.html

3. Jadad A R, Gagliardi A. Rating health information on the Internet. *JAMA* 1998; **279**(8):611-614.

4. Robinson T N, Patrick K, Eng T R, Gustafson D. An evidence-based approach to interactive health communication. *JAMA* 1998; **280**(14): 1264-1269.

5. Roscoe T. Two surveys of Internet use in primary care. *He@lth Information on the Internet* 1998;**3**:2-3. Available from: http://www.wellcome.ac.uk/healthinfo/pdfs/issue3.pdf

6. Federal Trade Commission. Remedies targeted in International Health Claim Surf Day: consumer protection, public health, private agencies from 25 countries assess over 1,200 Internet sites [news release], 1998. Available from: http://www.ftc.gov/opa/1998/9811/intlhlth.htm

7. Reuters Limited. Health experts repeat Web warning. 1998. Available from: http://www.news.com/News/Item/0,4,21606,00.html?st.ne.fd.mdh

8. Greenhalgh T. The Internet consultation. *He@lth Information on the Internet* 1998; **4**:2-3. Available from: http://www.wellcome.ac.uk/en/images/hioti4_pdf_694.pdf

9. Brown M S. Online communication gap between physicians and their cybersavvy patients. *Medicine on the Net* 1998; **4**(3):15-16.

10. McLellan F. Like hunger, like thirst: patients, journals and the Internet. *Lancet* 1998;**352**(S2):39-43. Available from: http://www.thelancet.com/newlancet/sub/supplements/vol352s2/article12.html

Section 1

Internet quick tour

This section provides a guided tour around the vast range of information sources that are currently accessible via the Internet. It is impossible to be comprehensive in this regard, but we have attempted to provide a taster of the variety of high quality and useful resources relevant to healthcare and medicine that are now available. We also provide some insight into what the Internet really has to offer – what it is good for, but also where it fares not so well and where a printed publication may be of greater benefit.

For those readers who are new to using the Internet, two types of information are referred to in this chapter. The first is information available via the World Wide Web (hereafter, the Web). The Web is essentially a vast collection of documents located on different networked computers around the world. These documents are connected together using (hypertext) links and are written in a language called Hypertext Mark-Up Language (HTML), which is discussed further in Chapter 22. HTML, aided by other tools such as the programming language Java, can be used to create not only text-based documents, but also multimedia and interactive resources. HTML is also used to define the links that connect different parts of the same resource, different resources within the same collection, or resources in entirely different locations.

In order to access the Web, a piece of software is required, often referred to as a browser, in addition to a connection to the Internet. The most commonly used browsers are Internet Explorer and Netscape Navigator (discussed in Chapters 20 and 21). Wherever a Web-based resource is referred to in the text, its address will be listed towards the end of the relevant section and will look something like this:

BMJ: www.bmj.com/

The above is the address for the *BMJ*. In order to access the site, open up your browser and in the address box (Internet Explorer) or location box (Netscape Navigator), simply type the address above, and press the enter key. Off you go! Once a Web page is displayed by your browser, you can follow links to other parts of the same resource or to another resource. You will recognise a link because either the text will be in a different colour and/or underlined, or when you move your mouse over some text or an image, a hand will appear, replacing the usual pointer. To follow a link, simply click once on it with your mouse.

The Internet is also used as a medium for communication. Communication between different Internet users interested in the same topic has resulted in the second type of information resource mentioned in this section – communication fora, such as mailing lists and newsgroups. These are described in general in Chapter 18. Mailing lists and newsgroups do not always publish material on the Web, but where this is available the Web page address is given.

Chapter 1

Desktop reference

If the Internet fulfilled all its promises it would never be necessary to leave your desk in search of information again. Whether this would be a positive change is a matter for debate, but one thing is certain: we are not there yet. Having a few decent reference books to hand and a good library to call upon is still often likely to produce higher quality results in less time. However, the Internet has expanded to become a major source of reference information. Internet users may now gain access to online reference works, such as dictionaries and encyclopaedias, access to geographical and travel information, such as maps and timetables, directory data, for example yellow pages, and users may even express their needs at online reference desks. This chapter will concentrate on these groups of resources, introducing some discrete, freely available, desktop reference materials that will help to answer specific factual queries.

Looking for words: dictionaries and thesauri

Dictionaries

Quickly checking the spelling of a word is not a task for which the Internet is an ideal tool. During the time taken to switch on, log in and find the relevant Web site, a paper dictionary could have been consulted several times. However, for more complex queries the retrieval features of an electronic dictionary are advantageous. As well as searching for an exact match, and words starting with a string (which could be accomplished with a paper dictionary), online dictionaries often have additional features, such as the ability to search for words ending with or containing a specified string. For example, the ALLwords service is an online dictionary provided by Arbour Media Inc. ALLwords does all of the above, will translate a word into several European languages and will even pronounce it for you.

Dictionaries of specialised terms are also available, although coverage may be patchy in some areas of medicine. Such dictionaries are best located via subject gateways (discussed in Chapter 14) which will list major services and differentiate between major works and the small, less useful collections that abound. One good example is the Online Medical Dictionary, which contains 65,000 terms and is extensively cross-referenced.

The Multilingual Glossary provides short definitions of medical terms in nine European languages. AltaVista, one of the tools used to search the Web (described in detail in Chapter 10) also provides a translation service that may be helpful.

Some types of specialised dictionaries are very common, for example, dictionaries of quotations such as the Quotations Archive. However, these are rarely as comprehensive as a high quality, commercially published resource.

The Internet excels in providing dictionaries that would not normally be widely available because of their obscurity. These are useful for one-off queries but can be time wasters! The Slang Dictionary is a good example of this, offering standard English interpretations of colloquialisms – for example, the definition of and origin of the word 'doobie' (Noun. A marijuana cigarette. 1960's. US).

ALLwords Dictionary: www.allwords.com/

AltaVista Translations: babelfish.altavista.com/

Multilingual Glossary: allserv.rug.ac.be/~rvdstich/eugloss/welcome.html

Online Medical Dictionary: www.graylab.ac.uk/omd/

Slang Dictionary: www.peevish.u-net.com/slang/

Quotations Archive: www.aphids.com/quotes/index.shtml

Thesauri

Thesauri are a little rarer than dictionaries. However, there is a full version of Roget's thesaurus online. Unfortunately it is the 1911 edition and suffers from not being up-to-date, especially with modern scientific terms. The Merriam Webster thesaurus is more up-to-date but uses American English.

It is useful to consult the US National Library of Medicine Medical Subject Headings (MeSH) online for medical terminology. The MeSH browser allows users to search for phrases, words or fragments in the MeSH vocabulary. Even more useful, but restricted to those with a license agreement, is the Unified Medical Language System (UMLS) which contains terms from 40 biomedical vocabularies (including MeSH) and provides links to different names for the same concepts. There are some implementations of UMLS available to non-licensees but these do not necessarily offer access to the full system. For example, CliniWeb International and the

Organising Medical Networked Information (OMNI) Thesaurus use UMLS to map keywords to MeSH terms.

CliniWeb International Search: www.ohsu.edu/cliniweb/search.html

Merriam Webster WWWebster Thesaurus: www.m-w.com/thesaurus.htm

NLM MeSH browser: www.nlm.nih.gov/mesh/99Mbrowser.html

OMNI Thesaurus: omni.ac.uk/search/thesaurus/

Roget's Thesaurus 1911 edition: www.thesaurus.com/

UMLS Knowledge Source Server: umlsks.nlm.nih.gov/

Looking for figures: statistical reference

Sources of statistical information abound on the Internet. International, regional and national sources are increasingly becoming available via the Web. Databases of health and medical statistics, in particular, are plentiful – see for example MedWebPlus, which brings together a wide range of statistical sources under the headings of Statistics and Vital statistics.

The WHO Statistical Information System provides a comprehensive collection of links through to numerous sources of statistical information. These include: basic Health Indicators from the World Health Report, country-reported data, Burden of Disease statistical tables, health personnel data (such as WHO estimates of numbers of doctors, dentists and nurses worldwide), international classifications, nomenclatures and terminology sources, HIV/AIDS and immunisation statistics, UN population data and links to several national health-related sites. The World Bank offers Development Data which includes several collections of health and population statistics such as access to health services, health expenditure, services and use.

In the US, the Centers for Disease Control and Prevention (CDC) provides links to several sources of scientific and laboratory data, as well as surveillance statistics for specific diseases such as tuberculosis. The CDC also operates the National Center for Health Statistics, which publishes tabulated state data and information on vital events (births, marriages, divorces and deaths), as well as data on health status and lifestyle, onset and diagnosis of illness and disability, and the use of healthcare. Also available from the CDC are the MMWR Disease Trends: State and Local

Health Statistics, which include searchable morbidity and mortality tables.

In the UK, the Government Statistical Service (GSS) makes available official statistics on the Web via the Source of UK facts and figures. This includes StatBase, which provides access to a comprehensive set of key statistics relating to the UK. StatSearch allows a search to be focused gradually through subjects and topics. Associated Web links are provided within the search results so that free publications may be downloaded directly from source. For example, a search for *back pain* produced an up-to-date Department of Health Statistical Bulletin, which was available electronically for free. The UK Office for National Statistics also maintains a set of Web pages.

Eurostat offers a similar facility for Europe and the information contained in the CIA World Factbook is a popular source of general statistical data on specific countries, including details of people, geography and government.

The National Library of Medicine in the US provides a guide to searching databases for health and medical statistics.[1]

Centers for Disease Control and Prevention (CDC) Data and Statistics: www.cdc.gov/scientific.htm

Centers for Disease Control and Prevention (CDC) MMWR Disease Trends: State and Local Health Statistics: www2.cdc.gov/mmwr/distrnds.html

Centers for Disease Control and Prevention (CDC) National Center for Health Statistics: www.cdc.gov/nchs/

CIA World Factbook: www.odci.gov/cia/publications/factbook/index.html

Eurostat: europa.eu.int/en/comm/eurostat/serven/home.htm

Government Statistical Service: www.statistics.gov.uk/

MedWebPlus Statistics: www.medwebplus.com/subject/Statistics.html

MedWebPlus Vital statistics: www.medwebplus.com/subject/Vital_Statistics.html

Office for National Statistics: www.ons.gov.uk/

StatBase: www.statistics.gov.uk/statbase/mainmenu.asp

StatSearch: www.statistics.gov.uk/statbase/ss.asp

WHO Statistical Information System: www.who.int/whosis/

World Bank Development Data: www.worldbank.org/data/

Looking for facts: directories and encyclopaedias

Business directories

Providers of business directories are prolific on the Internet and many of the most familiar sources have simply been transferred directly to this medium. The gains in functionality made by offering factual reference sources online, referred to above, are equally true for directories. However, there are also additional advantages where the directory is very large. For example, consider checking the Yellow Pages for a company that might be anywhere in the UK. Using the print version it would be necessary to check many volumes, but using the Electronic Yellow Pages only one search is necessary. The user does not lose the ability to identify local businesses – options to restrict a search by region are enhanced in the online version.

Some services now offered on the Internet are more familiar as resources offered previously in other electronic formats. The Kompass directory of businesses and products worldwide is produced by a company that has developed electronic as well as print directory information for many years, and is now simply offering these products in a different guise via a new medium.

Electronic Yellow Pages: www.eyp.co.uk/

Kompass: www.kompass.com/

Specialised directories

As well as large databases, there are numerous specialised directories. These include directories published by trade organisations or similar bodies (e.g. Private Health UK, a listing of private hospitals throughout the country), or made available by professional societies (e.g. Feet for Life, a directory of state-registered chiropodists published online by the Society of Chiropodists and Podiatrists).

Once again, familiar sources exist. For example, the National Health Service (NHS) Yearbook, a key source of directory information relating to the NHS, is available online to subscribers. Unfortunately, currently there is no comprehensive directory of NHS organisations and services available to the general public for free.

Local health and social welfare organisations, such as self-help and support groups for patients are difficult to find on the Internet, but many public libraries collecting this data as part of their community information remit are now disseminating the information online. The WELDIS service contains information about services in Westminster for older people, people with disabilities and their carers. Age Concern Croydon provides a similar service with their online directory of services in the London Borough of Croydon. Project CIRCE (Community Information Research resourCE) is investigating these types of services, and how community networks can co-operate to create a distributed network of local information of this kind.

Age Concern Croydon: www.croydon.gov.uk/ageconcern/

CIRCE: www.gloscc.gov.uk/circe/index.htm

Feet for Life: www.feetforlife.org/findchir.htm

Private Health UK: www.privatehealth.co.uk/

WELDIS: www.westminster.gov.uk/weldis/

Encyclopaedias

Online encyclopaedias range from the general to the very specific. For example, Paediapaedia is a collection of information, images and references on paediatric diseases. This is part of the huge Virtual Hospital resource based at the University of Iowa College of Medicine, which describes itself as a 'digital health sciences library' designed 'to help meet the information needs of healthcare providers and patients'. At the other end of the spectrum, Encyclopaedia Britannica offers a free online version of the famous general encyclopaedia.

Encyclopaedia Britannica: www.britannica.com/

Paediapaedia: www.vh.org/Providers/TeachingFiles/PAP/PAPHome.html

Virtual Hospital: www.vh.org/

Looking for help: reference services

The Internet is often described as a reference library online. Although many reference librarians would question this, there are some services that do act in much the same way. Two of these are Ask a Librarian and the Internet Public Library (IPL), both of which are well-known and highly recommended for general reference questions.

The Ask a Librarian reference service is provided by the Consortium for Public Library Networking (EARL), an organisation that exists to promote networking in public libraries. Internet users can send in requests for information on any topic and their question is fielded to one of over thirty participating public libraries around the country. Answers are sent by email and should be received in less than two working days. EARL claims that the service is used by everyone from children to university professors and you can see a sample of the sorts of questions that get asked on the Bouncing Answers page (where answers that are rejected by the email address given by the requester are posted).

A similar service is provided by IPL, which is staffed by individual volunteers throughout the US. IPL began as a project at the School of Information and Library Studies at the University of Michigan but is now an established service with salaried staff.

Ask a Librarian: www.earl.org.uk/ask/index.html

Internet Public Library: www.ipl.org/ref/QUE/

Looking for where to go: travel information

For those not lucky enough to have a travel agent on their doorstep, the Internet provides plenty of information about both UK and worldwide destinations. Times of departure, maps of destinations and ticketing may now be checked from your desktop.

The UK Public Transport Information (PTI) site provides an overall description of public transport in the UK, including rail, coach, air and ferry travel. Its comprehensive approach is useful for checking all of the options in an increasingly fragmented public transport system and there are many references to company Web sites and telephone hotlines where information is not available on the Web. The Railtrack Web site is a good example of what can be achieved and is an indispensable tool for regular rail travellers needing to verify departure and arrival times. As well as accessing data by type of transport, the PTI site also allows the user to zoom in on a geographical region within the UK and view all of the transport options for that region.

Information about UK locations is also available on a regional basis in the form of county or borough Web sites, with some regions, notably (and unsurprisingly) London, attracting coverage from commercial enterprises. Regional Web sites vary greatly in content and usefulness, sometimes being no more than a means of conveying a corporate image to the outside world. However, they may be the only source of street maps for towns outside London.

National services can be more useful, especially for road maps. The Multimap service covers the whole of the UK and provides maps at scales from 1:50,000 to 1:4,000,000 which are ideal for route planning, and have recently added street maps. Streetmap provides a similar service but at the time of writing was confined to London.

Worldwide, aeroplane companies and airports alike now provide extensive information for travellers. For example, the Heathrow Web site is exemplary in terms of the valuable information it provides about UK airports, including regularly updated flight arrival times.

Heathrow: www.heathrow.co.uk/BAAHome.htm

Multimap: www.multimap.com/

Railtrack: www.railtrack.co.uk/

Streetmap: www.streetmap.co.uk/

UK Public Transport Information: www.pti.org.uk/

Reference

1. Newman ML. Health statistics sources: searching bibliographic databases for health and medical statistics. 3rd ed. 1996. Available from http://www.nlm.nih.gov/nichsr/stats/database.html

Chapter 2

Teaching materials and continuing medical education

The use of the Internet as an academic and research network rapidly escalated following the introduction and widespread availability of the first multimedia browser for accessing the Web. With an increasing emphasis on student-centred learning, this growth is hardly surprising - the Internet offers an ideal mechanism to support learning through the provision of additional reading materials and multimedia interactive resources.

This chapter provides an overview of the types and variety of materials that are currently accessible to support both student learning and continuing medical education, with indicators of how they can be used, what their potential benefits are, and some of the pitfalls.

Medical education on the Internet

The widespread availability of the Internet means that one of its simplest uses for medical education is the dissemination of lecture notes. This can be beneficial to lecturers and students alike, allowing reading of materials prior to teaching sessions and providing a repository of materials for those who are unable to attend a session or have mislaid their notes. Potentially, these materials are accessible 24 hours a day and 7 days a week, easing the workload of lecturers and support staff, as well as being useful to health and medical students with a busy and sometimes erratic schedule.

Although the dissemination of such materials is often restricted to those within an organisation, there are some valuable materials that are more widely accessible. An example is a collection of virology lecture notes available from Leicester University. These are intended to accompany the courses running at the University's Departments of Microbiology and Immunology. A wide range of topics is covered, for example, viral immunopathogenesis, pathogenesis of AIDS, plant virology, emerging viruses, virus structure and virus replication.

Web-based delivery allows information to be presented in a range of formats and supports links to other materials. Therefore, in addition to the provision of lecture notes, the Internet is also being used to supplement lectures. The Leicester University virology lecture notes mentioned above include not only the text of teaching sessions, but also images. There is a link from each lecture to a searchable list of recommended reading materials and a link to a free Internet version of Medline. Likewise, although the lecture notes at LectureLinks at the Johns Hopkins University are only accessible from computers within the University, the site includes extensive links to external resources within the different subject areas for first and second year students, as well as other students.

A more recent development is the use of the Internet to deliver whole programmes. Greenhalgh[1] describes the development of a distance learning MSc in Primary Care to be delivered, monitored and assessed entirely via the Internet, with the exception of a preliminary one-week introductory session held at University College London. Pilot modules were underway from September 1999 with a view to the full programme commencing in September 2000. Greenhalgh asserts that the course was developed in response to recognition of the accessibility, flexibility and effectiveness of distance learning. It was also influenced by the practical constraints faced by students in attending lectures and other taught courses, and a 'high interest in Web-based courses'.

LectureLinks: omie.med.jhmi.edu/LectureLinks/

Leicester University virology lecture notes:
www-micro.msb.le.ac.uk/335/335Notes.html

Textbooks online

Several textbooks are now available online, either as a replica of a paper-based original or with supplementary features. Indeed, a glance at the medstudent.net site indicates how many textbooks are now available. Under anatomy alone, eight resources were listed at the time of writing. Textbooks are also listed for a wide range of other subjects including biochemistry, history of medicine, microbiology, obstetrics and gynaecology, pathology, paediatrics, psychiatry and surgery.

One example is the Merck Manual of Diagnosis and Therapy. A full text version of the seventeenth edition, published in April 1999, is available via the Internet free of charge, covering diseases, disorders and drug-related information. The text is divided into 23 sections, including nutritional disorders, immunology and allergic disorders, infectious diseases and psychiatric disorders. Each chapter is easily browsed for relevant information with links to tables or graphics. A significant advantage of accessing this information in an electronic format is not only the provision of links to related sections of text elsewhere in the book, but also the ability to search the full text of the Manual.

The Virtual Hospital (mentioned in the previous chapter) also contains an impressive volume of resources, including an extensive listing of textbooks for a range of different specialties and disciplines. In total, there were 41 textbooks listed at the time of writing. Not all of these are available in full text, and not all exploit fully the capabilities of the Internet. However, this is another useful guide to currently available textbooks.

It is also possible to purchase textbooks online – Amazon.com and Books OnLine (BOL) are possibly the best known online bookstores. Other booksellers may offer online purchasing. Traditional booksellers may also offer online purchasing. For example, at the Blackwell's Online Bookshop, users can buy books during a single transaction or register their details to speed up future purchases, and can buy using an account card.

Amazon.com: www.amazon.co.uk/ or www.amazon.com/

Blackwell's Online Bookshop: bookshop.blackwell.co.uk/

Books OnLine: www.bol.com/

medstudent.net: medstudent.net/

Merck Manual of Diagnosis and Therapy: www.merck.com/pubs/mmanual/

Virtual Hospital textbooks: www.vh.org/Providers/Textbooks/MultimediaTextbooks.html

---

Interactive learning

The ability to access interactive learning materials is one of the major benefits of the Internet for educators. There are now a number of freely accessible, high quality resources suitable for supporting medical education. The following is just a taster of two such examples.

The Interactive Patient, from the Marshall University School of Medicine in the US, is an interactive Web site that allows a user to simulate a patient encounter. The learning objectives are that, on completion, the user will be able to:

- assess relevant clinical features of abdominal pain with pertinent differential diagnosis and will have improved his/her diagnostic skills, with emphasis on history taking in patients with abdominal pain; and

- formulate criteria to determine a sound diagnostic approach and design a treatment plan in patients with the specific illness demonstrated.

The user chooses to view the patient's history, to conduct a physical examination, to view the relevant laboratory data and x-rays, or to submit their diagnosis. Selecting 'history' presents a brief history of the patient with space for the user to submit questions to them. For example, typing: *How long have you had the pain?*, results in the answer: *The pain started this morning at about 9am when I got to the office. It hasn't stopped since.* The user has three options for physical examination – to look at various areas of the patient, to examine areas of the patient, or to listen to their heart and lungs. This is achieved through clicking on a succession of images displaying different areas of the patient's body until further information is provided by the system – e.g. clicking on an image of the patient's back results in the statement: *The right costo vertebral angle is very sensitive to touch. Mild palpation causes the patient to flinch.* The user can then select various laboratory reports, including complete blood count and urine analysis, as well as x-ray images of the chest and abdomen. Following collation of all the relevant information, the user then selects their diagnosis and treatment plan from the list of available options and can make a comment or suggestion. This is submitted for analysis and users are notified by email of their results.

Trauma Moulage is a site providing 'moulages' or practice scenarios where the user has to assess and manage different patients. There are currently four scenarios available:

- initial assessment: in this moulage, the user is an emergency room doctor and must assess and adequately treat an injured patient;
- pre-hospital care: this is a pre-hospital scenario where the user must react to patients at the scene of a motorway accident;
- cervical spine clearance: the user is transferred to the spinal service where they assess and evaluate six patients with potential cervical spine injuries; and
- paediatric moulage: the user must manage a child injured in a vehicle accident.

There are also trauma leader decision scenarios, where the user is the leader of a trauma unit required to make decisions about patient care.

This site works differently to the Interactive Patient in that a description of the situation is provided at the top of the screen. The user must read the descriptions and make a selection of what action they wish to take next based upon the available information. As the user works through the system, an evaluation of their decisions is provided.

Simply accessing sites such as these indicates the value and usefulness of the Internet in supporting teaching and learning. Students can learn independently and work at their own pace, and they are provided with feedback. In addition, the multimedia nature of these materials means that they are both interesting to use and stimulating for students.

Interactive Patient: medicus.marshall.edu / medicus.htm

Trauma Moulage: www.trauma.org / resus / moulage / moulage.html

---

Other information for students and educators

The Internet can be an invaluable resource for prospective students in terms of assessing where to study and what courses are available. The Internet has been used for many years as an advertising vehicle in this respect and the information that is now available ranges from basic contact information, through email directories of staff and students to full details of the curriculum and access to the library catalogue. One example is the University of Wales College of Medicine, Cardiff. Like many other university sites, this site includes information about the college, its different departments, the courses that are available, areas of research, and information from the library.

An enormous number of journals are now available via the Internet, either in full or in part, for free or to subscribers only. These are discussed in detail in Chapter 16. However, it is worth mentioning here that both the *Student BMJ* and the *Medical Student JAMA* are available online. The *Student BMJ* is a monthly international journal for students with an interest in medicine. It contains both commissioned articles of interest to medical students as well as selected papers from the *BMJ*. The journal is compiled by a student who has taken a year out from their studies, in consultation with other students. The journal incorporates various sections covering not only scientific research but also educational issues and matters relating to the 'life' of a student (for example, where to go on an elective and avoiding debt). There is also a news section, letters, 'net.philes', and reviews. Similar resources are available from the *Medical Student JAMA*.

MED-STUDENT is an open mailing list 'set-up in order to provide a forum for medical students currently studying in the UK' although 'medical students worldwide are welcomed'. Topics are restricted to those with a medical slant. Unfortunately it is not possible to browse the archives of the list prior to subscribing, but clear guidelines about subscribing are available from the list's Web site.

There is also a mailing list, admin-medical, designed for all administrators involved in medical education and research, particularly those with a responsibility for medical or healthcare schools. It is designed to facilitate the exchange of news, information and advice between users. Similarly, medical-education is a list for those involved in teaching medicine. Browsing the archives of both lists indicates that there are few postings and that most messages are focused on conferences and meetings of interest to the audiences concerned.

---

admin-medical: www.mailbase.ac.uk/lists/admin-medical/

medical-education: www.mailbase.ac.uk/lists/medical-education/

Medical Student *JAMA*: www.ama-assn.org/sci-pubs/msjama/

MED-STUDENT: www.csosl.co.uk/sbmj/ml.html

Student *BMJ*: www.studentbmj.com/

University of Wales College of Medicine, Cardiff home page: www.uwcm.ac.uk/

Continuing Medical Education (CME) on the Internet

It is now widely recognised that in the fast-moving world of healthcare and medicine it is essential that practitioners keep up-to-date. In the UK, a framework of Continuing Medical Education (CME) supports a continuous process of updating knowledge and skills, through attending conferences, courses and other educational meetings. The scheme for physicians, for example, is jointly organised by the three UK Royal Colleges of Physicians of Edinburgh, Glasgow and London. The current requirement in the UK is to spend 50 hours per year on professional development. Within the 50 hours, roughly half of the time should be spent in the doctor's own organisation at teaching events, audit and interdisciplinary meetings, and the other half at events outside the hospital, such as conferences and study days.

Educational meetings must be approved beforehand to enable doctors to claim CME credits for attending them. A common system of CME approval has been developed in the UK for that purpose and those meetings and events approved for CME are listed in the Database of CME Events compiled by the Royal College of Physicians. There were over 3,500 events included in the database in December 1999, with over 90% of the events in medicine and over 25% of those in multi-specialties. The database contains the titles of events, the disciplines and the specialties covered. The site also provides information on how to seek CME approval for meetings and other events, and there is a sample attendance certificate and a sample evaluation questionnaire.

There is a wide range of other material available via the Internet that supports continuing medical education. In the US, it is now possible to earn CME credits through participating in courses and taking exams via the Internet. Medical Matrix lists 38 online CME courses. Many of these are free, while others require a submission fee for the appropriate CME credits. Users of the Interactive Patient (discussed earlier) can apply for CME credit for the American Medical Association Physician's Recognition Award. As both use of the Internet and CME continue to develop, this is a trend that is likely to spread internationally.

Database of CME Events: omni.ac.uk/cme/

Medical Matrix: www.medmatrix.org/

Information from the Royal Colleges

Not all of the Royal Colleges currently have a Web site, but those that do provide an invaluable source of information, particularly with regard to membership and fellowship. For example, the Royal College of Anaesthetists includes details about the college, its newsletter, information on training, including the relevant registration forms, details of courses and meetings and the associated CME credits, and guidelines relating to professional standards. With regard to the examinations, the regulations, dates, syllabus and application forms are all available online.

The Royal College of Pathologists uniquely includes past papers on its Web site. Papers are available for chemical pathology, haematology, histopathology and medical microbiology, and they include comments and advice on answering the questions. In the absence of formal collections of examination papers on the other Royal College Web sites, more informal approaches have been developed. For example, the 'MRCP p@rt 1 question bank' is a searchable databank of about 1200 multiple choice questions (MCQs) of the type found in the Membership of the Royal College of Physicians (MRCP) part one multiple choice exam in the UK, with answers. This MCQ question bank has been growing since 1992 and first appeared on the Web in 1996. The MCQs are collated from those who have taken the exam and are made available via the Web by three medical professionals, based in Wales, with an interest in how the Internet can be used for learning, particularly in hospitals which are at a distance from the local teaching hospital. Information is also available about the Royal Colleges and the MRCP exam, as well as information for those taking the exam abroad and places for study.

MRCP p@rt 1 question bank: mrcppart1.co.uk/

Royal College of Anaesthetists: www.rcoa.ac.uk/

Royal College of Pathologists: www.rcpath.org/contents.html

Accessing evaluated resources

This chapter has given only an indication of the volume and variety of resources that are available to support teaching and learning within healthcare and medicine. However, as with any type of material available via the Internet, there are serious discrepancies in terms of quality. This is particularly worrying in relation to educational resources where students may be misled by 'glamorous' sites with potentially inaccurate or out-of-date information.

CTI-Biology is one of 24 centres aiming to promote the effective use of technology in supporting teaching and learning within higher education in the UK, by reviewing resources and disseminating information about them. The initiative is supported by the Higher Education Funding Councils. Specially designed criteria and guidelines are used to review software that may be valuable in teaching and learning, and information about the software is provided in resource guides. From April 2000 CTI-Biology, and the other subject-based CTI centres, became part of the Learning and Technology Support Network.

As discussed in Chapter 14, there are a number of different tools for finding information available via the Internet, including those that pre-select high quality material using predetermined criteria. One such tool is OMNI, a gateway to high quality Internet resources within medicine, biomedicine, allied health, health management and related topics. The service is funded primarily through higher education resources, and therefore, although its coverage is much wider, it includes a large number of resources of interest to students and teaching staff within UK higher education.

CTI-Biology: www.liv.ac.uk/ctibiol.html

Learning and Technology Support Network: www.ilt.ac.uk/ltsn/index.htm

OMNI: omni.ac.uk/

Some pitfalls

Commentators in this area have highlighted various risks associated with using the Internet in medical education. For example, Pallen[2] suggests that for the 'weak-willed or poorly motivated student, the Internet may present another distraction from their studies' or students 'may become addicted'. Furthermore, he suggests 'the unscrupulous might exploit the online opportunities for cheating in essays and projects'.

The possibility of becoming distracted by the Internet is a reality. Similarly, copying sections of text from the Internet must be a real threat. Previously educators were able to identify plagiarism more easily because there were a limited number of textbooks within an area that were accessible to groups of students. With an ever-increasing volume of information, it is almost impossible for educators to assess whether an assignment is written by a student or copied in part or whole from elsewhere. In the US, it is now possible for students to access directly sites such as schoolsucks.com or cheater.com that are designed to enable students to plagiarise by copying and pasting chunks of text into their own work. However, in a recent Chronicle of Higher Education article, Carnevale[3] highlights sites that are designed to assist educators in identifying cheating. For example, plagiarism.org runs any paper against a database of 'answers'. The service then outputs an 'originality report' which identifies copied text.

It is possible to identify disadvantages with any medium for delivering education materials. However, the few resources highlighted within this chapter indicate the benefits of this medium to both lecturers and students alike.

cheater.com: www.cheater.com/
plagiarism.org: www.plagiarism.org/
schoolsucks.com: www.schoolsucks.com/

Looking for images

Although image quality is sometimes suboptimal, and no single source exists that brings collections together comprehensively, there is a proliferation of sources available via the Internet that provide access to images.

Collections of health and medical images

The Dermatology Online Atlas (DOIA) from the Friedrich Alexander University, Erlangen, Nuremberg brings together images that apply to an individual specialty. It allows retrieval by known diagnosis or by morphological specification, which can be given by localisation, lesion, age of patient, gender and skin colour. Over 3,000 high quality images of more than 600 dermatological diagnoses and differential diagnoses are available via DOIA. Morphological features of the images have been described by dermatologists and an indication is given of the quality of individual images for teaching. Direct links are given to possible differential diagnoses and to related images. Links are provided to several external sources, which include disease-related information in databases such as Medline and Online Mendelian Inheritance in Man (OMIM), as well as links to relevant Web sites. More than 500 Internet links are described and evaluated.

A search for *Rothmund* in DOIA retrieved thumbnails of several relevant images. On selecting a thumbnail, a larger version of the selected image was displayed and it was possible to select the relevant external links. These allow the user to search the published research literature (a search for the synonym *Poikiloderma Congenitale* was submitted to PubMed, limited to major MeSH headings) and learn more about the genetic background of the Rothmund-Thomson syndrome via OMIM. A search for *hemangioma* also produced a link through to PubMed, as well as a link to a relevant patient information Web page: AAD Patient Information Pamphlets: Vascular Birthmarks, from the American Academy of Dermatology.

Bristol Biomed (the Bristol Biomedical Image Archive) was first created in the form of a videodisc in the early 1990s, from teaching slides donated by medical, dental and veterinary teaching staff from several universities worldwide. Around 15,000 slides have since been made available on the Web. Thumbnail sized versions of the images and larger versions of selected images can be browsed for free. Brief annotations are given to accompany the images. Copyright in the individual images resides with the donors.

Martindale's Health Science Guide – 2000: the Virtual Medical Centre provides links to numerous teaching resources, including image banks and atlases. Among those provided for dermatology, DOIA featured again, as well as a Dermatology Image Bank from the University of Utah. Multimedia courses including text and images included one on the Language of dermatology: fundamentals of morphologic description.

Images from the History of Medicine is the catalogue of the prints and photographs collection of the National Library of Medicine (NLM). Its purpose is to assist users in finding illustrative material for private study, scholarship, and research. The NLM note that it is the responsibility of those using the catalogue to ensure that their use of the material is in compliance with copyright law.

Vesalius Clinical Folios and Image Archive includes images, illustrations, photographs, animations, and multimedia resources, all of which are freely available for downloading, non-commercial use, and non-commercial redistribution. The Clinical Folios are a collection of short educational narratives on surgical anatomy and procedures designed for online reference and study. Content in the Vesalius Clinical Folios is presented under the headings: anatomy, procedures and transparencies. Anatomy modules explain the anatomy relevant to one or more surgical procedures. Procedures describe the key steps in a surgical procedure. Transparencies present a layered or rotational view of surgical anatomy in the form of active programs or movies (using Macromedia's ShockWave or Apple's QuickTime). The Image Archive includes anatomical and surgical illustrations, photographs and radiological images that form a free source of images for education and reference.

Searching for images generally

Generic search engines and directories are discussed in detail in later chapters. However, it is worth mentioning here that AltaVista and Lycos, both generic search engines, provide support for image-related information retrieval. Words in the 'ALT' text (text describing the image which may be included in the Web page containing the image), file names and words on the page are indexed and subsequently returned as a result of a search. AltaVista results contain thumbnail pictures of images it has found, making it easy to select relevant matches, whereas Lycos displays only text descriptions. AltaVista also offers a facility to conduct image searches independently of text association. For example, selecting to view images that are visually similar to an image of a teaching stethoscope returned many more images of stethoscopes but also numerous unrelated images as well. Using AltaVista, it is possible to retrieve more images by selecting additional options, as available, including types of image (black and white images are not included by default), shape choices (small buttons, wide banners and very tall thin pictures are excluded by default) or image sampling (more than one picture may be shown from each matching page).

Many of the pictures retrieved via AltaVista originate from Corbis, a company that maintains one of the world's largest collections of digital images – four out of five images retrieved as a result of a search for *Joseph Lister* originated from Corbis. A search for *Lister antiseptic* retrieved an image of 'Women with Sprayguns of Antiseptic for Crowd Hygiene at Wimbledon, 1951. Wimbledon, London, England, UK, June 1951', once again from Corbis.

However, because most material is not held or maintained centrally, there is no overall quality control. The thumbnails often do not expand to an image of adequate size or resolution and the image material is often not accompanied by detailed descriptive information. This may reduce its utility for wider use and application.

AltaVista Photo & Image Finder: image.altavista.com/

Bristol Biomed (the Bristol Biomedical Image Archive): www.brisbio.ac.uk/

Corbis: www.corbis.com/

Dermatology Online Atlas (DOIA): dermis.net/bilddb/index_e.htm

Images from the History of Medicine: wwwihm.nlm.nih.gov/

Lycos Pictures & Sound: www.lycos.co.uk/search/options.html#cat

Martindale's Health Science Guide - 2000: the Virtual Medical Centre: www-sci.lib.uci.edu/HSG/Medical.html

OMIM: www.ncbi.nlm.nih.gov/omim/

Vesalius Clinical Folios and Image Archive: www.vesalius.com/

References

1.   Greenhalgh T. Delivering an MSc in Primary Care via the Internet. *He@lth Information on the Internet* 1999 Feb; (7):10-11. Available from: http://www.wellcome.ac.uk/en/images/hioti7_pdf_2254.pdf

2.   Pallen M. Medical education on the Internet. *He@lth Information on the Internet* 1998 Aug; (4):8-9. Available from: http://www.wellcome.ac.uk/en/images/hioti4_pdf_694.pdf or http://www.wellcome.ac.uk/en/1/homlibinfacthiiarc4med.html

3.   Carnevale D. Web services help professors detect plagiarism. *The Chronicle of Higher Education* 12 November 1999: A47. Available from: http://www.chronicle.com/free/v46/i12/12a04901.htm

Chapter 3

Using the Internet to support evidence-based healthcare

The paradigm shift towards evidence-based healthcare has resulted in a proliferation of paper-based materials on the subject and it is no surprise that the Internet reflects this. The Internet provides access to resources concerned with explaining the concepts of evidence-based healthcare, as well as tools to critically appraise materials and sources of evidence. In addition, local guidelines and information on producing local guidelines are becoming widely available. This chapter provides an overview of the types of Internet-based materials that will assist readers in finding and using some of the best available sources of evidence to support healthcare decision making.

Organisations

There are now numerous organisations involved in developing evidence-based healthcare and a variety of materials are accessible via their Web pages.

The NHS Research and Development Centre for Evidence-Based Medicine was established in Oxford, UK, as the first of several centres whose aim is broadly to promote evidence-based practice and to provide support and resources. The Centre's Web site provides a calendar of evidence-based health and other related events – conferences and meetings are listed by date with the title, venue and contact information. Other resources include teaching materials, a toolbox (discussed below), CATBank (a creation, storage and retrieval facility for Critically Appraised Topics), as well as links to other relevant sites. There are also links to other centres for evidence-based practice, such as the Centre for Evidence-Based Child Health and the Centre for Evidence Based Mental Health.

The NHS Centre for Reviews and Dissemination (CRD) is commissioned by the NHS Research and Development Division to produce and disseminate reviews concerning the effectiveness and cost-effectiveness of healthcare interventions. The aim is to identify and review the results of research and to disseminate the findings. Available from their Web site is further information about the CRD, details of systematic reviews undertaken by the CRD (either completed or in progress), and the CRD guidelines for undertaking a systematic review. Links to publications produced by the CRD are provided (*Effectiveness Matters* and *Effective Health Care* bulletins are discussed below). There are also three searchable databases produced by the CRD – the Database of Abstracts of Reviews of Effectiveness, NHS Economic Evaluation Database, and Health Technology Assessment database, discussed further below.

Other important organisations are the National Institute for Clinical Excellence (NICE) and the Cochrane Collaboration. NICE was established as a Special Health Authority in the UK in April 1999 to provide the NHS in England and Wales with authoritative, robust and reliable guidance on current best practice. The site currently includes information about NICE with access to the NICE database (information on quality improvement and related subjects). The Cochrane Collaboration was established 1992. It is an international organisation that aims to enable people to make well informed decisions about healthcare by preparing, maintaining and ensuring the accessibility of systematic reviews of the effects of healthcare interventions. Again, their Web site provides information about the Collaboration, as well as access to several information resources, some of which are discussed below.

Centre for Evidence-Based Child Health: www.ich.ucl.ac.uk/ebm/ebm.htm

Centre for Evidence-Based Medicine: cebm.jr2.ox.ac.uk/

Centre for Evidence Based Mental Health: www.psychiatry.ox.ac.uk/cebmh/

Cochrane Collaboration: www.cochrane.org/

National Institute for Clinical Excellence: www.nice.org.uk/

NHS Centre for Reviews and Dissemination: www.york.ac.uk/inst/crd/welcome.htm

---

Evidence-based journals

Electronic journals are discussed in detail in Chapter 16. However, there are a number of journals that are used specifically to disseminate the best available research findings into practice, which are worth highlighting here.

The *ACP Journal Club* contains abstracts of research-based articles that have been drawn from the published journal literature. Experts in the area evaluate the articles in terms of their methodological basis and clinical relevance and provide commentaries. The journal, published bi-monthly by the American College of Physicians, is designed to assist practitioners in keeping apace with developments of medical research and its implications for their practice. The contents pages and selected articles are available via the Web with subscription information.

Bandolier, produced by the Oxford and Anglia NHS region in the UK, is a newsletter designed to keep purchasers up-to-date with local and national initiatives on the effectiveness of healthcare interventions. The whole of *Bandolier*, since the journal was first launched, is accessible either by browsing by issue or via a search tool.

The NHS Centre for Reviews and Dissemination produces both *Effective Health Care* bulletins and *Effectiveness Matters*. *Effective Health Care* bulletins are designed to help decision makers in the health service make more informed decisions by providing effectiveness information on different interventions. The information is based on systematic reviews of the literature on clinical effectiveness, cost effectiveness and acceptability of different interventions. *Effectiveness Matters* summarises the results and implications of systematic reviews and is available on the Web from volume 2 onwards.

Other journals providing similar information which are also accessible via the Internet are *Health Evidence Bulletins Wales* and *Evidence-Based Medicine*. Journal Club on the Web is an interactive 'journal club', where the editor summarises and comments on articles from the published research literature and readers are invited to submit comments which are subsequently appended to the article summaries. The articles are primarily in the field of adult internal medicine and mainly from the *New England Journal of Medicine, Annals of Internal Medicine, JAMA* and *The Lancet*.

ACP Journal Club: www.acponline.org/journals/acpjc/jcmenu.htm

Bandolier: www.jr2.ox.ac.uk/bandolier/

Effective Health Care bulletins: www.york.ac.uk/inst/crd/ehcb.htm

Effectiveness Matters: www.york.ac.uk/inst/crd/em.htm

Evidence-Based Medicine: www.bmjpg.com/data/ebm.htm

Health Evidence Bulletins Wales: www.uwcm.ac.uk/uwcm/lb/pep/

Journal Club on the Web: www.journalclub.org/

Finding the evidence

Finding information via the Internet, including using bibliographic databases, is discussed in detail in Chapters 10 to 17. However, it is worth highlighting here those databases covering resources to support evidence-based healthcare.

The Cochrane Library is generally considered to be the premier resource for accessing evidence-based information. It consists primarily of four databases:

- Cochrane Database of Systematic Reviews (CDSR)
- Database of Abstracts of Reviews of Effectiveness (DARE)
- Controlled Clinical Trials Register (CCTR)
- Cochrane Review Methodology Database (CRMD)

The CDSR is a full text database of systematic reviews of randomised controlled trials (RCTs) that have been conducted by the Cochrane Collaboration. The database includes the statistical analysis (meta-analysis) for each review with a diagrammatic representation of the results (the odds ratio diagrams). Protocols of reviews in progress are also included. DARE contains structured abstracts of systematic reviews conducted elsewhere with commentaries provided by the NHS Centre for Reviews and Dissemination on the quality of the reviewing process. CCTR is a register of RCTs that have been published or reported elsewhere – the database is the most extensive of its type as it includes both published and unpublished research. Lastly, the CRMD contains papers relating to conducting reviews and is designed to assist those involved in the process.

The Cochrane Library has traditionally been available only in a CD-ROM format but it is now possible for subscribers to access all of the material via the Internet, for example from Update Software. The abstracts of the Cochrane Reviews are accessible and searchable for free and you can view comments and criticisms of the reviews. In the UK, NHS regional research and development offices or library units may provide region-wide subscriptions to the Cochrane Library for NHS personnel, and the databases are likely to become available via the National electronic Library for Health (NeLH). Members of selected information services, for example Doctors.net in the UK, may also receive free access.

The UK NHS Centre for Reviews and Dissemination (CRD) makes available three databases:

- the Database of Abstracts of Reviews of Effectiveness (DARE), which is also included in the Cochrane Library;
- the Health Technology Assessment Database (HTA); and
- the NHS Economic Evaluation Database (NHS EED).

An additional database of reviews in progress, details for which are collected by the UK NHS CRD, is the National Research Register (NRR). The NRR is the most comprehensive single register of information about current and ongoing research in the NHS, with information on approximately 64,000 research projects, and is further referred to in Chapter 7.

ScHARR has produced an introduction to free databases of interest to UK healthcare practitioners.

Cochrane Collaboration: www.cochrane.org/

Cochrane Reviews, abstracts: www.cochrane.org/cochrane/revabstr/mainindex.htm

Cochrane Reviews, search the abstracts: www.update-software.com/abstracts/

Cochrane Reviews, current comments and criticisms: www.cochrane.org/cochrane/currcrit.htm

DARE (Database of Abstracts of Reviews of Effectiveness): nhscrd.york.ac.uk/

Doctors.net: www.doctors.net.uk/

HTA (Health Technology Assessment Database): nhscrd.york.ac.uk/

NeLH: www.nelh.nhs.uk/

National Research Register (NRR): www.doh.gov.uk/nrr.htm

NHS EED: nhscrd.york.ac.uk/

Trawling the Net: a ScHARR introduction to free databases of interest to NHS staff on the Internet: www.shef.ac.uk/~scharr/ir/trawling.html

Update Software: www.update-software.com/

Online tools for critical appraisal

The need to critically appraise the quality of any information is central to evidence-based practice and there are various tools to guide in this process. McMaster University has made its Users' Guides available via the

Internet. Originally published in *JAMA*, these guides aim to assist clinicians in critically appraising different types of information. The guides are created by the Evidence-Based Medicine Working Group, a group of clinicians at McMaster and colleagues across the US. They include advice on how to use primary studies about therapy or prevention, diagnosis, prognosis, and harm, and how to use integrative studies of practice guidelines, outcomes analyses, overviews, and decision analyses.

The Critical Appraisal Skills Programme (CASP) develops educational interventions to help health service decision makers and those who influence health service decisions develop skills in the critical appraisal of evidence about effectiveness. The CASP site includes information on how to understand and appraise different types of research, including randomised controlled trials (RCTs), economic evaluations, and qualitative research studies. CASP also has a mailing list, critical-appraisal-skills. This is a low-volume list, used primarily for announcing meetings and workshops, with little discussion and debate.

---

critical-appraisal-skills: www.mailbase.ac.uk / lists /
critical-appraisal-skills /

Critical Appraisal Skills Programme: www.phru.org / casp /

McMaster University: hiru.mcmaster.ca / epc /

McMaster Users' Guides: www.cche.net / ebm / userguid /

Creating the evidence: guidelines for conducting high quality research

In addition to guidelines on critically appraising existing research, the Internet provides access to materials for producing the evidence, or conducting high quality research that ultimately will have an impact on patient care. These include:

- the Cochrane Handbook for producing high quality systematic reviews of the medical research literature;
- the CRD guidelines for those carrying out or commissioning reviews; and
- the NHS Research and Development Centre for Evidence-based Medicine, 'Evidence-based Medicine Toolbox' (mentioned earlier).

Cochrane Reviewers' Handbook: www.cochrane.org/cochrane/hbook.htm

Evidence-based Medicine Toolbox: cebm.jr2.ox.ac.uk/docs/toolbox.html

NHS CRD Guidelines for carrying out or commissioning reviews: www.york.ac.uk/inst/crd/report4.htm

Local guidelines

The Internet is also becoming an invaluable resource for information on guidelines relating to the local implementation of evidence-based healthcare. For example, the National Guideline Clearinghouse is a US-based resource for evidence-based clinical practice guidelines. It is both searchable and browsable and covered 640 guidelines at the time of writing. Clinical Practice Guidelines (CPG) 'at your fingertips' is a browsable directory of guidelines which are available on the Internet in full text. They have been produced or endorsed in Canada by a national, provincial or territorial medical or health organisation, professional society, government agency or expert panel. It is possible to browse the guidelines by category list, alphabetically by title, or by developer, and there is a link to the full text of each. In addition, there are various materials for assisting those involved in the development of guidelines. These include: Tools for guideline development and evaluation, and Guidelines for guidelines.

ScHARR also offers a list of guidelines.

CMA Infobase: www.cma.ca/cpgs/

Guidelines for guidelines: www.msd-newzealand.com/guidelines.html

National Guideline Clearinghouse: www.guidelines.gov/

ScHARR listing of guidelines: www.shef.ac.uk/~scharr/ir/guidelin.html

Tools for guideline development and evaluation: www.nzgg.org.nz/tools.htm

Guides to Internet-based resources

As with almost any subject area, there is now so much information available via the Internet on evidence-based healthcare that it is has become almost overwhelming. However, there are a number of useful guides within this area.

Netting the Evidence: a ScHARR Introduction to Evidence-Based Practice has been developed for a number of years by Andrew Booth, Head of Information Services at the School of Health and Related Research (ScHARR), University of Sheffield in the UK. It now constitutes an invaluable guide to Internet-based resources concerned with evidence-based practice for a range of professional groups. Material is listed in alphabetical order with an informative paragraph describing each of the sites.

The A to Z of Evidence-based Healthcare has been produced by Ann Pickering, a lecturer at King's College School of Medicine and Dentistry in the UK. It is part of the Doctor's Desk, which describes itself as 'an integrated desktop information and communications system' that 'seeks to be the ultimate home page for General Practice'. The A to Z itself is part of a resource pack designed to support evidence-based practice. The guide covers Internet and non-Internet based resources, and although it does not cover more resources than Netting the Evidence, it includes useful contact information for each resource (in addition to the Internet address). As with Netting the Evidence, it is not aimed at any one professional group but attempts to encompass all professions and disciplines.

Both of these guides provide details of a much larger number of resources than can be described here and are invaluable in assisting practitioners in identifying quickly and easily the most useful materials that are currently available via the Internet.

Several virtual libraries are under construction under the aegis of the NeLH initiative, with the remit to select and provide access to information for patients, carers, practitioners and commissioners. The National electronic Library for Mental Health (NeLMH) is one of the first NeLH virtual libraries, and aims to provide easy access to best current knowledge within fifteen seconds for clinicians. According to its inclusion criteria, material will be selected only if it has been critically appraised and abstracted in a way that allows the user to quickly find an answer to their question. As a result, it is anticipated that the NeLMH gateway will include evidence-based clinical practice guidelines, evidence-based patient information produced by the Centre for Health Information Quality, as well as links to the journal *Evidence-Based Mental Health* and the Cochrane Library. Other summaries of evidence such as *Effective Health Care* bulletins, *Clinical Evidence, Bandolier, DEC Reports* and CATs (Critically Appraised Topics) may also be included.

A number of searchable databases of Web-based effectiveness resources have been compiled, most of which are listed in the Netting the Evidence guide. However, few of these offer cross searching. Exceptionally, Turning Research Into Practice (TRIP) from the Centre for Research Support (CeReS) provides a single search interface to 26 datasets of relevance to evidence-based practice, few of which are indexed by Medline or other bibliographic databases. Searching is by title only.

In addition, SUMSearch offers a pre-determined model for evidence-based searching. SUMSearch has been designed to search 'the best resources' for a question, to format the question appropriately for each resource, and to generate additional searches depending on results. Sources searched include the 17th edition of the Merck Manual of Diagnosis and Therapy, PubMed, the US National Guideline Clearinghouse and the DARE database from the UK NHS Centre for Reviews and Dissemination. Depending on the focus requested, SUMSearch will search PubMed using the highly sensitive filters developed by Haynes *et al*.[1]

A different selection of additional sources is searched depending on the query. For example:

- the AIDS Knowledge Base is searched for AIDS related queries;
- Bedside Diagnosis: an Annotated Bibliography of Literature on Physical Examination and Interviewing is searched for queries relating to physical examination;
- the Food and Drug Administration (FDA) site or the FDA 'Dear Healthcare Professional' Letters are searched for queries involving adverse treatment effects;
- the Canadian Task Force for Preventive Services Handbook is searched for screening or prevention related queries; and
- CancerNet is searched for cancer related queries.

SUMSearch employs a variety of strategies for narrowing a search so that fewer than 100 hits are returned. More matches are sought and the search is broadened if fewer than ten or twenty hits are returned, depending on the source, or an attempt is made to offer helpful search tips.

A to Z of Evidence-based Healthcare: drsdesk.sghms.ac.uk/ Starnet/atoz.htm

AIDS Knowledge Base: hivinsite.ucsf.edu/akb/1997/

Bedside Diagnosis: an Annotated Bibliography of Literature on Physical Examination and Interviewing: www.acponline.org/public/bedside/

Canadian Task Force for Preventive Services Handbook: www.ctfphc.org/

CancerNet: cancernet.nci.nih.gov/

CeReS: www.ceres.uwcm.ac.uk/

Doctor's Desk: drsdesk.sghms.ac.uk/

FDA: www.fda.gov/search.html

FDA 'Dear Healthcare Professional' Letters: www.fda.gov/medwatch/safety.htm

Merck Manual of Diagnosis and Therapy: www.merck.com/pubs/mmanual/

NeLH: www.nelh.nhs.uk/

NeLMH: www.nhs.uk/mentalhealth/

Netting the Evidence: www.shef.ac.uk/uni/academic/R-Z/scharr/ir/netting.html

SUMSearch: sumsearch.uthscsa.edu/

TRIP: www.ceres.uwcm.ac.uk/frameset.cfm?section=trip

Reference

1. Haynes R B, Wilczynski N, McKibbon K A, Walker CJ, Sinclair JC. Developing optimal search strategies for detecting clinically sound studies in MEDLINE. *Journal of the Medical Informatics Association* 1994 Nov-Dec; **1** (6) :447-458.

Chapter 4

Diseases, rare diseases and outbreaks

Although the Web is a key resource for all aspects of disease information for the public, the patient and also the healthcare practitioner, it is particularly useful in drawing together what would otherwise be hard-to-find or hard-to-monitor information on rare diseases and disease outbreaks. The benefit of instantaneous access by specialist practitioners to information on the Web on the rarest of diseases or conditions has been documented in a letter to the *BMJ*.[1] Twenty-four hour access increases the availability of such valuable information, at times when it may be most required.

Rare diseases

Useful resources for rare diseases include Online Mendelian Inheritance in Man (OMIM), developed for the Web by the National Center for Biotechnology Information (NCBI). This brings together textual information, pictures and reference information on human genes and genetic disorders from a catalogue that is authored and edited by Dr Victor A McKusick and colleagues at Johns Hopkins University in the US and elsewhere. Additionally, the Office of Rare Diseases from the US National Institutes of Health, provides information on more than 6,000 rare diseases, 'including current research, publications from scientific and medical journals, completed research, ongoing studies, and patient support groups'. The National Organization for Rare Diseases, Inc. (NORD) also provides a Web-accessible database, the Rare Disease Database (RDB), that contains information on over 1,100 rare diseases. Access to the NORD documents is available only for a fee, although abstracts are currently available for free.

The potential use of Web sites that are being established by organisations or associations for patients with rare or uncommon diseases has also been discussed widely. It has been suggested that such sites might, indeed, offer:

> Immediately accessible sources of up-to-date knowledge (for example, evidence-based texts, clinical guidelines, contacts and treatment centres, caveats for emergency care, literature searches,

etc.), which their medical expert advisory panels might voluntarily provide.[2]

In the UK, NHS Direct Online provides links to patient organisations, several of which will provide information on specific rare diseases.

The National Organization for Rare Diseases, Inc. (NORD): www.rarediseases.org/

NHS Direct Online: www.nhsdirect.nhs.uk/

Office of Rare Diseases: rarediseases.info.nih.gov/ord/

OMIM: www.ncbi.nlm.nih.gov/omim/

Disease outbreaks and emergencies

Numerous sources address issues of disease outbreaks. As would be expected, key international and national organisations provide online, up-to-date sources of information on disease outbreaks anywhere in the world. Key among these are the World Health Organization (WHO) publications *Weekly Epidemiological Record* (which provides international coverage) and *Disease Outbreak News*. *Eurosurveillance* provides European coverage, and governmental organisations within each country, for example the Centers for Disease Control and Prevention (CDC) in the US and the Public Health Laboratory Service (PHLS) in the UK, offer bulletins and information relating specifically to their respective geographical domains. In the US, the CDC produces the well-known *Morbidity and Mortality Weekly Report (MMWR)*, as well as the journal *Emerging Infectious Diseases*. The UK PHLS produces a regular bulletin on communicable diseases, *CDR Weekly*. The CDC also offers links to international bulletins.

For timely communication, sources such as those referred to above offer email updating services. For example, the WHO offers an email table of contents service for the *Weekly Epidemiological Record*, together with other short epidemiological bulletins. *Eurosurveillance* offers a weekly update service, which gives the titles of the week's reports.

The role of mailing lists and newsgroups is of central importance for rapid dissemination of information in the case of disasters, and possibly none more so than in the case of disease outbreaks. Key among these has been ProMED, an initiative by the Federation of American Scientists to promote the establishment of a global programme for monitoring emerging diseases, and the only 'total public global electronic network for reporting outbreaks of infectious human, plant and animal diseases'.

Like outbreaks, greater speed of communication via email can offer significant advantages in relation to emergencies. One example of this was documented by Hernandez-Borges AA *et al.*,[3] who describe a case in Haiti where a batch of locally produced acetaminophen was contaminated with diethylene glycol and several children were intoxicated and a number died. Discussion of the case on the PEDNEPH mailing list[4] allowed a rapid response from paediatric nephrology departments at a number of US centres, and the timely evacuation of several children with renal failure. The first announcement on PEDNEPH preceded publication of details of the event in US newspapers by nine days.

CDC links to international bulletins:
www.cdc.gov/mmwr/international/world.html

Communicable Disease Report: www.phls.co.uk/publications/cdrw.htm

Disease Outbreak News: www.who.int/emc/outbreak_news/

Emerging Infectious Diseases: www.cdc.gov/ncidod/EID/

Eurosurveillance: www.eurosurv.org/

Eurosurveillance weekly update service:
www.eurosurv.org/update/

Morbidity and Mortality Weekly Report (MMWR): www.cdc.gov/mmwr/

ProMED: www.fas.org/promed/

ProMED archives: www.promedmail.org:8080/promed/promed.folder.home

Weekly Epidemiological Record: www.who.int/wer/

Disease and conditions information from specialist organisations

Almost every organisation imaginable now seems to have a Web presence, and where specialist healthcare organisations are concerned, this can be an invaluable source for information on diseases and conditions. There are too many examples to list here, but the search tools discussed in later chapters, and the gateways described in Chapter 14 in particular, will prove invaluable in finding such sites.

For example, a search for *diabetic retinopathy* using any of the information gateways described in Chapter 14 is likely to retrieve resources provided by the National Eye Institute (NEI) of the National Institutes of Health, as well as other key specialist organisations in the field. Sites such as the NEI can provide a wealth of insight on specific conditions for the healthcare professional as well as the health consumer. Highly specialist resources may be made available in the form of searchable databases, which cannot be tapped directly via Web search engines or directories (such as the NEI search option, for example).

A number of services attempt to identify searchable databases of this kind, and gateways like those referred to in Chapter 14 can be most useful in highlighting their existence. Medical Matrix has created two compilations of links to such sources with its Clinical Searches and Search Hub pages. OMNI indexes databases with the headings 'Databases, Bibliographic' or 'Databases, Factual', for example, a search for *eye AND keywords=databases* retrieved the Rare Diseases Clinical Research Database, which included ophthalmological diseases.

Medical Matrix: www.medmatrix.org/

National Eye Institute (NEI): www.nei.nih.gov/

OMNI: omni.ac.uk/

References

1. Dearlove OR, Sharples A, Stone C. Internet is useful for information on rare conditions. *BMJ* 1997 Aug 23;**315**(7106):491. Available from: http://www.bmj.com/cgi/content/full/315/7106/491/a

2. Briggs M, Bennett J. Doctors should have ready access to sites about rare diseases on World Wide Web. *BMJ* 1998 Jul 18;**317**(7152):211. Available from: http://www.bmj.com/cgi/content/full/317/7152/211/b

3. Hernandez-Borges AA, Pareras LG, Jimenez A. Comparative analysis of pediatric mailing lists on the Internet [electronic article]. *Pediatrics* 1997 Aug;**100**(2):e8. Available from: http://www.pediatrics.org/cgi/content/full/100/2/e8

4. Pediatric Nephrology Discussion List USA (pedneph-request@bio-3.bsd.uchicago.edu).

Chapter 5

Consumer health information

There is no doubt that health consumers are using the Internet as an information source. In one survey, 95% of respondents agreed that useful information could be found on the Internet and 83% felt that it was easy to find health information in this way.[1] Material published with patients in mind abounds and health consumers have themselves become information providers, exploiting the potential of the Internet as a cheap and easy publishing medium.

In addition, the distinction between information designed for consumers and information published for health professionals is blurring. When the then US Vice President Al Gore launched the National Library of Medicine's PubMed service (a freely available version of Medline, see Chapter 15) he searched for references to a condition he had once suffered and compared the treatments described in the results to the treatment his physician had recommended.[2] In effect, the National Library of Medicine has made Medline available to millions of health consumers in the US and worldwide. For the first time patients are able to access some of the same sources used by physicians to plan their treatment.

With the creation of NHS Direct, a national telephone enquiry number for health consumers, and its Web counterpart, NHS Direct Online, the UK government signalled its view of the importance of informing patients. In this light, the existence of health information on the Internet is a positive development. However, there is also a downside: the quality of the information can vary considerably and misinformation may result in risks to patients and an increased workload for health professionals who must spend time refuting inaccurate statements.

This chapter describes the types of resources available on the Web, who publishes the information and why. Quality issues relating to consumer health information are also considered (evaluation of health and medical information generally is discussed in Chapter 19).

NHS Direct Online: www.nhsdirect.nhs.uk/

PubMed: www.ncbi.nlm.nih.gov/PubMed/

What is available?

The Internet offers resources covering a wide range of topics in various formats and styles.

Access to the Internet puts patients in easy reach of:

- Health promotion information: advice on issues such as quitting smoking, diets, exercise and avoiding stress. For example, part of the remit of HEBSWeb, the Health Education Board for Scotland Web service, is health promotion and education. The HEBSWeb site contains online versions of their published information in formats which can be easily downloaded and printed.

- Data about diseases: information about specific conditions, their manifestations, diagnosis and prognosis. For example, the collaboration between the Royal National Institute for the Blind (RNIB) and the Royal College of Ophthalmologists to produce information on eye diseases. A consumer health organisation and a professional organisation have together published this excellent group of patient-oriented documents, which are made available to the public via the RNIB's Web service. They contain concise information on various eye conditions, including retinal detachment, cataracts, diabetic retinopathy and glaucoma.

- Information on treatments and procedures: patients can locate explanations of particular medical procedures or drugs in non-technical language. For example, Questionable Cancer Therapies is a collection of documents describing alternative cancer treatments with summaries of published research into their effectiveness. This resource is part of Quackwatch, a site that aims to expose 'quackery' and 'health fraud'.

- Peer support and experience: patients are able to access knowledge and support from other health consumers. For example, the Terrence Higgins Trust (THT) is a UK charity which provides information and support to people living with HIV and AIDS, including patients, their friends and relatives. As an independent organisation, the information it provides has a different value to that published by, say, a Royal College or government department. The THT Web site offers information for patients on all aspects of AIDS and HIV and is an ideal way to find information about AIDS issues.

- Directory information: lists of support groups, general practitioners and hospitals, whether national or local. For example, the Information Network for Croydon Health (INCH) is produced by a partnership between local libraries, the health authority and voluntary organisations, providing a local view of health and social welfare services and a mechanism for local organisations to reach Croydon residents via the Internet.

As the above examples illustrate, consumer health information available via the Internet may be presented in many different formats. As well as documents, such as simple online versions of patient handouts or leaflets, the health consumer may find searchable or browsable collections of data, as well as interactive resources such as mailing lists, online chat fora or newsgroups.

HEBSWeb: www.hebs.org.uk/

Information Network for Croydon Health: www.croydon.gov.uk/ healthinfo/

Quackwatch: www.quackwatch.com/

Terrence Higgins Trust: www.tht.org.uk/

Understanding your eye condition: www.rnib.org.uk/info/ eyeimpoi/welcome.htm

---

Who produces it?

Consumer health information on the Internet is published by a number of different types of organisations and individuals:

- Commercial companies: consumer health information may be published by commercial organisations such as pharmaceutical companies, either as a marketing tool for their products, as a means of attracting visitors to the company site, or arising from philanthropic motives;
- Patients, relatives and carers: setting up a Web site is one way to share experience, and personal Web pages detailing an individual's story of illness or treatments are common;
- Healthcare organisations/personnel: information may be published at the regional or local level within a national or private health service; and
- Organisations with a health education role: the Internet offers an additional mode of dissemination to organisations who already have a role in offering information to health consumers, and some have produced extensive collections of data online.

Evaluating the quality of consumer health information

Quality issues and the evaluation of Internet-based information sources are discussed in detail in Chapter 19. However, this chapter looks specifically at the quality of consumer health information - for the lay person, this issue may be of paramount importance. Indeed, misleading or inaccurate information could place lives in danger. While it is impossible to assess how much of the information aimed at patients is accurate, one study suggests that it may be as little as 12%.[3]

Key issues for evaluation of consumer health information are:

*   the authority of the information provider, and
*   the intended purpose of the information.

An authoritative source (whether this is determined by the author or the publisher) may give an indication of the quality of the information being offered. The motive of the publisher may be important also. A commercial company, for example, may have a very different motivation for making information about a certain treatment available, when compared to a health professional or healthcare organisation. Both may be less authoritative sources than an official health education organisation, such as the UK's Health Development Agency, or a professional association, such as the British Dental Association. Even organisations such as these may produce materials with inappropriate cultural or national overtones, or material that is only relevant locally.

Assessing whether a source is authoritative is only one side of the coin. It is also necessary to consider the needs of the information seeker and their intended use of the information. A leaflet published by the most authoritative organisation may be unhelpful for a patient looking for a support group or seeking information on alternative remedies. In these cases, more than ever, it is up to the end user to make the final judgment.

A US Food and Drug Administration (FDA) Consumer Reprint proposes a number of questions for consumers to use in judging the reliability of information:[4]

*   Who maintains the site?
*   Is there an editorial board or another listing of the names and credentials of those responsible for preparing and reviewing the site's content?
*   Does the site link to other sources of medical information?
*   When was the site last updated?
*   Are informative graphics and multimedia files such as video or audio clips available?

- Does the site charge an access fee?

The US Federal Trade Commission (FTC) also offers a number of tips to avoid health fraud:[5]

- If it sounds too good to be true, it probably is.

- Beware of products or treatments that are advertised as a quick and effective cure-all for a wide range of ailments or for an undiagnosed pain.

- Be cautious of testimonials claiming amazing results.

- Watch out for promoters who use phrases such as 'scientific breakthrough', 'miraculous cure', 'exclusive product', and 'secret ingredient'.

- Before you purchase, consult your pharmacist, doctor or other health professional.

The FTC also recommends that all information should be validated through other sources (such as medical databases or journal articles) and ultimately discussed with a physician. They also emphasise the importance of judging the quality of health information from the Internet according to the reliability of the providing organisation.[6]

Guides to quality consumer health information

In response to concerns about the quality of medical information that is freely available from the Internet, guides to identifying quality information and aids to evaluation have been developed. These include codes of conduct for those writing or publishing on the Internet, evaluation guidelines used by intermediaries such as librarians to select Internet resources, and rules of thumb for the Internet user. These are discussed in detail in Chapter 19.

However, some tools and guidelines are designed specifically for consumer health information. For example, a Policy Paper issued by the Health Summit Working Group presents a set of seven criteria developed for use in evaluating the quality of health information on the Internet.[7] The criteria primarily address health information Web sites aimed at the general public under the headings: credibility, content, disclosure, links, design, interactivity and caveats.

Centre for Health Information Quality (CHiQ)

In the UK, the Centre for Health Information Quality (CHiQ) is funded by the NHS to promote the production of good quality patient information. CHiQ, which is run by the Help for Health Trust, has produced a bulletin devoted to health information quality on the Internet, which is available from their Web site.

Centre for Information Quality Management (ChiQ): www.hfht.org/
chiq/

Centre for Information Quality (ChiQ) Management Topic Bulletin
2: Quality assessment of Internet sites: www.hfht.org/chiq/
download_pdf.htm

SciPICH

The Science Panel on Interactive Communication in Health (SciPICH)
site includes a bibliography of work on health information quality and a
listing of evaluation guidelines in health and medicine. An Interactive
Health Communication checklist is provided, as well as an interactive
Web site evaluation drill encouraging users to practice evaluating Internet-
based resources.

SciPICH: www.scipich.org/

SciPICH Interactive Health Communication checklist:
www.scipich.org/IHC/checklist.htm

SciPICH Web site evaluation drill: www.scipich.org/IHC/
webdrill.htm

DISCERN

The DISCERN Project, originally funded by the British Library and the
NHS Research and Development Programme in the UK, has developed
quality criteria for written consumer health information on treatment
choices.[8] The experiences gained from this work have recently been transferred to consumer information on the Internet. The emphasis of the
DISCERN quality criteria is on assisting consumers in assessing the content of information and is therefore likely to be a valuable tool.

DISCERN: www.discern.org.uk/

References

1. Health on the Net Foundation. HON's Fourth survey on the use of
   the Internet for medical and health purposes: March-April 1999.
   Available from: http://www.hon.ch/Survey/ResumeApr99.html

2. National Library of Medicine. Vice President Al Gore Launches Free
   Medline. *NLM Newsline* 1997;**52**(2-4). Available from: http://
   www.nlm.nih.gov/pubs/nlmnews/maraug97.html

3. McClung H J, Murray R D, Heitlinger L A. The Internet as a source for current patient information [electronic article]. *Pediatrics* 1998 Jun;**101** (6):e2. Available from: http://www.pediatrics.org/cgi/content/full/101/6/e2

4. US Food and Drug Administration. Health information on-line. FDA Consumer Reprint. 1998. Available from: http://www.fda.gov/fdac/features/596_info.html

5. Federal Trade Commission. Remedies targeted in International Health Claim Surf Day: consumer protection, public health, private agencies from 25 countries assess over 1,200 Internet sites [news release]. 1998. Available from: http://www.ftc.gov/opa/1998/9811/intlhlth.htm

6. World Health Organization. The World Health Assembly adopts a resolution on the sale of medical products through the Internet. 50th World Health Assembly, press release WHA/6. 1997 May 12. Available from: http://www.health.fgov.be/WHI3/periodical/months/wwhv1n8tekst/180797b3.htm

7. Health Summit Working Group. Criteria for assessing the quality of health information on the Internet: policy paper. Available from: http://hitiweb.mitretek.org/docs/policy.pdf

8. Charnock D. The DISCERN Handbook. Abingdon: Radcliffe Medical Press; 1998. Available from: http://www.discern.org.uk/

Chapter 6

Data to support biomedical research

Developing beyond its origins as a military network, the Internet became a place where academia communicated and research was carried out. In 1991, *Nature* published an editorial exhorting readers to:

> Hook our computers into the worldwide network that gives access to daily changes in the databases and also makes immediate our communications with each other.[1]

The databases referred to were huge repositories of molecular biology data, the basic tools of biomedical research. Sharing data and experience via the Internet is much more than merely convenient – it has facilitated truly collaborative, international research programmes such as the Human Genome Project.

More recently, the Internet has been extensively exploited by the commercial sector and commercial domain names (addresses ending in '.com', or containing 'co', e.g. 'co.uk') are now the most common type. Advertising of products and services, establishing and promoting a corporate image, and online ordering and payment are all now commonplace activities on the Web.

The aim of this chapter is to introduce the most significant resources for researchers in three areas: databases used in biomedical research, buying materials for research online, and patent information.

Research databases

Understanding biomedical research databases on the Internet is often difficult for the uninitiated because:

- they are numerous,
- they often overlap,
- they appear repeatedly under different guises, and
- they are frequently integrated with other data sources.

In addition, this is an area where jargon abounds. These factors together result in a complex and often confusing information landscape, and the new user desperately needs a good atlas!

Molecular biology for beginners

A basic knowledge of the science underpinning molecular biology is invaluable. Help in the form of a plethora of introductions, primers and guides is at hand. The resources in this chapter are listed in order of increasing complexity, so absolute beginners should start here.

Researchers at the Rothamsted Experimental Station of the BBSRC (the Biotechnology and Biological Sciences Research Council) have developed the Beginner's Guide to Molecular Biology. This resource concentrates on the basic science of cells, DNA and proteins.

As well as coordinating data services (described later) for the UK's Human Genome researchers, the UK Human Genome Mapping Project Research Centre (HGMP-RC) offers training for researchers and others. Online notes are provided for several courses, which can be downloaded freely from the HGMP Web site. For example, at the introductory level, there is a series of notes from a 1996/1997 UK Online User Group (UKOLUG) course for librarians, entitled 'Molecular biology concepts and terminology'.

First published in the early 1990's, the Primer on Molecular Genetics is still a good introduction. As well as sections on DNA, genes and chromosomes, mapping a sequence and the impact of the Human Genome Project, it has a section on data collection and interpretation which serves as an ideal supplement to this chapter.

Finally, the notes accompanying the HGMP Introductory Biocomputing course are more extensive.

Beginner's Guide to Molecular Biology:
www.iacr.bbsrc.ac.uk/notebook/courses/guide/

Introductory Biocomputing:
www.hgmp.mrc.ac.uk/Courses/Intro_3day/index.html

Molecular biology concepts and terminology:
www.hgmp.mrc.ac.uk/Courses/UKOLUG/buzzwords.html

Primer on Molecular Genetics:
www.bis.med.jhmi.edu/Dan/DOE/intro.html

Major research databases

The main features of this landscape are the datasets themselves. However, knowing the name of a dataset is not enough. To work in this subject area efficiently, it is also necessary to have some knowledge of:

- its relationship with other datasets, and
- access issues, such as the software to query the data, its location, etc.

For convenience, the datasets described in this chapter are divided into sequence datasets, genomic datasets, disease information and structure data.

Sequence datasets

The EMBL nucleotide sequence database is a comprehensive collection of DNA and RNA sequences collected from the scientific literature, patent applications and directly submitted from researchers around the world. The database is produced by the European Bioinformatics Institute (EBI), which is an outstation of the European Molecular Biology Laboratory (EMBL). It is for most purposes equivalent to the GenBank database, from the National Center for Biotechnology Information (NCBI) in the US, and the DNA Database of Japan (DDBJ), which is produced by the National Institute of Genetics (Japan). Data is exchanged between these major centres daily. The EMBL database may be used via several access points worldwide. A complete description of the database, previously published in *Nucleic Acids Research*, is available online.

EMBL (and its near equivalents GenBank and DDBJ) are produced collaboratively by the European Bioinformatics Institute (EBI), the National Centre for Biotechnology Information (NCBI) in the US and the National Institute of Genetics (Japan). A complete description of the database, previously published in Nucleic Acids Research is available online.

SWISS-PROT is a database of protein sequences produced collaboratively by researchers at the University of Geneva and the European Bioinformatics Institute. SWISS-PROT may be accompanied by TrEMBL, which can be thought of as a database of items awaiting publication in SWISS-PROT.

DDBJ: www.ddbj.nig.ac.jp/

EMBL: www.ebi.ac.uk/embl/

EMBL, Description of: www.ebi.ac.uk/embl/Documentation/NAR/gkc070_gml.html

GenBank: www.ncbi.nlm.nih.gov/Genbank/

> SWISS-PROT: www.ebi.ac.uk/swissprot/
>
> SWISS-PROT, Description of: www.ebi.ac.uk/swissprot/ Information/information.html

Genome datasets

The Human Genome Sequencing Index (HGSI) provides the 'big picture of sequencing activity'. It records which regions of the human genome have been or are being sequenced around the world. HGSI is produced by the NCBI (see Major organisations).

Genome DataBase (GDB) was orginally located at Johns Hopkins University in Baltimore and was the official repository for genomic mapping data resulting from the Human Genome Initiative. The management of GDB passed to the Bioinformatics Computing Centre at the Hospital for Sick Children in Ontario, Canada in 1999 after public funding from the US government ceased. GDB contains a variety of information relating to human genome sequencing. The help files are worth visiting in themselves as they are a mine of information about the jargon associated with this dataset.

There are many other datasets holding genome information for other organisms. Usually, these are created by researchers who are looking for similarities between an organism's genome and the human genome. For example, the FUGU Project in the UK is creating a map of the genome of the puffer fish *Fugu rubripes* that has approximately the same number of genes as are present in the human genome, but has a much shorter sequence.

> FUGU: fugu.hgmp.mrc.ac.uk/
>
> GDB: www.gdb.org/
>
> HGSI: www.ncbi.nlm.nih.gov/HUGO/

Disease information

Online Mendelian Inheritance in Man (OMIM) is a catalogue of human genetic disorders containing clinical information cross-referenced with genetic, sequence, structural and bibliographic data. These cross-references make it possible to search OMIM for a disease, locate the gene thought to be responsible, and find relevant references in the literature, all from one system. OMIM is produced by the NCBI.

The Human Gene Mutation Database (HGMD), at the University of Wales College of Medicine, Cardiff in the UK, is a database of sequences relating to human genetic disease (i.e. genetic mutation). Data in HGMD is linked to related records in OMIM and GDB.

Similar datasets relating to specific diseases are sometimes seen. For example, HAMSTERS is a dataset containing similar information for the genetic mutation leading to haemophilia.

HAMSTERS: europium.rpms.mrc.ac.uk/

HGMD: www.uwcm.ac.uk/uwcm/mg/hgmd0.html

OMIM: www.ncbi.nlm.nih.gov/omim/

Structure data

Structural datasets, as their name implies, contain information on the spatial characteristics of biological molecules. The Protein Data Bank (PDB) and the Molecular Modelling Database (MMDB) are the most commonly encountered structural databases and are closely interlinked.

- PDB is an archive of three-dimensional structures of biological macromolecules, determined experimentally by techniques such as x-ray crystallography and nuclear magnetic resonance.

- MMDB contains three-dimensional structures from PDB that have been compared for similarity in three-dimensional space. Records are cross-referenced to sequence and bibliographic data via Entrez (see Integrated services below).

MMDB is produced by the NCBI and PDB by the Research Collaboratory for Structural Bioinformatics.

MMDB: www.ncbi.nlm.nih.gov/Structure/

PDB: www.rcsb.org/pdb/

PDB (UK mirror site): pdb.ccdc.cam.ac.uk/

Integrated systems

Multi-database access systems are commonplace in biological research and most of the databases mentioned above offer access to relevant data in other databases. Below are some systems that are well-known and will be encountered frequently by anyone seeking molecular biology data on the Internet.

Sequence Retrieval System (SRS) is a tool for accessing many sequence, genome and structural datasets. It is based at the UK's HGMP-RC (see Major Organisations below).

Entrez provides integrated access to many NCBI sources, including MMDB, OMIM and the PubMed version of Medline. It is probably the best known of the integrated systems as it was the first to offer free access to a subset of Medline on the Web.

GeneCards is a database of all types of information about human genes, produced at the Weizmann Institute in Israel using various data mining techniques. GeneCards includes references to information in OMIM and GDB, as well as links to clinical information such as diagnosis and therapy.

Entrez: www.ncbi.nlm.nih.gov / Entrez /

GeneCards: bioinformatics.weizmann.ac.il / cards /

SRS: srs.hgmp.mrc.ac.uk /

Major organisations

A few national and international organisations dominate this field, the most significant of which are described below.

The National Center for Biotechnology Information (NCBI) is part of the National Library of Medicine, one of a group of organisations under the US government's National Institutes of Health. NCBI provides research database services for the US and world audiences and also has a training and education role. Major databases produced by the NCBI include OMIM and HGSI.

The Human Genome Mapping Project Resource Centre (HGMP-RC) is funded by the Medical Research Council to support the research community in the UK and to undertake research in its own right. Database services are a large part of this remit, but the HGMP-RC also educates new users in the use of molecular biology datasets at courses around the UK. HGMP-RC also maintains a useful database of all types of biological research databases. The European Molecular Biology Laboratory (EMBL) is a group of four collaborating organisations located in Europe conducting research and offering database services to the scientific community in general. It is supported financially by fourteen European countries and Israel. EMBL is not to be confused with the European Bioinformatics Institute (EBI), which is based at the Wellcome Trust Genome Campus in Cambridge.

The Institute for Genomic Research (TIGR) was created in 1992 and is based in Baltimore in the US. It was funded by the biotechnology company, Human Genome Sciences, for the first five years of its existence, which retained the intellectual rights in TIGR's work. The partnership ended in 1997 and now TIGR operates as a not-for-profit research institute. TIGR has been involved in the sequencing of the human genome.

European Bioinformatics Institute (EBI): www.ebi.ac.uk/

European Molecular Biology Laboratory (EMBL): www.embl-heidelberg.de/

Human Genome Mapping Project Resource Centre (HGMP-RC): www.hgmp.mrc.ac.uk/

National Center for Biotechnology Information (NCBI): www.ncbi.nlm.nih.gov/

The Institute for Genomic Research (TIGR): www.tigr.org/

Other frequently encountered jargon

Once you have discerned the type of data in your dataset, found the organisation responsible for it and located the most appropriate access point (integrated or otherwise), there may still be more to learn before accessing the data itself. Different algorithms for querying sequence and other molecular biology data exist – the more common ones are: BLAST, FastA and GCG. It is beyond the scope of this work to list and describe them but services making use of a particular algorithm will usually direct you to background information about it.

Readers needing to stay abreast of developments in this area should consider joining the lis-genome mailing list at Mailbase. This list was established to support library and information service staff in the UK serving researchers using major genome and sequence databases. It is an excellent source of announcements about courses, books and services, as well as a non-threatening environment in which to ask questions.

lis-genome: www.mailbase.ac.uk/lists/lis-genome/

Keeping abreast of databases

Nucleic Acids Research (NAR) publishes an annual guide to molecular biology databases, and numerous similar compilations can be found on the Web from individual researchers. The *NAR*'s Molecular Biology Database Collection for 2000 serves as a searchable, up-to-date launchpad to relevant Web sites. Databases are included especially if new value is added to the raw data through curation, new data connections or other innovations. The databases are listed alphabetically by name or by category of database. Indicatively, the following categories are available: comparative genomics, gene expression, gene identification and structure, genetics maps, genomic databases, intermolecular interactions, major sequence repositories, metabolic pathways and cellular regulation, mutation databases, pathology, protein databases, protein sequence motifs, proteome resources, RNA sequences, retrieval systems and database structures, structure, transgenics and varied biomedical content.

> *Nucleic Acids Research (NAR)*. Molecular Biology Database Collection: www.oup.co.uk/nar/Volume_28/Issue_01/html/gkd115_gml.html

Reagents and catalogues

Those involved in biomedical research, particularly in genetics and molecular biology, are well served on the Internet by commercial services. Online commerce in equipment and supplies for basic medical research is widespread.

Product catalogues

Product catalogues on the Internet vary greatly in size, availability and usefulness. Smaller companies may not have their own Web site, and so their catalogues will not be available in stand alone format (but see Shopping malls and combined catalogues, below). Large companies may offer more information online than is available in print.

What's available?

The researcher aiming to buy products online may find:

- Chemicals – basic organic and inorganic solvents, reagents and catalysts e.g. the Sigma-Aldrich service where keyword searches of six brands or catalogues may be carried out online. One of these is the Aldrich catalogue that is widely used in chemical research. Online ordering is available for account holders.
- Biological products – enzymes, proteins and DNA vectors, etc. e.g. the Invitrogen Web service, where customers may search or browse the catalogue, request printed information to be mailed and order online. The catalogue often provides pointers to extensive background material, e.g. references in the literature, manuals, etc.
- Equipment – including hi-tech research equipment and disposables e.g. the Amersham Pharmacia Biotec catalogue, which specialises in cell and molecular biology equipment and techniques such as chromatography, electrophoresis and spectrophotometry.

Amersham Pharmacia Biotec: www.apbiotech.com/

Invitrogen: www.invitrogen.com/catalog.html

Sigma-Aldrich: www.sigma-aldrich.com/

Shopping malls and combined catalogues

As well as individual companies selling their wares the Internet is home to a number of useful services offering information on products from different vendors. These include:

- shopping malls, i.e. hosts that provide a shop window for several companies in an integrated site,
- comparative services, i.e. organisations producing reviews or comparisons of products, and
- pages listing company Web pages for easy access.

In contrast to the catalogues described above, these services may offer the opportunity to search for a single product across many catalogues or to read critical evaluations of products.

A good example of this type of service is Anderson's Webalog, or ATCG (formerly Anderson's Timesaving Comparative Guides). Anderson's Webalog aims to make life simpler for the biomedical researcher by bringing together product information from diverse sources into one location. Products include books, equipment and office supplies, as well as chemicals, enzymes and vectors. This service allows users to search by product name across data from over 2,400 companies. Guest access is available but registered customers may open accounts and also buy purchasing services.

Also serving the biomedical research market is BioSupplyNet. Recommended by the Federation of American Societies for Experimental Biology (FASEB), BioSupplyNet is similar in intention to Anderson's Webalog. Using BioSupplyNet it is possible to search or browse by product name or supplier and also to order catalogues from individual companies.

Many other smaller services cover niche markets. For example, the Lab Pages service offers a searchable database of company Web pages that may help in locating information about smaller UK firms and their products.

There are also some comparative sites of interest to clinicians, e.g. the Surgical Materials Testing Laboratory's (SMTL) Dressing Data Cards provides detailed information on surgical dressings available on the UK market. SMTL was once publicly funded but is now a wholly commercial enterprise, selling services to, amongst others, health authorities.

For dentists, the British Dental Trade Association, a long established trade organisation, maintains an online database of companies and their products.

Anderson's Webalog: www.atcg.com/

BioSupplyNet: www.biosupplynet.com/ or biomednet.com/ biosupplynet/

British Dental Trade Association: www.bdta.org.uk/

Lab Pages: www.labpages.com/

Surgical Materials Testing Laboratory: www.smtl.co.uk/

Which service?

Which of the many online catalogues and combined services should you use? In the final analysis, the decision whether to buy via the Web or not will probably be taken at the organisational level. Indeed many companies insist on an agreement or an account being established in advance.

As with all online purchases there may be issues of security to consider – you may want to assess prior to ordering whether any security measures, such as data encryption, are in place to ensure safe transactions (see Chapter 20 for more information about secure transactions on the Web).

Even if online purchasing is not an option, online catalogues may be useful as a method of locating materials that may then be purchased using more conventional methods. The effectiveness of the service will then depend on its ease of use compared to other routes to the same information. Many online catalogues are merely electronic versions of the bulky, paper catalogues often located in laboratories. In such cases, a paper version may be more convenient for regular consultation. However, a good search feature will offer functionality that paper cannot provide and electronic versions of a catalogue may be more regularly updated than their paper equivalent.

There is no one combined service that covers all the available material in this area. It is crucial therefore to ask if the service you use contains information from the catalogues that you might expect. If not, a visit to the individual company sites will be necessary.

Reference

1.   Gilbert W. Towards a paradigm shift in biology [editorial]. *Nature* 1991 Jan 10;**349**(6305):99.

Chapter 7

Finding out about research funding and research projects

The Internet can now be used to gather background information before a funding application is submitted, to request information online, and in a few cases, to submit the application.

Many organisations offering funding to researchers have an Internet presence, including:

- research councils, e.g. the Medical Research Council,
- other government sources, e.g. the Department of Health,
- international organisations, e.g. the European Union, and
- charities, e.g. the Wellcome Trust.

In addition, there are databases that present information from many funding bodies in a searchable format. This chapter highlights some of the resources that are currently available.

Several tools are also described that may be used to locate details about research already in progress. This is approached from three perspectives: finding projects by source of funding, by project type and by project location. Many of the services described here were not freely available to Internet users until recently. However, while there has been much advancement in this particular area of information provision, there are still many key databases not yet accessible via the Internet – Current Research in Britain being one such example. Therefore, the tools listed should be used together with existing paper, CD-ROM or traditional commercial online host services.

Research councils

The research councils are government agencies that have within their remit the distribution of central funding to researchers located in universities and elsewhere. The combined research councils budget for 1998/9 was over one thousand million pounds.

The Medical Research Council (MRC) supports entire laboratories, programmes, projects and individuals carrying out biomedical research in the UK. It also awards funding within the particular areas of research it is promoting, as well as for specific one-off items, such as equipment or new clinical trials. The MRC Web site offers extensive background information on its grants, data on current award holders, and advice on how applications are assessed. Those wishing to submit applications by email may download the electronic grant application (EGA) form (IBM PC compatible users only).

The Biotechnology and Biological Sciences Research Council (BBSRC) supports research in the field of biological sciences including animal science and agriculture. As well as supporting individuals, the Council funds a number of research centres, such as the Roslin Institute famous for being first to clone an adult mammal, Dolly the sheep. The BBSRC Web site outlines eligibility criteria for awards, provides advice on making applications, and offers a facility for downloading application forms.

The remaining UK research councils are the Economic and Social Research Council (ESRC), Particle Physics and Astronomy Research Council (PPARC), Natural Environment Research Council (NERC) and Engineering and Physical Sciences Research Council (EPSRC). Their details are listed at the joint home page of the UK research councils.

Biotechnology and Biological Sciences Research Council (BBSRC): www.bbsrc.ac.uk/

Joint home page of the UK research councils: www.nerc.ac.uk/research-councils/

Medical Research Council (MRC): www.mrc.ac.uk/

Other UK government sources

The Department of Health's Research and Development Directorate advises the Secretary of State for Health on NHS research and development, as well as its relationship to other centrally funded research. The Research and Development Directorate's home page is therefore a good starting point and can be used to locate requests for proposals for particular Department of Health initiatives.

Local research and development units are a key source of information for those working in the NHS sector. For a typical example, see the units listed at the regional research and development directorate for the North West.

Department of Health Research and Development Directorate:
www.doh.gov.uk/research/

Department of Health Research and Development Directorate -
North West: www.doh.gov.uk/nwro/rddnwro.htm

International organisations

Funding from the European Union (EU) has become increasingly important to UK researchers. EU funding is distributed within a series of
frameworks, each lasting several years. The Fifth Framework is the present
funding programme, running beyond the end of 2000.

The COmmunity Research and Development Information Service
(CORDIS) is the EU's online service for research, and is a vast store of
information on European research funding. Some of the services available via CORDIS include:

* information on specific initiatives and research programmes,
* a current awareness service, and
* background information about EU institutions.

As well as information published by the EU, there are several other key
sources dealing with EU funding. For example, the UK has its own pages
on CORDIS, carrying information of special interest to the UK community. Under the direction of the Office of Science and Technology, this
venture aims to provide information about UK involvement in EU funded
research, concentrating on information for UK researchers about the Fifth
Framework. The site also contains a summary of the UK's involvement in
the Fourth Framework.

The United Kingdom Research Office (UKRO) alerts registered organisations to EU funding news, programme and policy information. Many UK
universities are subscribers and all subscribing organisations are listed
publicly on the UKRO Web site. Various services are offered to participating organisations, including email notification of funding news. UKRO
is sponsored by all six of the research councils as well as the British
Council.

For those ineligible for UKRO's services, the Mailbase mailing list, lis-
european-programmes, also provides regular updates.

Finally, the REFUND service (discussed below under 'Databases of funding sources') offers extensive coverage of EU funding sources.

CORDIS: www.cordis.lu/

CORDIS UK: www.cordis.lu/united_kingdom/

lis-european-programmes: www.mailbase.ac.uk/lists/lis-european-programmes/

United Kingdom Research Office (UKRO): www.ukro.ac.uk/

Charities

There are many charities in the UK that fund research on widely differing scales.

The Wellcome Trust is possibly the biggest benefactor of medical research in the UK. The Trust supports research in three areas: history of medicine, biomedical research and research into the relationship between medicine and society. The Wellcome Trust Web site offers advice to applicants and allows online applications for funding in some cases.

Other charities fund research into specific diseases or interventions. For example:

- The Cancer Research Campaign funds research into treatments for cancer and publishes extensive information on applying for funds on the Web.
- The Muscular Dystrophy Campaign funds research into treatment of neuromuscular conditions. Their Web site is used as a vehicle for fundraising and to inform about previous and ongoing research.
- Lasers for Life is a small charity which raises funds to support research into the benefits of laser therapy.

There are obviously many more charities supporting medical research in the UK than can be listed in the space available here. In addition, the amount of information given for researchers seeking funding differs widely from Web site to Web site. Fortunately, there are sources that bring together relevant information – some of the databases listed under 'Databases of funding sources' include references to funding from charities.

As a first port of call, a visit to the umbrella organisation, the Association of Medical Research Charities (AMRC) is worthwhile. The AMRC aims to further medical research in the UK and increase the effectiveness of its member charities. It provides information to assist those seeking funds as part of this remit. The AMRC Web site has a grants database that enables users to browse charities by category of applicant or type of award (postgraduate, travel, etc.) and gives plenty of detail about the charities included.

Association of Medical Research Charities: www.amrc.org.uk/

Cancer Research Campaign: www.crc.org.uk/

Lasers for Life: www.mersyworld.com/lasers/

Muscular Dystrophy Campaign: www.muscular-dystrophy.org/

Wellcome Trust: www.wellcome.ac.uk/

Databases of funding sources

The Wellcome Trust, in addition to providing funding itself, also publishes the Schemes database. This includes data on funding schemes run by over 100 UK organisations. The database may be searched by organisation name, scheme name or keyword.

RDInfo is a 'digest of health-related research funding and training opportunities'. Supported by a consortium of higher education and NHS organisations, the service is based at Leeds University. RDInfo lists organisations likely to offer funding with contact details and some award data, listing funding opportunities by closing date where appropriate. The database may be searched by keyword and the service is currently free.

REFUND is a Web-based service offered on a subscription basis to the academic and research community. It is created by the Research Services Unit at the University of Newcastle-upon-Tyne. Many UK universities have already subscribed and a list of subscribers is publicly available on the REFUND Web site.

Aiming to be a one-stop-shop for researchers from all disciplines, REFUND offers:

- a continuously updated research funding news bulletin,
- email alerts,
- background information on major sponsors and their awards, and
- summaries of useful information for particular categories of researcher.

REFUND covers funding from research councils, government departments, industry, major charities and the EU. All information is searchable.

RDInfo: www.leeds.ac.uk/rdinfo/

REFUND: www.refund.ncl.ac.uk/

Schemes: wisdom.wellcome.ac.uk/wisdom/fundhome.html

Finding research projects by source of funding

Several databases exist that contain details of all projects funded by an agency, be it a government department, research council or charitable trust. Knowing the source of funding of a project is, therefore, a great help in locating more information about it.

The National Research Register (NRR), mentioned in Chapter 3, is the register of research projects funded by the NHS. It also includes entries from the Medical Research Council's Clinical Trials Register, and details of reviews in progress collected by the NHS CRD. NRR contained information on approximately 64,000 research projects at the time of writing, including both completed and ongoing projects. The database is freely accessible and is published by Update Software Ltd on behalf of the UK Department of Health.

A database of all MRC funded projects may be consulted online at the Community of Science (COS). The MRC Funded Projects Database allows searches by title, keyword, investigator, institution or any combination of these, and therefore provides an opportunity to locate researchers working in a particular field. The Funded Projects Database is updated annually.

COS is a commercial Web publisher that originated at Johns Hopkins University in the US. It also publishes registers of research projects funded by the US National Institutes of Health (NIH) and National Science Foundation (NSF). COS is also a good source of personal details of North American researchers and academics – it claims to be the largest Web database of researchers in North America and contains about 500,000 profiles. Access to COS information is via subscription.

Another key source of US project information is CRISP, a database of information on research supported by the US Department of Health and Human Services. It includes NIH data, and therefore overlaps with material available from COS. However, it also includes details of projects funded by other US government agencies such as the Centers for Disease Control and Prevention, the Food and Drug Administration, the Health Resources and Services Administration and the Agency for Healthcare Policy and Research.

Outside the US and the UK, it may be less easy to find comprehensive, English language, national sources. CORDIS is again useful for projects funded by the EU. The best place to start for other projects is often the government Web site, or local medical research council or equivalent, if this is known.

Projects underway in Europe will be easier to locate once the ERGO database, now a pilot, is developed (possibly during the present Fifth Framework Programme). The project has conducted research into the technological and human challenges involved in creating a Europe-wide projects database. The ERGO pilot database contains details of over 80,000 projects across all disciplines.

Community of Science (COS): www.cos.com/

CORDIS: www.cordis.lu/

CRISP: www-commons.cit.nih.gov/crisp/

ERGO: www.cordis.lu/ergo/home.html

Medical Research Council (MRC) Funded Projects: fundedresearch.cos.com/MRC/

National Research Register: www.doh.gov.uk/nrr.htm

Finding projects by project type

Some databases have been compiled to allow users to rapidly locate specific types of projects. For example the UK Clearing House Outcomes Activities Database is a database of projects engaged in measuring health outcomes. It was compiled by the UK Clearing House on Health Outcomes, an organisation based within the Nuffield Institute for Health, at the University of Leeds and funded by the UK government. The database may be searched by keyword and information given includes the project title, aims, outcome measures, study group, setting, duration and contact details. It is now no longer updated.

Similarly, the National Database of Telemedicine, a joint project of the University of Portsmouth and the Department of Health, is a database of telemedicine projects in the UK based on a series of surveys commissioned by the Research and Development Division of the Department of Health.

One key type of research project, information about which may be required, is controlled drug trials. Some of the databases mentioned above, such as the NRR, contain details of these. There is also a new service dedicated to listing controlled trials called mRCT or meta Randomised Controlled Trials. mRCT is a venture being undertaken by the publisher Current Science Group. It includes details of controlled trials from several sources, including the MRC and the NRR, but also pharmaceutical companies such as Glaxo Wellcome plc and Schering Healthcare Ltd. Although the inclusion of commercial trials will mean that the database has international scope, its focus will be on UK trials.

Chapters 3 and 15 give further guidance on locating evidence-based medicine resources, including randomised controlled trials, on the Web.

mRCT: www.controlled-trials.com/

National Database of Telemedicine: www.dis.port.ac.uk/ndtm/

Outcomes Activities Database: www.leeds.ac.uk/nuffield/infoservices/UKCH/oad.html

Searching by location

Knowing the location of a project is a step towards finding information about it since most publicly funded organisations involved in research like to publicise their projects on the organisational Web site. For example, the National Institute for Medical Research, one of the laboratories funded by the MRC, publishes short descriptions of projects by research division.

Frequently, organisations will also list key personnel involved in projects. This may be via a separate database or linked with project details. For example, the Division of Microbiology and Infectious Diseases at the University of Nottingham lists staff and gives details of their current research interests and publications.

National Institute for Medical Research: www.nimr.mrc.ac.uk/

University of Nottingham Division of Microbiology and Infectious Diseases: www.nottingham.ac.uk/microbiology/

Chapter 8

Finding a job

The Internet is cheap to use on an individual or departmental level (if not for the organisation) once a connection has been established, compared to traditional methods of publishing. It allows various forms of information dissemination, from proactive distribution to a large number of known addresses via email to the more passive act of publication on a Web site. The process of publication can also be relatively rapid compared to other media. These characteristics make it an ideal medium for the circulation of time-sensitive information that needs to be issued regularly to a large but specific audience. Job adverts are a prime example of this type of data and this chapter gives tips for finding and disseminating them online.

Advantages of online job seeking

The Internet is now a key resource for job seekers and for organisations seeking to fill vacancies. Organisations can save paper (and money) by:

- publishing job adverts on an organisational Web site;
- distributing the necessary application forms to potential applicants electronically;
- circulating adverts by email or newsgroup; and
- accepting expressions of interest by email.

Individual job seekers can:

- publish their CVs on the Web;
- look for vacancies in a specific profession, organisation or locality;
- seek information about prospective employers unobtrusively; and
- gain access to online versions of key print sources of vacancies, such as newspapers.

The Internet also provides a number of entirely new services with no equivalent. Key email and Web-based resources are highlighted below.

Email/newsgroups

Joining a few relevant email lists is perhaps the easiest way to look for new vacancies. Adverts are frequently circulated in this way, especially those with an information or technology/computing component.

For employers, email represents a low cost, efficient, timely method of reaching a potentially global audience. However, while email is a means of reaching out to more people, it should not be overlooked that it also allows very specific audiences to be targeted. After all, email lists and newsgroups effectively address millions of email users as they are usefully arranged by subject or common interest.

The existence of Mailbase as the UK higher education sector's provider of email list facilities is discussed in Chapter 18. However, it is worthy of a mention here as a key tool for recruitment. Mailbase's portfolio of over 2,000 mailing lists includes nearly 200 on topics related to medicine and the biosciences, the majority open to organisations wishing to post job advertisements. Often notification of a post becoming vacant may reach Mailbase list members first before the advert appears in journals or other print media. Figure 8.1 displays a page from the archive of the list medical-it, a list for those interested in the use of technology in medical education, showing several adverts appearing in one month.

Figure 8.1: Vacancies on medical-it

medical-it archives - February 1998 (by date)

Previous month | Next month | Other months | Search | **List Homepage**

Sort by: Thread | Subject | Author

Messages

- BMiS Meeting @city.ac.uk - Fri, 27 Feb 1998
- Seminars on medical visualization and imaging (Manchester UK, 18/3/98) @afs.mcc.ac.uk - Wed, 25 Feb 1998
- Conference - WWW in Lab Medicine - Tue, 24 Feb 1998
- C&IT Developer Post - Job Ad - Thu, 19 Feb 1998
- Fw: Call for Abstracts - Sun, 15 Feb 1998
- New CAL post - Tue, 10 Feb 1998
- VHP announcements - Mon, 9 Feb 1998
- BMIS Workshop on PG Education @city.ac.uk - Fri, 6 Feb 1998

Newsgroups may be useful also, particularly for posts in biomedical research, which are frequently sought and offered in the groups bionet.jobs and bionet.jobs.wanted. The latest postings may be viewed on the Web, and it is also possible to post messages via the Web. In contrast to Mailbase, bionet is used by an international audience and usually the majority of jobs posted are based in the US.

---

bionet.jobs: www.bio.net/hypermail/EMPLOYMENT/

bionet.jobs.wanted: www.bio.net/hypermail/EMPLOYMENT-WANTED/

Web resources

The Web presents the job-seeker with an immense choice of sources.

Organisational Web sites

Writing to companies and other organisations to ask if they have vacancies may become a thing of the past as so many organisations are now placing adverts on their Web sites. Publicly funded bodies such as universities and hospitals are particularly good at doing this and many have extensive and well-organised vacancy lists available on the Web. For example, Brighton Healthcare Trust, one of the first hospital trusts to establish a Web site, has a list of vacancies permanently displayed online, updated fortnightly.

At University College London, jobs are listed at the university level and often also at the departmental level – see the pages for the Medical Research Council (MRC) Laboratory for Molecular Cell Biology, for example. Consequently the provision of job information is not uniform and in some cases may not be offered at all, or there may be more than one page where jobs are listed.

Brighton Healthcare Trust: www.rsch.org.uk/rsch/jobs1.htm

Medical Research Council (MRC) Laboratory for Molecular Cell Biology jobs: www.ucl.ac.uk/LMCB/jobs.html

University College London vacancies: www.ucl.ac.uk/personnel/job.htm

---

Newspapers and periodicals

Many publishers are now providing online access to their journal titles. Frequently, a selection of material is made available for free as a taster to advertise the whole. Vacancies sections are ideal for this type of promotion because they are ephemeral and because their usefulness is greatly enhanced by the addition of a simple keyword search facility.

The Guardian newspaper, for example, has placed all of its job advertisements published throughout the week on Jobs Unlimited. Job seekers can see adverts arranged as they would be in the printed newspaper (divided into broad sections such as education, public, science and technology, each section corresponding to a day of the week), or browse jobs by sector. Adverts may also be searched by keyword or phrase, which can be invaluable for locating a specific vacancy.

Some medical journals have also followed this route. One of the most important sites for UK medicine must be the full online version of the *BMJ* Classified section. It is unrivalled as the place to look for UK hospital and community health posts and also carries some advertising of overseas appointments. In addition, the *BMJ* Classified section offers the full text of Career Focus, a regular column tackling career, accreditation and training issues affecting UK doctors. Vacancies may be browsed by job type but there is no search facility.

> *BMJ* Classified: classified.bmj.com/
>
> Jobs Unlimited: www.jobsunlimited.co.uk/

Databases: general

Perhaps the most exciting developments in the recruitment field are those being offered by publishers seeking to break the mould and create totally new services with no printed equivalent. These seek to replace existing methods of recruitment and are becoming more common: in the UK, the academic sector alone is served by several major sites.

Jobs.ac.uk is a service funded by income and a consortium of UK higher education bodies. Organisations pay to advertise posts at a commercial rate and job seekers can view advertisements for free. Jobs.ac.uk carried approximately 1,000 vacancies at the time of writing which may be searched or browsed by discipline. After looking around jobs.ac.uk, you may be surprised to encounter the NISS Vacancies Service. Like jobs.ac.uk, NISS is funded by the higher education community, and, like jobs.ac.uk, the Vacancies Service lists academic posts in subject categories with a search option. Unlike jobs.ac.uk, NISS offers this service freely to both job seekers and employers.

Outside academia, the same trend towards centralisation is evident. In the commercial sector, a number of organisations are jostling for pole position. One of the largest is Monster, a global online recruitment company with sites in the UK, Canada, the USA, the Netherlands, Belgium,

Australia and France. Monster have a healthcare section which frequently advertises NHS posts.

Coordinated online recruitment is also becoming more common in local government. In the London Borough of Croydon the JobMart service, maintained by Croydon Council, advertises local jobs in council departments, schools, further education colleges and hospitals and is also used by local recruitment agencies.

---

jobs.ac.uk: www.jobs.ac.uk/

Croydon JobMart: www.croydon.gov.uk/jobmart/

Monster Healthcare: healthcare.monster.co.uk/

NISS Vacancies Service: www.vacancies.ac.uk/

Databases: medicine and the biosciences

There are also specific services serving the medical and biological research communities. These sites can carry a greater variety and number of opportunities than jobs.ac.uk and similar national services, and many advertise overseas posts as well as those available in the UK.

A well-established service, Biomedical Research Vacancies, is part of the Wellcome Trust's WISDOM suite of databases. The database advertises posts in the UK for biomedical research assistants, studentships and technicians, but not permanent positions. The database cannot be browsed but it can be searched by keyword and searches can be restricted according to type of vacancy and location.

The BioMedNet Jobs Exchange claims to be international, but as so often happens, this implies an emphasis on North America. On the plus side, Jobs Exchange is so well-stocked that it is still useful for UK vacancies, and it is also set out clearly, with a browsable section making it possible to view vacancies by type of post, location or specialty. There is also a good search feature. Registration is required to use all BioMedNet services.

Professional organisations often maintain smaller lists of vacancies in specific disciplines or specialties. For example, the British Society for Immunology or the Dental Practice Board of England and Wales, which lists vacancies as part of its Dentanet service. Visiting the Web sites of a few key professional organisations in your chosen subject area is therefore always worthwhile when job seeking.

Biomedical Research Vacancies: wisdom.wellcome.ac.uk/wisdom/jobshome.html

BioMedNet Jobs Exchange: jobs.bmn.com/

British Society for Immunology posts vacant: immunology.org/jobs.htm

Dentanet recruitment: www.dentanet.org.uk/dentanet/recruit/recruit.html

Chapter 9

Keeping up-to-date

Recent years have witnessed a growth in integrated information products promising to feed information to the desktop. Such services typically
offer key databases, access to selected Internet sites, and added extras
such as job 'marts' and online shopping. The essence of such services is
that they assist the user in seeking out timely, relevant information. This
chapter examines ways of keeping up-to-date, covering: popular news,
health news, current awareness, official news and conference news. Both
free and commercial resources are highlighted and how they might be
brought together on the desktop.

Popular news: reading all about it

The Internet-ready inhabitants of the UK are peculiarly blessed by having
online all of the main, national 'quality' daily broadsheets. *The Guardian,
The Independent, The Daily Telegraph* and *The Times* are freely available on
the Internet. That is equivalent to saying that the principal output of four
independent news gathering organisations may be accessed in minutes
from the desktop, giving the Internet user four different views of the popular news, updated daily.

Free access, without even the need to register, is also available to a fifth
source containing information from the largest, and probably most highly
respected news gathering organisation in the world, the BBC. The BBC
News service has the added advantage of being continuously updated
throughout the day.

It is also possible to search several news sources in one go. An example of
such a search tool is NewsTracker, which searches more than 300 online
newspapers and magazines that are available for free on the Web.
NewsTracker can be set to track up to 50 pre-established topics, the most
current articles from which may be viewed by visiting personalised
NewsTracker pages. My NewsPage from Individual.com on the other hand,
offers a personalised electronic news service consisting of daily headlines and news briefs that match a custom news profile and are delivered
by email every weekday.

BBC: news.bbc.co.uk/

Electronic Telegraph (*The Daily Telegraph* and *Sunday Telegraph*): www.telegraph.co.uk/

Individual.com: www.individual.com/

News Unlimited (*The Guardian*): www.newsunlimited.co.uk/

NewsTracker: nt.excite.com/

The Independent: www.independent.co.uk/

The Times Internet Edition: www.the-times.co.uk/

Health news and current awareness

Some of the popular news services have a dedicated health section. These may bring together health-related news in one place, or give access to longer, feature-type articles. Reuters Health provides daily news, and its consumer-oriented health news sources remain viewable for free for ten days via its Health eLine archive. CNN also provides daily updated pages relating to health. The BBC News Health site is another good example. There are also sites that offer digests of health-related topics from a range of sources, for example Health News.

The above services are aimed at the general public and tend to define health too narrowly, often concentrating on health in the sense of well-being, not including other items such as those on disease outbreaks or regulatory news. UK medical professionals can gain access to a set of integrated news pages drawn from both popular and professional sources via Doctors.net. (Doctors.net also gives members access to closed discussion groups, a bookshop, databases and vacancies.)

Other services include Reuters Medical News, a subscription service bringing together news gathered from over 100 key medical journals plus other database services. Reuters Medical News is compiled from scanning key research journals as they are published. With a little ingenuity and some hard work it is possible to set up a current awareness system of this kind for yourself. Many research journals now offer Internet users the option of receiving tables of contents by email. This may be offered either by the particular journal, or by a publishing house that carries many titles and offers the service en masse. *The Lancet* emails table of contents data to anyone registering for this service at their Web site, *The Lancet* Interactive.

Many journals can be covered at once using Contents Direct that covers Elsevier, Pergamon, North Holland and Excerpta Medica imprints.

A little more sophisticated, and perhaps even aspiring to the level of service libraries have provided for the past few decades, is Customised @lerts from the *BMJ*. The user submits an email address and selects from several services, including email alerts of articles published in the *BMJ* in a list of approximately 100 clinical and non-clinical topic areas.

Journals are also making it easier for journalists to home in on breaking news of research findings, as many now provide press release pages online. Like other journals in health and medicine, *JAMA* offers consumer-orientated Medical News Headlines from Reuters and the American Medical Association.

EurekAlert! offers a centralised service for news releases announcing the latest research advances in science, medicine, health, and technology. EurekAlert! is produced by the American Association for the Advancement of Science (AAAS), with technical support provided by Stanford University. Contributors include universities and colleges, scientific and medical journals, companies, government agencies, and nonprofit organizations. Different embargo policies apply for the scientific journals that post to EurekAlert!, and registration for access to the embargoed areas is open only to journalists and public information officers. Releases may also relate to grant announcements, prizes awarded to scientists or journalists, press conferences, scientific meetings and newly published books and may include links to supplementary material. Fees are levied for posting information via EurekAlert!.

MedWebPlus offers a comprehensive collection of links to health and medicine news sites.

BMJ Customised @lerts: www.bmj.com/cgi/customalert/

CNN Health: www.cnn.com/HEALTH/

Doctors.net: www.doctors.net.uk/

Elsevier Science Contents Direct: www.elsevier.nl:80/homepage/ about/contentsdirect/Menu.shtml

EurekAlert!: www.eurekalert.org/

Health News: www.health-news.co.uk/

JAMA Medical News Headlines: For example, at www.ama-assn.org/insight/gen_hlth/med_news.htm

---

MedWebPlus: News:
www.medwebplus.com/subject/News_[Publication_Type].html

Reuters Health: www.reutershealth.com/

Reuters Medical News: www.reutershealth.com/uk/

The Lancet: www.thelancet.com/

Official news

It is now possible to follow the progress of a piece of legislation from green paper into law via the Internet. Keeping up-to-date with government business is also facilitated by a number of official sites and services.

The House of Commons Select Committees place reports and press releases online, including those of the Health and Science and Technology select committees.

Substantial official documents are very often made available online by the Stationery Office. The Stationery Office Web site lists official publications by date and by government department so that it is possible to see listed all online material published on behalf of the Department of Health (DoH). This includes new green and white papers (e.g. Our Healthier Nation), inquiry reports (e.g. the Acheson report into Inequalities in Health), government responses to select committees and reports of special advisory committees (such as the Spongiform Encephalopathy Advisory Committee). Those particularly needing to stay up-to-date with publications from the Stationery Office should use the online Daily List.

The DoH itself publishes a substantial amount of up-to-date material. As well as press releases (updated daily), the DoH Web site now offers a searchable database of all recent Departmental Circulars (including Executive Letters) called Circulars on the Internet or COIN. Another recent innovation is 'Publications on the Internet', or POINT, a database of all DoH publications available online from 1996 onwards. This is invaluable for ferreting out recently published material.

COIN: www.doh.gov.uk/coinh.htm

Daily List: www.national-publishing.co.uk/d_listfr.html

Government press releases: www.coi.gov.uk/

House of Commons Select Committees: www.parliament.uk/
commons/selcom/CMSEL.HTM

POINT: www.doh.gov.uk/publications/pointh.html

Stationery Office: www.the-stationery-office.co.uk/

Conferences

The best way to ensure you receive news about forthcoming conferences
and other events is undoubtedly to find a forum, whether email,
newsgroup, or Web-based, covering your subject area (see Chapter 18 for
more information). Posting a call for papers or an announcement to relevant fora has become an essential part of any conference organiser's
publicity strategy.

As far as the Web is concerned, sadly, there are few free central sources of
information. The best place to look will depend upon your field, and
some fields are better served than others. This is not to say that there is a
lack of event-related information on the Internet – far from it. Many conferences have their own Web sites with information about the conference
venue, programme and sometimes online booking procedures. One such
example is the Web site for the 8th International Congress on Medical
Librarianship (ICML 2000).

Traditional commercial online hosts make available conference databases,
which may be accessed on a pay-as-you-go basis. For example, Dialog
make the EventLine database, published by Elsevier Science and traditionally accessed via commercial online host services, available through
the medicine section of their DialogSelect Open Access service on the
Web. Users searching for *Upcoming Meetings* are presented with the titles
of records from the EventLine database and may view full details for
$1.75 per record (at the time of writing). No registration is necessary (pay-
ment is by credit card) but users who do wish to register receive a discount.

DialogSelect Open Access - Medicine: openaccess.dialog.com/
med/

ICML 2000: www.icml.org/

Tools for current awareness

There are so many sources of up-to-date information on the Web that it
can be difficult to keep track of them all. For users who wish to revisit sites

methodically, it is possible to set up a browser to do some of the work. Chapter 20 describes the features of the most popular browsers, and Chapter 21 describes online bookmark services that could also be used.

For more traditional current awareness services, covering the published biomedical literature, see Chapters 15 and 16.

Section 2

Finding information on the Internet

The temptation simply to click on the 'search' button provided by Internet Explorer or Netscape Navigator (see Figures 10.1 and 10.2) can be irresistible, and it is often assumed that clicking on this button is the way to search the Internet. While this offers one approach to searching, success in finding the information you seek may be compromised by this arbitrary choice.

Clicking on the Netscape Navigator Search button causes a page of generic search tools to be displayed (the Netscape Netcenter Net Search page), as selected by Netscape Communications Corporation, the company that produces Netscape Navigator. A random choice is offered and search results will vary depending on which tool is selected. Clicking again on the Search button will produce a different choice. An additional choice of search engines is offered at the Netscape Communications Corporation home page itself, or Netscape Netcenter, which can be reached by clicking on the Netscape Navigator browser's N logo (see Figure 10.1).

Figure 10.1 Netscape Navigator version 4.7 and Netscape Netcenter

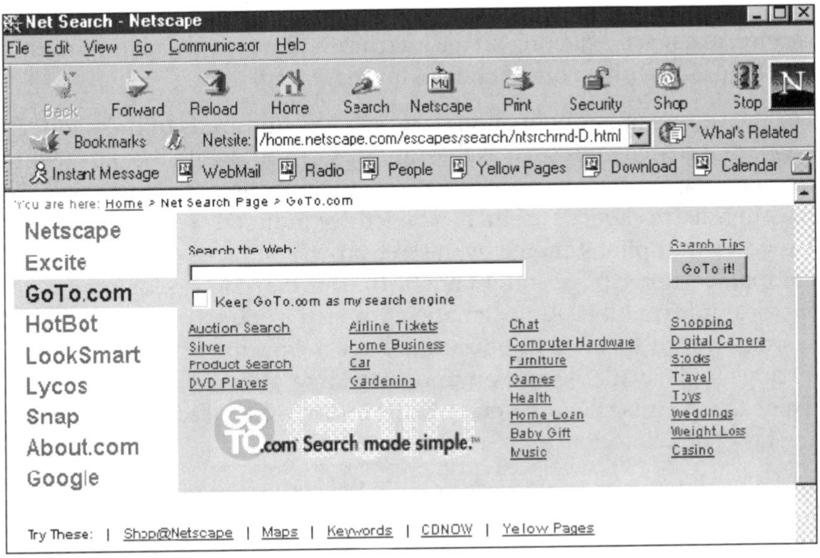

Figure 10.2 Internet Explorer version 5 and the Microsoft Network (MSN)

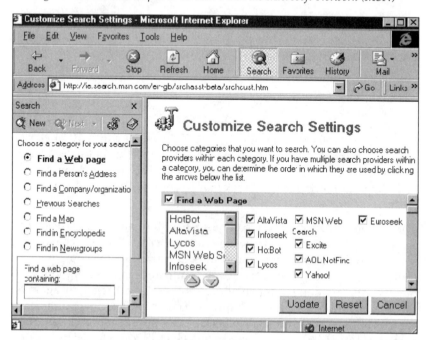

Clicking on the Microsoft Internet Explorer Search button produces a similar effect: an Explorer search bar appears offering the option to choose a search tool from those displayed. Microsoft Corporation, the company that produces Internet Explorer, has selected these. Though by no means complete, the list of search tools provides searchers with several starting points, depending on the type of search required. Microsoft's msn.com service, reached by clicking on the Internet Explorer default Home button (see Figure 10.2), also offers choices for searching.

For those who are patient enough to scan the hundreds of links to Web pages that search tools such as these may return, and with the persistence to connect to each one separately in order to assess its value, this approach may reveal a number of useful hits directly or indirectly related to a query. However, the options offered by the Web browser utilities or at the browser companies' home pages might not be the optimal choices for health and medical information. A systematic approach is likely to achieve better results and for this it is important to have a working knowledge of the various tools available and an understanding of how they are created. This section aims to equip you with the information needed to approach the task with confidence.

Chapter 10 looks at how to use generic Web search engines for the purpose of identifying relevant information quickly. Metasearch engines, which allow the user to query several search tools simultaneously, are covered in Chapter 11. Chapter 12 provides an overview of generic Web directories and review sites. Health and medical search tools and information gateways were developed to identify and describe resources likely to be of greater value to health education, research and clinical practice. Chapters 13 and 14 provide insights into how these subject-based tools can be exploited so that information seekers can begin a fruitful exploration of available resources.

Traditional sources for accessing the medical literature, namely journals and bibliographic databases, usually need to be accessed separately because their content is inaccessible via search engines and other Internet search tools. It is easy to envision the Internet as an online library, but research-based information continues to be locked mostly within traditional sources, and this seems likely to continue for the foreseeable future. Chapters 15 and 16 therefore provide an outline of approaches to retrieving information from a range of such sources.

Lastly, many of the skills needed to use a search tool are transferable. While Chapter 10 includes an examination of common search features that apply across a range of different tools, Chapter 17 outlines a more strategic approach to searching.

Microsoft Network (msn.com): home.microsoft.com/;
also available via international sites worldwide e.g. msn.co.uk/

Netscape Netcenter: home.netscape.com/

Netscape Netcenter. Net Search: home.netscape.com/escapes/search/

Chapter 10

Search engines

This chapter discusses one of the more common ways of searching for information on the Internet: using Web search engines.

There are many Web search engines from which to choose – a selection of the larger ones is listed below. Web search engines are compiled with the aid of programs called robots, crawlers or spiders, that visit Web sites collecting page addresses and capturing the words that make up the pages. Indexing software then indexes each instance of every word from the captured pages, and records information such as the use of capitalisation, the position of the word within the page and the address of the page. These details allow searchers to retrieve individual words, phrases in specific word order, and words or phrases with specific capitalisation.

The spiders visit sites regularly and the indexes are updated recording any changes that may have been made since the last visit. Different search engines index different numbers of pages per day. AltaVista, for example, indexes up to 10 million pages daily and 'continuously crawls and indexes the 2,000 most active sites on the WWW as well as selected public service and government sites to provide even fresher search results for the most popular sites'.[1]

Most search engines are generic and do not attempt to restrict their coverage to health and medicine alone. Search engine indexes cannot be browsed: their sheer size and lack of subject organisation makes that impractical.

AltaVista: www.altavista.com/ (or simply av.com/)
Also provides a search only interface via Raging Search:
www.raging.com/
A text-only search page is also available: www.altavista.com/cgi-bin/query?text

Excite: www.excite.com/

FAST Search: www.alltheweb.com/

Google: www.google.com/

HotBot: www.hotbot.com/

Northern Light: www.northernlight.com/

AltaVista: an example of a Web search engine

AltaVista is one of the better known Web search engines, estimated at the time of writing to cover over 350 million Web pages.[2] Its size, frequency and regularity of updating, and flexibility of search options are AltaVista's prime advantages. Northern Light, Excite and HotBot provide comparable breadth of coverage and similar flexibility of search options. More recently, FAST Search and Google have become available, and their coverage may at times be competitive compared to that of AltaVista.

AltaVista, like most Web search engines, offers a Simple Search interface and an additional Advanced Search interface, each of which offers a search form of varying complexity. Unlike many other search engines, AltaVista requires different search notations to be used with each interface and each search approach is likely to produce a different set of results. In contrast, other search engines, such as Northern Light, allow search queries to be employed interchangeably in both their simple and advanced search interfaces. Tables 10.1 and 10.2 summarise a range of search features, as available in AltaVista and Northern Light, for comparison. A sample query is displayed in the right-hand column, with indicative numbers of hits returned given in square brackets.

Table 10.1: Sample search queries using AltaVista

AltaVista Simple Search	
<ul><li>Use +- notation: + indicates that a term must be present - indicates that a term must not be present</li><li>Use truncation (*)</li><li>Search for phrases using double quotation marks (" ")</li><li>Exclude commercial sites, e.g. using -host:com -host:co.uk</li></ul>	*+zinc +gluconate +lozenge* +cold* +child** [460] *+"zinc gluconate" +lozenge* +cold* +child** [418] *+zinc +gluconate +lozenge* +cold* +child* -host:com -host:co.uk* [74] *+"zinc gluconate" +lozenge* +cold* +child* -host:com -host:co.uk* [103]
AltaVista Advanced Search	
<ul><li>Use truncation (*)</li><li>Search for phrases using double quotation marks (" ")</li><li>Use Boolean operators (AND, OR, AND NOT)</li><li>Arrange the search terms in concept groups using parentheses</li><li>Exclude commercial sites, e.g. using AND NOT (host:com OR host:co.uk)</li><li>Restrict to educational sites, e.g. using AND (host:edu or host:ac.uk)</li></ul>	*("zinc gluconate" OR "zinc lozenge*") AND cold* AND (child* OR infant*) AND NOT (host:com OR host:co.uk)* [377] *("zinc gluconate" OR "zinc lozenge*") AND cold* AND (child* OR infant*) AND (host:edu OR host:ac.uk)* [77]

Table 10.2: Sample search queries using Northern Light

Northern Light Simple or Power Search	
• Use +- notation: + indicates that a term must be present - indicates that a term must not be present • Use truncation (*) • Search for phrases using double quotation marks (" ") • Use Boolean operators (AND, OR, [AND] NOT) • Arrange the search terms in concept groups using parentheses • Exclude commercial sites, e.g. using *NOT url:com NOT url:co.uk*; the same result can be achieved using *NOT (url:com OR url:co.uk)* • Restrict to educational sites, e.g. using *AND (url:edu OR url:ac.uk)*	*+zinc +gluconate +lozenge* +cold* +child* NOT url:com NOT url:co.uk* [128] *+"zinc gluconate" +lozenge* +cold* +child* NOT url:com NOT url:co.uk* [120] *+"zinc gluconate" +lozenge* +cold* +child* NOT (url:com OR url:co.uk)* [120] *("zinc gluconate" OR "zinc lozenge*") AND cold* AND (child* OR infant*) NOT (url:com OR url:co.uk)* [358] *("zinc gluconate" OR "zinc lozenge*") AND cold* AND (child* OR infant*) AND (url:edu OR url:ac.uk)* [80]

AltaVista Simple Search

Figure 10.3 illustrates the AltaVista Simple Search interface. AltaVista Simple Search allows language to be set as a search option: only one language can be chosen at a time from the preselected list (click on the down arrow next to 'any language' to see the drop-down menu and the available choices). Search terms can be entered as a question, as single words, as a phrase or using the +- notation (see Table 10.1). Up to 200 hits are returned in ranked order.

Figure 10.3 AltaVista Simple Search

Typing one word will usually result in an unmanageable number of matches to sift through – searching for *tuberculosis* will generate tens of thousands of hits. In addition, searching for a single word increases the chances of retrieving matches to pages that use the word out of the intended context. For instance, searching for *discern* will return pages that contain the word in any context. Fortunately, AltaVista and other search engines allow case specific queries – a search for *DISCERN* in upper case will select only those pages where the term is entered entirely in upper case. Included will be those pages that refer to DISCERN: the assessment instrument for the critical appraisal of written consumer health information. The difference in numbers of pages returned is significant, even though using all upper case will still return pages out of context (e.g. where page creators have simply entered the word in upper case for emphasis).

The alternative is to compose a search query that is specific enough to return a manageable number of hits, using features such as those indicated in Table 10.1.

To search for the effectiveness of zinc gluconate lozenges in treating the common cold in children using AltaVista Simple Search, the following might be entered:

+zinc +gluconate +lozenge* +cold* +child*

The +- notation simply requires a + or - to be placed directly before a search term (word or phrase) that is specifically required (+) or conversely not required (-). All terms in the above query would be required to be present in the pages retrieved. To exclude Web pages produced by international or UK commercial organisations it is possible to enter the following query:

+zinc +gluconate +lozenge* +cold* +child* -host:com -host:co.uk

However, care should be exercised when excluding sources. For example, a search for *"multidrug resistant tuberculosis"* retrieved 1,541 hits at the time of writing. A search for *"multidrug resistant tuberculosis" -host:com* reduced the number to 1,044. Among those missed with this search query were the tables of contents from six issues of the *BMJ*, simply because the address of the *BMJ* is http://www.bmj.com/. One of the articles to which these linked, the full text of which was available for free online, was an editorial titled: Diagnosing multidrug resistant tuberculosis in Britain: clinical suspicion should drive rapid diagnosis.[3]

A different type of search query would need to be used with AltaVista Advanced Search for the same search topic (see below).

AltaVista Advanced Search

To switch from Simple to Advanced Search, simply click on the tab marked Advanced Search. As well as allowing language to be specified, the Advanced Search interface also allows the selection of a range of dates and the option to show only one result per Web site (see Figure 10.4). Two search boxes are displayed, each serving a different purpose. The upper box is reserved for entering Boolean expressions (using the AND, OR and AND NOT Boolean operators, see below). When search queries are entered in this box alone, AltaVista Advanced Search returns matches in no particular order and over 200 may be returned. If terms are entered in the lower box, matches will be returned in ranked order and the number of hits returned will be restricted to no more than 200. The choice of terms entered in this lower search box will influence the ranking of the results. Any search term can be used for the purpose of ranking, if necessary repeating the same terms used in the Boolean search expression (omitting the Boolean operators), or introducing new ones.

Figure 10.4 AltaVista Advanced Search

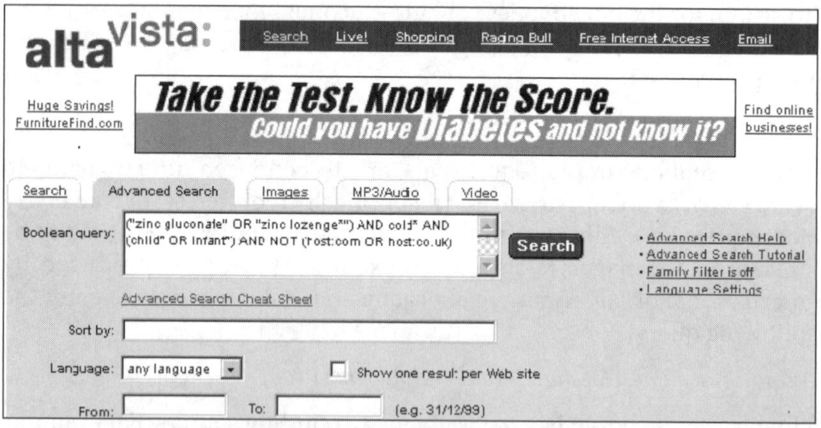

To search for information about the effectiveness of zinc gluconate lozenges in treating the common cold in children using AltaVista Advanced Search, the following query may be typed in the Boolean query box:

("zinc gluconate" OR "zinc lozenge*") AND cold* AND (child* OR infant*)

Entering this alone as a Boolean search query produced 1,621 matches in no particular order. Additionally entering *gluconate* as the ranking term produced 89 pages in ranked order.

Entering *("zinc gluconate" OR "zinc lozenge*") AND cold* AND (child* OR infant*) AND NOT (host:com OR host:co.uk)* as a Boolean search query produced 377 matches in no particular order. Entering *gluconate* as the ranking term produced 85 pages in ranked order.

A search conducted using AltaVista Advanced Search will often produce a different set of matches compared to Simple Search because the search logic is different. AltaVista Advanced Search generally allows a more sophisticated logic to be applied: the use of Boolean expressions as well as the NEAR proximity operator allows a search query to be specified precisely (see Boolean expressions below). For example, the Boolean OR operator makes it possible to search for search term synonyms using AltaVista Advanced Search, which would be impossible to specify precisely using the +- notation in AltaVista's Simple Search.

Searching with other Web search engines: common search features

Table 10.2 illustrates how similar search queries could be submitted to Northern Light which, together with AltaVista, FAST Search and Google, was reported to be among the largest search engines at the time of writing (2). Both the +- notation and Boolean searching are supported. Using Northern Light, either form of search query can be employed interchangeably in both the Simple and Power Search interfaces. Support for key search features can differ significantly between search engines, as indicated in Table 10.3.

Table 10.3: Web search engines: comparison of key search features
(featuring on following page)

+- notation

Most major search engines support the use of +- notation:

- a + placed directly before a search term (word or phrase) indicates that the term is required to be present in pages retrieved; and
- a - placed directly before a search term (word or phrase) indicates that the term is required to be absent from pages retrieved.

For example, the expression *+zinc +gluconate +lozenge* +cold* +child** requires that all search terms are present. The expression *+zinc +gluconate +lozenge* +cold* +child* -host:com -host:co.uk* requires that no pages are retrieved that contain com. or co.uk in the host name.

Inevitably, excluding international and UK commercial sites would also exclude potentially useful pages, so this feature would need to be used with caution. For example, the above search query would miss a journal article[4] available online from Medscape, which reviewed new approaches to the treatment of the common cold and concluded that 'further investigation is essential before concluding that zinc is useful'.

Medscape: www.medscape.com/

Table 10.3: Web search engines: comparison of key search features

	Uses + -	Uses Boolean / proximity operators	Uses phrase searching	Truncation
AltaVista Indexes 350 million pages	Yes (only in Simple Search)	Yes (only in Advanced Search) AND (&) OR (|) AND NOT (!) Proximity operator NEAR (~) allows a search for terms up to 10 words apart	Yes	* (0 or more characters) Can be used within a word, though at least three non-wildcard characters must be present before the * notation The wildcard replaces a maximum of five characters
FAST Search Indexes 340 million pages	Supports searches for "all of the words", "any of the words" or "the exact phrase". Up to three search terms may be specified	No	Allows searching for an exact phrase	Not supported
Google Indexes 580 million pages fully and 500 million pages partially	Yes	No	Yes	Not supported
Northern Light Indexes 260 million pages	Yes	Yes AND OR NOT; may also use AND NOT	Yes	* (0 or more characters) % (single character) Can be used within a word, though at least 4 non-wildcard characters must be present before the * notation

Boolean expressions

If a search engine allows the use of Boolean operators, it is possible to specify that:

- a page must be included if all the search terms separated by AND occur in the same page; for example, a search for *"zinc gluconate" AND "common cold"* will retrieve only those pages that include both the phrase *"zinc gluconate"* and the phrase *"common cold"*.

- a page must be included if any of the search terms connected with OR occur in the page; for example, a search for *"zinc gluconate" OR "zinc lozenge*"* will retrieve pages that include either of the two phrases.

- a page must be excluded if the search terms following NOT occur in the page; for example, a search for *"zinc gluconate" AND NOT (host:com OR host:co.uk)* will retrieve pages that include the phrase *"zinc gluconate"* but which are not provided by international or UK commercial organisations.

Note: using NOT rather than AND NOT in AltaVista Advanced Search returns a 'Syntax error(bad query)' message.

AltaVista Advanced Search supports the use of the NEAR proximity operator, allowing a search to be conducted for terms up to ten words apart. For example, a search for *sildenafil NEAR citrate* using AltaVista Advanced Search will find those pages in which the two terms occur sufficiently close as to avoid retrieval out of context, though not necessarily side by side. At the time of writing, proximity operators were not widely supported by other search engines.

Complex search queries

Multiple Boolean operators can be used within a search query. It is advisable to arrange the search terms in concept groups using parentheses to keep the search logic clear. For example, consider the search for information about the effectiveness of zinc gluconate lozenges in treating the common cold in children.

Table 10.4: Developing a search query: arranging search terms in concept groups

Population		Intervention	Source filter
common cold	age group	zinc product	type of provider institution
cold*	child* OR infant*	"zinc gluconate" OR "zinc lozenge*"	host:edu OR host:ac.uk

Table 10.4 illustrates how concept groups might be derived, based loosely on the idea of the three-part clinical question.[5]

Each of the four different concept groups may include synonyms as search terms. The search terms for each concept group are combined together using the OR operator and each concept group is bounded by parentheses. The different concept groups are linked together using AND.

```
(child* OR infant*) AND ("zinc gluconate" OR "zinc lozenge*")  ...

|___ Concept 1 ___|        |_____ Concept 2 _____|  ...
```

The resulting search query might become: *cold* AND (child* OR infant*) AND ("zinc gluconate" OR "zinc lozenge*") AND (host:edu OR host:ac.uk)*.

Phrase searching

All three search engines allow searches for a phrase by using double quotation marks to bound the words that make up the phrase. Entering terms without quotation marks may retrieve pages in which the words do not necessarily occur in the same context. For example, a search for *sildenafil citrate* without the double quotation marks may retrieve pages containing the word sildenafil, but with citrate in a completely different context, as in the following extract from a page retrieved using Northern Light: 'The FDA has approved the marketing of fentanyl citrate "lollipops" for cancer patients with severe breakthrough pain'.[6]

AltaVista Advanced Search supports automatic phrase searching, leading to more precise hits being returned.[7] For example a search for *zinc lozenge* returned 3,035 matches, the same number of matches as for a search for the phrase *"zinc lozenge*"*. By comparison, a search for *zinc NEAR lozenge* returned 3,961 matches, whereas a search for *zinc AND lozenge* returned 5,353 matches. As may be expected, phrase searching is likely to produce the most precise results, while the use of NEAR can be expected to produce more precise results than the use of AND.

Truncation and wildcards

Most major search engines allow the use of truncation. Most commonly, the asterisk (*) can be used for right-hand truncation (i.e. at the end of a search term) to retrieve different word endings, as in *lozenge**. AltaVista requires at least three non-wildcard characters to be present before the * notation, whereas Northern Light requires at least four.

Many search engines also allow the asterisk to be used within a search term as a wildcard, replacing zero or more characters, to account for variant spellings. For example, a search for *thalass*emia* retrieves occurrences of both thalassemia and thalassaemia. A search for *thal*emia* would retrieve the same, and also a variety of misspellings (e.g. thalecemia, thalessemia, thallassaemia, thallasaemia, thalasemia and so on) which might otherwise be missed.

Northern Light additionally allows the use of the % wildcard, permitting a single character to be masked. For example, searching for *"necroti%ing fasciitis"* returns the same number of matches as *"necrotising fasciitis"* OR *"necrotizing fasciitis"*.

Note: a search for *beclomet** using AltaVista will not retrieve pages about beclomethasone that do not also refer to beclomet or beclometasone, although it will retrieve occurrences of beclometasona, if non-English pages are included in the search. The wildcard replaces a maximum of five characters in AltaVista, so it would be necessary to truncate at *beclometh** in order not to miss the majority of matches for beclomethasone: searching for *beclomet** (English-language pages) retrieved 157 hits, whereas a search for *beclomethasone* retrieved over 3,763 hits at the time of writing.

Word stemming

Northern Light automatically stems most common plural and singular forms of words;[8] for example, a search for *"zinc lozenge"* will also return results containing *"zinc lozenges"*, and *vice versa*. Support for word stemming is variable across search engines.

Capitalisation

AltaVista allows searches for terms with mixed capitalisation, and will treat an all-lower case search query as non-case sensitive. For example a search for *"Multidrug Resistant Tuberculosis"* using AltaVista returned 350 matches, compared with 1,541 matches found for *"multidrug resistant tuberculosis"*. A search for *mdr-tb* retrieved 1,414 pages whereas a search for *MDR-TB* returned 1,400, missing some pages which included the abbreviation spelled with mixed case: MDR-Tb. The mixed case query *MDR-Tb* returned just fourteen matches. Entering all-lower case search queries may be preferred for comprehensive retrieval, unless capitalisation can help to eliminate occurrences of a search term out of the intended context, e.g. AIDS. Most other search engines do not recognise mixed capitalisation.

Fielded searching

Fielded searching exploits the structure of Web pages as described by HTML tags. To view the HTML source of a page, simply select the browser's View option, then select Source (using Internet Explorer) or Page Source (using Netscape Navigator). A number of relevant HTML tags, including meta tags, are likely to appear between the opening <head> and closing </head> tags. (A fuller description of the structure of simple HTML documents and the most commonly used tags is given in Chapter 22.)

For example, at the time of writing, the HTML source for the Jamaican Sickle Cell Unit detailed sickle cell information: index Web page[9] included the following between the <head> and </head> tags:

```
<head>

<meta name="description" content="The Jamaican Sickle
Cell Unit provides a selection of unpublished infor-
mation on aspects of sickle cell disease. To be used
in conjunction with our published articles online.">

<meta name="keywords" content="sickle cell disease,
sickle cell, anaemia, anemia, thalassaemia,
thalassemia, haematology, hematology, Jamaica, jamaica,
Jamaican, jamaican, trait, haemolytic anaemia, hemolytic
anemia, homozygous, SS disease, SC disease, SCD">

<title>Jamaican Sickle Cell Unit Detailed Sickle Cell
Information: Index</title>

</head>
```

A description, a range of keywords and the title are given here. The title information is displayed in the browser title bar (the blue bar displayed right across the top of a browser window). The meta description and keywords are not displayed by the browser, so may contain variable spellings, as above.

Web search engines usually allow the words that appear in the meta tags (both description and keywords) to be searched. A general search for *thalassaemia* using AltaVista will therefore potentially retrieve the above page, even though the word does not appear on the Web page as it is displayed by the browser.

Fielded search queries are entered as a *fieldname:value* expression. For example, the words making up the title can be searched using the *title:* expression, a feature that is common across several search engines. So a general search for *thalassaemia* will potentially retrieve the Jamaican Sickle Cell Unit page in the matches found, whereas a search for *title:thalassaemia* will not. Restricting a search to the *title:* words in this way will produce a far smaller number of hits compared to a general search.

Different search engines provide a different range of fielded searches. Most search engines support search expressions that allow parts of a URL to be specified in a search (*url:, host:* or *domain:*) and support search expressions that allow linking pages to be retrieved (*link:*). Details of the available options for fielded searching are given in the search engine help pages (several of which are referenced at the end of this chapter)[8, 10, 11].

Restricting by domain

Information seekers in health and medicine often wish to restrict a search to just sources that have traditionally been associated with the production of high quality information, for example educational institutions or not-for-profit organisations (though see article by McClung *et al.*)[12]. At the very least, limiting the results of a search to such sources can often help reduce the sheer number of hits returned to a manageable number. Imposing such a limit can be a crude exercise, however, since many reputable sources (including journals such as *Scientific American*, with the URL: http://www.sciam.com/) will also be excluded.

AltaVista and Northern Light both support the *url:* expression, used to specify strings of characters that may appear as any part of a URL in a search query. AltaVista additionally supports the *host:* and *domain:* expressions, whereas HotBot supports only the *domain:* expression.

Sample URL:

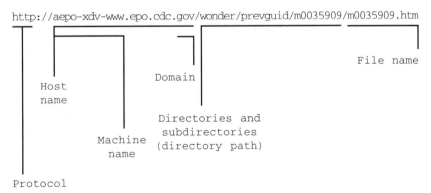

```
http://aepo-xdv-www.epo.cdc.gov/wonder/prevguid/m0035909/m0035909.htm
```

File name

Domain

Host name

Directories and subdirectories (directory path)

Machine name

Protocol

Using AltaVista or Northern Light, the entire URL can be searched using the *url:* expression (though it is necessary to drop the protocol element when searching with AltaVista).

Using AltaVista, the *host:* expression restricts the search to any part of the host name but is not extended to the remainder of the URL (e.g. directories, subdirectories and file names). The search query *host:aepo-xdv-www.epo.cdc.gov* in AltaVista retrieves all pages from the aepo-xdv-www.epo.cdc.gov host. A search for *host:aepo-xdv-www* retrieves all pages from servers with the machine name aepo-xdv-www. The *domain:* expression, on the other hand, restricts the search to the top level domains and country codes only (see, for example, HotBot Help,[13] for a list of these). Consequently, a search for *domain:ac.uk* using AltaVista would return 0 hits, whereas a search for *domain:uk* would be successful. The expression *host:ac.uk* would need to be used to search for hosts ending in ac.uk, i.e. UK academic sources.

When a *url:* expression is used in Northern Light, the stage at which it is used in a search query can have a significant effect. The Northern Light help pages warn: 'if you search against one or more field, you *must* include the TEXT: parameter if you also wish to search within the text of documents or Web sites'.[8] For example, a search for *"multidrug resistant tuberculosis" AND url:ac.uk* returned 21 hits. The search query *url:ac.uk and "multidrug resistant tuberculosis"* returned 0 hits, and would need to be recast as *url:ac.uk AND text:"multidrug resistant tuberculosis"* in order to return matches consistently.

Finding linking pages

Pages that link to documents of key interest may be useful in identifying other more recent documents or collections of additional relevant resources. They may also indicate the importance of an original key document, if trusted sources are among those linking to it. Pages providing links to the Virtual Hospital's Adult pulmonary care curriculum,[14] for example, might be expected to include collections of educational resources. Indeed, a search for pages linking to its URL identified a range of sources of CME resources, including a page of useful links from the Radiological Society of North America, as well as a number of lists of links to radiology teaching resources:

Using AltaVista (Simple or Advanced Search), the search query:
link:www.vh.org/Providers/TeachingFiles/PulmonaryCoreCurric/PulmCoreCurric.html
will produce a list of pages linking to the resource.

Using AltaVista Simple Search, the query:

+link:www.vh.org/Providers/TeachingFiles/PulmonaryCoreCurric/
PulmCoreCurric.html -host:www.vh.org -host:uiowa.edu
will exclude pages linking to the resource from the Virtual Hospital itself
or the University of Iowa which hosts it.

Alternatively, using AltaVista Advanced Search, the equivalent query can
be entered as:
link:www.vh.org/Providers/TeachingFiles/PulmonaryCoreCurric/
PulmCoreCurric.html AND NOT (host:www.vh.org OR host:uiowa.edu)

Linking pages can be identified in a similar way using HotBot (Simple or
Super Search) by typing:
link:http://www.vh.org/Providers/TeachingFiles/PulmonaryCoreCurric/
PulmCoreCurric.html -domain:www.vh.org -domain:uiowa.edu
which will identify linking pages other than those originating from the
Virtual Hospital or the University of Iowa.

Increasingly, search engines are including a 'search for links to this URL'
feature (though Northern Light did not support searching for linking
pages at the time of writing). Google, for example, is a search engine that
uses information about links between pages in order to rank results.

Currency / invalid links

According to the Search Engine Watch search engine EKGs,[15] most large
search engines are relatively fresh, i.e. their indexes are refreshed regularly. Both AltaVista and Northern Light allow searching by date last
modified, and Northern Light also allows date sorting of results. Northern Light was found in 1998 to be less effective than AltaVista or HotBot
at eliminating invalid links[16] but since mid-1999 had been improving
continuously, while in contrast AltaVista had become less effective.[17]

Refining search results

Northern Light and AltaVista allow a search to be further refined beyond
an initial query. Further terms can be added or additional search options
chosen. Northern Light also offers an innovative document categorisa-
tion approach. Northern Light dynamically creates 'custom search
folders', which are presented alongside search results, grouping results
together. A Northern Light search for *"zinc gluconate"* retrieves over 3,500
hits. Northern Light suggests a range of custom search folders alongside
the hits that are generated specifically as a result of this search (see Figure
10.5).

Selecting a folder will return a subset of the original documents, as well
as further sub-topics. Clicking on the 'all others…' folder icon reveals a
further set of folders, and so on until all results in a category have been

displayed. Clicking on the top-most folder will redisplay the main results list. Custom search folders are created for subjects (as they relate to individual search queries), type of document (e.g. press releases), source (e.g. commercial Web sites) and language.

Figure 10.5 Northern Light. Custom search folders and subfolders

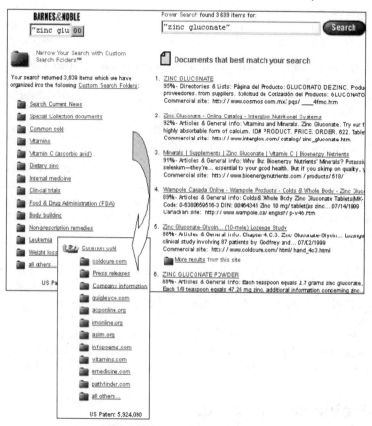

In practice it is often difficult to arrive at just the results of interest by using the custom folders. Although folders with a subject orientation are created, they tend to be very general (e.g. *Common cold* in Figure 10.5). Custom folders may be of greater use for homing in on different types of domains (e.g. *Commercial sites* may be available for some searches), or for identifying sites with large clusters of pages on the topic (e.g. *coldcure.com* in Figure 10.5).

Results display

The display of results varies among search engines. AltaVista and Northern Light provide a total number of hits found. The hits are individually numbered in succession so that it is possible to know which matching hit is displayed at any time out of the total hits returned. AltaVista allows pages of hits to be skipped (e.g. to go straight to the 20th page of hits and view hit number 200 directly), and FAST Search allows hits to be selected in clusters of ten at a time. Northern Light allows only the next or previous pages to be accessed in succession. AltaVista, FAST Search and Northern Light return 10 hits at a time. All major search engines return the basic display elements: title, brief text extract, URL. Each search engine may offer additional display features, some of which are summarised in Table 10.5:

Table 10.5: Web search engine display features

	Detail returned	No of hits returned / no displayed per page
AltaVista	Detailed Includes page size, title, URL, date last modified, language	Yes / 10 Can skip pages of results
FAST Search	Brief Includes URL, title, brief text extract	Yes / 10, with choice of 10, 25, 50, 75, 100 Can skip pages of results
Google	Brief Includes URL, title, words in context, size of cached copy, link to similar pages	Yes / 10, 30, 100 Can skip pages of results
Northern Light	Detailed Includes URL, title, brief text extract, ranking score, date last modified, document type (e.g. article), document source (e.g. commercial site)	Yes / 10 Cannot skip pages of results

Ranking: how results are returned

AltaVista Simple Search returns up to 200 hits in ranked order, i.e. by the closeness of match to the words entered as the search query. However, closeness of match does not guarantee appropriateness of search results and the 'best' match in terms of quality of content may not appear among the highest ranked hits. AltaVista Advanced Search returns matching hits in no particular order if no ranking words are specified, i.e. when only a Boolean expression is used, and more than 200 of these may be displayed if available. If ranking is required, then terms must be entered in the 'Sort by' search box for this purpose, and up to 200 hits may then be displayed in ranked order.

The following influence the ranked output of results by most search engines:

- the number of search terms (words or phrases) contained in a page;
- the frequency of search terms in a page;
- the location of terms in a page, particularly if the search terms occur in the title, meta tags, or the first few lines of a page;
- the proximity of search terms within a page; and
- the uniqueness of search terms.

Unscrupulous practices are prevalent as Web page creators strive to ensure their pages are retrieved and displayed among the top hits returned irrespective of their relevance to a search query. Meta tags are often implicated in such efforts. As mentioned earlier, meta tags provide information about the content of a page and are part of the HTML source – they are not viewed unless the HTML code itself is displayed. For example, a glance at the Jamaican Sickle Cell Unit detailed sickle cell information: index page[9] would suggest no immediate reason why it should be retrieved following a search for *thalassaemia*. Checking the HTML for the page, however, reveals that thalassaemia and thalassemia have both been listed as keywords:

```
<meta name="keywords"
content="sickle cell disease, sickle cell, anaemia,
anemia, thalassaemia, thalassemia, haematology,
hematology, Jamaica, jamaica, Jamaican, jamaican, trait,
haemolytic anaemia, hemolytic anemia, homozygous, SS
disease, SC disease, SCD">
```

This is an example of legitimate use of meta keywords since the articles that are available online from this site include a number about thalassaemia. However, other Web page creators are not as scrupulous in their keyword allocation and a number of practices are used to manipulate search results.[1] These include:[18]

- filling the meta keywords tag with keywords that do not relate to the site's actual content;
- repeating the same keyword by including it in comment tags;
- adding keywords, sometimes repeated, with the text set to the same colour as the page background, or using minute font; and

- using a meta refresh tag to lead a viewer away from a dummy page to a target page.

In response, search engines have devised guidelines to deal with this problem, some of which are more successful than others.

Web search engines: special features

Different search engines offer a range of special features that are often unique to the individual search engine. Below are some examples.

AltaVista

AltaVista supports a translation feature[19] offered as a matter of course with each matching hit returned. English, French, German, Italian, Portuguese and Spanish are the languages supported, as well as Russian to English. It is possible to request a translation by clicking on the Translate hypertext link, or by entering the full URL of the page to be translated at the AltaVista Translations site, and then selecting the language pair required. It is also possible to type or paste text directly into the translation box for automatic translation.

AltaVista also offers a Related Searches feature. For example, a search for *glomerulonephritis* using AltaVista Simple Search returned the following suggestions for Related Searches:

- postinfectious glomerulonephritis
- membranoproliferative glomerulonephritis
- rapidly progressive glomerulonephritis
- fibrillary glomerulonephritis
- acute glomerulonephritis

However, suggestions such as these cannot be relied on to be provided systematically and prior knowledge of appropriate terminologies would still be required.

Finally, AltaVista often offers the option to display Related Pages: pages that are similar to the original page are then retrieved. A 'Facts about…' option is sometimes also offered, giving information about host institutions, which are usually US-based.

AltaVista Translations: babelfish.altavista.com/

Google

Clicking on Google's Show matches (Cache) link, it is possible to see the cached contents of a Web page as of the time it was indexed by Google. This feature may allow the display of content from servers that may be temporarily unavailable, although using cached content would be inappropriate when currency is important. Google also offers a Similar pages option, which can be used to identify related content.

Google is best known for its ranking of Web pages. Drawing on the principle that a page that is linked to by many other pages is likely to be of interest to a random user, Google uses a PageRank approach to results display. However, such a simple measure as popularity of linking may provide only a very rough guide to relevance for health and medicine.

In June 2000 Google announced full coverage of 580 million pages and additional partial coverage of 500 million more, making it the largest Web search engine at the time.

HotBot

A search for *"zinc gluconate"* (exact phrase) returned the invitation to *Get the Top site for "zinc gluconate"*. This feature is provided by Direct Hit, which claims to determine the most popular and relevant sites for a search request by tracking the sites that are selected from lists of search results. The usefulness of such an approach for health and medicine may be limited, since popularity of a site may not reflect its appropriateness.

Northern Light

Northern Light makes available a Special Collection – information from over 6,000 business magazines, trade journals, newswires, academic journals and health publications. In health and medicine, however, the quality of these may not match that of peer-reviewed research journals, such as those indexed by Medline and other medical bibliographic databases, and even where high quality resources are made available, Northern Light may not offer the most cost-effective method of access.

For example, Northern Light retrieved hundreds of hits for the search *"multidrug resistant tuberculosis" OR "drug resistant tuberculosis"* from its Special Collection. The journals *Chest*, *The Lancet* and the *BMJ* all feature here. However a charge of between $1.00 and $4.00 is levied for material that can possibly be retrieved for free from the originating site. At the time of writing, all of the *BMJ* articles were available in full text from the *BMJ* site directly for no fee. Particular care should be taken not to assume that the most recent articles of interest will necessarily be available through such a source or that retrieval from a particular source will be complete. For example, two references from the *BMJ* that matched the query were not found to be included in the Special Collection for the year 2000, and electronic material that is freely available on the *BMJ* Web site was similarly not available via the Special Collection.

Regional search engines

AltaVista operates an international search network, that includes a UK site and several other European sites (France, Germany, Italy, Netherlands, Sweden). Lycos and Excite also offer alternative services globally, including UK-oriented services.

Neither HotBot nor Northern Light operate regional sites, although Inktomi, which powers HotBot, is searchable via a number of services other than HotBot. Inktomi partners are many and varied internationally, and from mid-2000 were expected to tap in to a much larger index, amounting to 500 million pages.[20] Search Engine Watch offers a chart that details search engine alliances,[21] which at the time of writing included MSN Search, Yahoo! and UKMax as Inktomi partners.

All search services that target the UK market offer the option to limit the search results to sources originating from the UK, although search options are also available to tailor the choice of origin of the hits returned and to retrieve worldwide matches (see UKMax, for example).

AltaVista International: doc.altavista.com/international.shtml

AltaVista UK: www.altavista.co.uk/

Excite UK: www.excite.co.uk/

Lycos UK & Ireland: www.lycos.co.uk/

Microsoft Network (UK): msn.co.uk/

UKMax: www.ukmax.co.uk/

Yahoo! UK & Ireland: www.yahoo.co.uk/

References

1. Digital's AltaVista search site unveils largest and freshest Web index [press release]. Maynard, Mass.; 1997 Oct 14. Available from: http://www.altavista.com/av/content/pr101497.htm

2. Search Engine Watch. Search engine sizes. Available from: http://www.searchenginewatch.com/reports/sizes.html

3. Drobniewski FA. Diagnosing multidrug resistant tuberculosis in Britain: clinical suspicion should drive rapid diagnosis. *BMJ* 1998;**317**:1263-1264. Available from: http://www.bmj.com/cgi/content/full/317/7168/1263

4. Pitkäranta A, Hayden FG. What's new with common colds? complications and management. *Infection Medicine* 1998;**15**(2):117-118,121-122,124-128. Available to subscribers from: http://www.medscape.com/SCP/IIM/1998/v15.n02/m4581.hayd/m4581.hayd.html

5. Richardson WS, Wilson MC, Nishikawa J, Hayward RS. The well-built clinical question: a key to evidence-based decisions. *ACP Journal Club* 1995 Nov-Dec ;**123** (3) :A12-A13. Available also from: http://www.cche.net/principles/education_all.asp

6. University of Washington, Department of Pharmacy Services, Pharmacy Resources Network. UWMC/HMC Drug Information Center. UWMC/HMC Drug Alerts! Available from: http://weber.u.washington.edu/~druginfo/Alerts/dralerts.html

7. Search Engine Watch. How AltaVista works. Available to subscribers from: http://www.searchenginewatch.com/subscribers/altavista.html

8. Northern Light. Search help: optimize your search. Available from: http://www.northernlight.com/docs/search_help_optimize.html

9. Jamaican Sickle Cell Unit detailed sickle cell information: index. Available from: http://mrcjamaica.nimr.mrc.ac.uk/detailed.htm

10. AltaVista. Help: basics. Available from: http://www.altavista.com/av/content/help.htm

11. HotBot. Help search tips: advanced search features. Available from: http://www.hotbot.com/help/tips/search_features.asp

12. McClung HJ, Murray RD, Heitlinger LA. The Internet as a source for current patient information [electronic article]. *Pediatrics* 1998 Jun ;**101**(6) :e2. Available from: http://www.pediatrics.org/cgi/content/full/101/6/e2

13. HotBot. Help: top level domains. Available from: http://www.hotbot.com/help/domains.asp

14. Peterson MW, Kline JN. Virtual Hospital: Adult pulmonary core curriculum. Available from: http://www.vh.org/Providers/TeachingFiles/PulmonaryCoreCurric/PulmCoreCurric.html

15. Search Engine Watch. Search engine EKGs. Available from: http://www.searchenginewatch.com/reports/ekgs/index.html

16. Lawrence S, Giles CL. September 1998 search engine coverage update. Available from: http://www.neci.nj.nec.com/homepages/lawrence/websize98.html

17. Notess GR. Search engine statistics: dead links report. Available from: http://www.notess.com/search/stats/9911dead.shtml

18. Piquet L. Search engines battle the new spam. *ZDNet* 1998 Sep 24. Available from: http://www.zdnet.com/products/stories/reviews/0,4161,1600389,00.html

19. Digital announces first Internet translation capability: AltaVista Search Services delivers free Web translation service in Spanish, French, German, Portuguese and Italian [press release]. Maynard, Mass.; 1997 Dec 9. Available from: http://www.altavista.com/av/content/pr120997.htm

20. SearchEngineWatch. Inktomi reenters battle for biggest. Available from: http://searchenginewatch.internet.com/sereport/00/06-inktomi.html

21. SearchEngineWatch. Search engine alliances chart. Available from: http://searchenginewatch.internet.com/reports/alliances.html

Chapter 11

Metasearch engines

When seeking information on a rare disease, e.g. alveolar microlithiasis, where the instances of any mention are relatively rare even in sources accessible via the Web, the searcher may well wish to retrieve anything that refers to the disease. However, individual Web search engines only cover a small part of the indexable Web.[1,2] Metasearch engines attempt to address this and other search engine limitations by submitting search queries to multiple Web search engines simultaneously. Their main attraction is their ability to aggregate results from a range of search engines, so they may help to identify matches that might otherwise not be found by using a single search engine. A selection of metasearch engines is listed below.

Of the metasearch engines listed, only Dogpile and Megasearch allow full retrieval from a range of search engines. In contrast, most metasearch tools submit their queries to a range of search engines, typically retrieve only the first 10 to 30 hits from each search engine, and return the results integrated and ranked by relevance.

At the time of writing, no metasearch engine submitted queries to Northern Light and very few submitted queries to HotBot, although alternative Inktomi powered search engines were sometimes queried instead (e.g. Snap or GoTo). Table 11.1 indicates which of the major Web search engines are queried by a selection of metasearch engines.

Table 11.1: Major search engines: coverage by metasearch engines

	Dogpile	Mega-search	MetaCrawler	ProFusion	Search.com
AltaVista	Yes	Yes	Yes	Yes	Yes
HotBot (or other Inktomi powered search engine)	(GoTo)	(GoTo)	(GoTo)	(GoTo, Snap)	Yes (GoTo, Snap)
Google	Yes		Yes		
Excite	Yes		Yes	Yes	Yes
Infoseek	Yes	Yes	Yes	Yes	Yes
Lycos	Yes	Yes	Yes	Yes	Yes

Dogpile: www.dogpile.com/

Megasearch: www.thebighub.com/

MetaCrawler: www.metacrawler.com/

MetaCrawler PowerSearch:
www.metacrawler.com/index_power.html

ProFusion: www.profusion.com/

Search.com: savvy.search.com/

Types of metasearch engine

Just as there is a proliferation of search engines, there is also a proliferation of metasearch engines. Two discrete types can be distinguished and their main differences are summarised in Table 11.2. Table 11.3 summarises the main features of a selection of metasearch engines.

Non-ranking metasearch engines

Metasearch engines such as Dogpile and Megasearch return potentially all hits from each contributing search engine source, maximising the numbers of hits returned, by submitting search queries to a wide range of search engines.

Metasearch engines in this category employ no ranking mechanism of their own but report the results from each search engine as delivered. Links are provided to each search engine that allow potentially all hits to be viewed in turn.

Ranking metasearch engines

Metasearch engines such as MetaCrawler, ProFusion and Search.com, provide selective, integrated and ranked output from contributing search engine sources and emphasise optimal ranking of results rather than comprehensiveness of retrieval.

Some metasearch engines in this group offer the option of extending the search directly to the search engines. MetaCrawler allows this, whereas ProFusion and Search.com offer no direct links to the search engines originally queried, nor a clear statement of precisely how a search query may have been submitted. MetaCrawler, on the other hand, does not report the total number of hits returned from each search engine, nor whether any search engines are unavailable. However, this information could be gleaned indirectly from the results display pages.

Table 11.2: Types of metasearch engine

	Number of hits retrieved from each search engine	Search results integrated and duplicates removed	Search results ranked
Non-ranking (e.g. Dogpile, Megasearch)	All hits returned from each search engine	No	No
Ranking (e.g. MetaCrawler, ProFusion, Search.com)	Selected hits only returned from each search engine	Yes	Yes

Table 11.3: Metasearch engine features

	Major Web search engines queried	Can customise?	Provides direct links to each reporting search service	Reports number of hits per search engine? / how much info displayed?
Dogpile	Yahoo!, GoTo.com, Lycos, InfoSeek, AltaVista	Option to select which search engines to include and order of search engines Maximum search time: 10, 20 seconds (default), 30, 40, 50, 60 seconds Requires cookies	Yes: can simply click on a link generated for each search engine and repeat the search exclusively with one specific search engine	Yes / Detail varies depending on the search engine queried, e.g. for AltaVista results: title; brief text; URL; date last modified; page size; language
Mega-search	AltaVista, Infoseek, Lycos, Yahoo!	Option to select which search engines to include Maximum search time: 5, 10 (default), 15, 20 seconds	No: may be possible to work out how a search was submitted but only indirectly	No / Brief entry returned: title, short extract and URL alone

Meta-Crawler	AltaVista, Excite, Infoseek, Lycos, WebCrawler, LookSmart, Thunderstone,	PowerSearch: Option to select which search engines to include Timeout 5 seconds (default) - 10 - 15 - 30 - 60 - 2 minutes Search mode: any, all, phrase Limit results by domain Results per page 10 - 20 (default) - 30 Results per source 10 (default) -20-30	Yes: can click on link to search engine following each hit displayed, which will cause the search to be executed directly with the specific search engine	No / Brief description given (separate description from each search engine); overall ranking score; title; URL
Pro Fusion	AltaVista, LookSmart, Infoseek, Excite, Lycos, WebCrawler, Yahoo!	Option to select which search engines to include Search mode: Simple, All (AND), Any (OR), Boolean, Phrase Check links (No, 1-10, 1-20, 1-50, 1-99, All) Search engine selection criteria: best 3, fastest 3, all, you choose Show results (All, 1-10, 1-20, 1-50, 1-99, All)	No link is provided to search engines	Yes / Title, brief summary, URL, ranking score
Search. com	AltaVista, Excite, HotBot, Google, GoTo, Infoseek, Lycos, Snap, WebCrawler	Option to select which search engines to include	No link is provided to search engines	Yes / Title; brief description; URL; source of hit

Search features

Search queries submitted to a metasearch engine are likely to be more effective if they use features that are commonly recognised by the majority of source Web search engines, otherwise they may be interpreted in an unpredictable manner. Most metasearch engines will attempt to translate search queries into a form that can be recognised by an appropriate group of search engines. However, the more complex a search query, the more likely it is that some of the search engines will not support the full range of search features used, or the metasearch engines will not translate the search query appropriately, and irrelevant hits will be returned.

Table 11.4: Search query translations: queries as submitted to AltaVista by a range of metasearch engines

	zinc gluconate cold child	"zinc gluconate"	+zinc +gluconate +cold +child	zinc and gluconate and cold and child	"zinc gluconate" or "zinc lozenge" or "zinc lozenges"
Dogpile	Submits as *zinc gluconate cold child* to AltaVista Simple Search	Submits as +*"zinc gluconate"* to AltaVista Simple Search	Submits as *zinc gluconate cold child* to AltaVista Simple Search	Submits as *zinc gluconate cold child* to AltaVista Simple Search	Submits as *"zinc gluconate" "zinc lozenge" "zinc lozenges"* to AltaVista Simple Search
Mega-search	Submits as *zinc gluconate cold child* to AltaVista Simple Search	Submits as *"zinc gluconate"* to AltaVista Simple Search	Submits as +*zinc +gluconate +cold +child* to AltaVista Simple Search	Submits as *zinc and gluconate and cold and child* to AltaVista Simple Search	Submits as is to AltaVista Simple Search
Meta-Crawler	Submits as *zinc gluconate cold child* (when ANY chosen) or +*zinc +gluconate +cold +child* (when ALL chosen) to AltaVista Simple Search	Submits as *"zinc gluconate"* to AltaVista Simple Search	Submits as +*zinc +gluconate +cold +child* to AltaVista Simple Search	Submits as *zinc and gluconate and cold and child* to AltaVista Simple Search (when ANY chosen)	Submits as *"zinc gluconate" "zinc lozenge" "zinc lozenges"* or or [sic] to AltaVista Simple Search (when ANY chosen)
Pro-Fusion	Submits as *zinc AND gluconate AND cold AND child* to AltaVista Advanced Search	Submits as *"zinc gluconate"* to AltaVista Simple Search	Submits as +*zinc +gluconate +cold +child* to AltaVista Simple Search	Submits as *zinc and gluconate and cold and child* to AltaVista Simple Search	Submits as is to AltaVista Simple Search
Search.com	Submits as +*zinc +gluconate +cold +child* to AltaVista Simple Search	Submits as +*"zinc gluconate"* to AltaVista Simple Search	Submits as +*zinc +gluconate +cold +child* to AltaVista Simple Search	Submits as +*zinc +gluconate +cold +child* to AltaVista Simple Search	Does not execute

Indicatively, Table 11.4 documents the wide variability in search query translation among metasearch engines for a range of queries, as submitted to AltaVista.

Metasearch engines often claim to support a full range of search query features, including:

- phrase searching,
- +- notation,
- Boolean expressions, and
- complex queries.

Not all explain as clearly as Search.com what might happen if a particular search feature is not supported by the target search engines: 'You may improve your results through […] advanced search techniques, but many engines do not support these options, so sometimes your results may appear to be exactly the same as they would be without them'.[3]

Precise, simple queries using commonly supported search features, such as the +- notation, are more likely to be handled successfully by metasearch and search engines. The more search features that are included in a query, the more likely it is that individual search engines may be excluded that cannot handle the complexity of the search query. In order of relative breadth of support by the search engines, the following search features can be employed with metasearch engines (with caution):

- Entering a series of search terms with no additional notation: this is roughly equivalent to a search query implicitly employing the Boolean OR operator. Most search engines, when a search query such as this is directly submitted, will return Web pages that contain all the search terms near the top of the list of results, while pages that refer to just one of the search terms are likely to appear lower in the results. However, metasearch engines may translate such search queries inappropriately prior to submission to the search engines.
- Phrase searching: the use of double quotation marks to bound the search query is fairly widely supported by search engines, and metasearch engines generally do not attempt to translate phrase searching prior to submission of a search query.
- The +- notation is generally interpreted correctly by metasearch engines and will usually be recognised by the major Web search engines.
- Boolean expressions are less likely to be correctly translated by metasearch engines prior to submission of a query to a search engine. The search engines are also less likely to support the comprehensive use of Boolean expressions. ProFusion and Search.com, for example, attempt to translate this type of query

prior to submitting it to the search engines (see Table 11.4). Search.com uses the + notation and submits the query to AltaVista Simple Search. ProFusion employs the Boolean AND operator, and also submits the query to AltaVista Simple Search (even though AltaVista Simple Search does not support the use of Boolean expressions).

- Complex search queries: not many search engines support the use of parentheses, so search queries that use such a feature are likely to be handled less successfully by metasearch or search engines.

Specialist search features

Metasearch engines are restricted in their ability to offer novel search features since they rely on a range of disparate search engines for results. A couple only are mentioned here:

- MetaCrawler allows search queries to be restricted roughly by continent – or by domain in the case of US educational, commercial and government sources.
- ProFusion offers a broken link detection facility that checks for pages which are no longer available. Link checking can be particularly time-consuming.

Results display

Dogpile reports the total number of hits returned by each search engine in succession. Not all metasearch engines, however, provide such information. Valuable contextual information may therefore be lost.

Tips for better retrieval

Different metasearch engines allow different search features to be selected. Consult up-to-date help pages to discover specialist search features. The following tips may help optimise search results generally:

- Increase the maximum search time, if the option is available, otherwise a number of search engines may return no hits.
- If a metasearch engine allows the range of search engines to be specified, ensure you include the major search engines, otherwise hits from smaller search engines may skew the results.
- For comprehensive retrieval, choose a non-ranking metasearch engine, such as Dogpile.
- For ranked output of just a few, possibly highly relevant hits, choose a ranking metasearch engine, for example Search.com.
- Resubmit queries, as a few minutes may make a difference to the results retrieved.

- Keep search queries simple – over-reliance on complex queries may cause unanticipated results to be returned, either because the metasearch engine has translated the query in some unpredicted manner, or because one or more of the search engines does not support the full range of search features used.

References

1. Lawrence S, Giles CL. September 1998 search engine coverage update. Available from: http://www.neci.nj.nec.com/homepages/lawrence/websize98.html

2. Lawrence S, Giles CL. Accessibility of information on the web. *Nature* 1999 Jul 8; **400**(6740):107-109.

3. Search.com. Help: Advanced search tips. Available from: http://savvy.search.com/help/index.html#advanced

Chapter 12

Web directories

Web directories differ from Web search and metasearch engines in that they lend themselves to browsing, although most can also be searched. Directories offer hierarchically organised lists of links, sometimes with either brief or expansive annotations. Inevitably the coverage of directories is much reduced compared to that of the Web search engines because they require an element of human intervention in their creation – they typically cover hundreds of thousands of Web sites rather than millions of Web pages.

By far the most popular generic directory of Web sites is Yahoo!,[1] originally created as a means of collecting and sharing favourite sites on the Web.[2] Yahoo! captured the imagination of Internet users as it provided an easy to browse, hierarchically organised view of the Web. Yahoo! has now been joined by other Web directories, all of which share the same key features: a hierarchical structure of numerous topic categories, populated by listings of pages, services and sites. With some directories approaching two million listings, such as LookSmart and Open Directory, browsing through the hierarchy of categories is becoming increasingly cumbersome. As a result, Web directories also offer the option of directly searching the directory contents.

Furthermore, Web directories have now become hybrid services, allowing not only browsing and searching of their own databases of category names, listings titles and descriptions, but also searching via large generic search engines, particularly AltaVista and Inktomi (the Web index that also powers HotBot). When no hits are returned from a directory, results are displayed directly from the associated Web search engines. Table 12.1 summarises the coverage of the four main Web directories, Yahoo!, LookSmart, Open Directory and Snap, and their associated Web search engines.

Table 12.1: *Web directories: associated Web search engines*

	Associated Web index or search engine
Yahoo!	Inktomi, Google
LookSmart	Inktomi, AltaVista
Open Directory	Google, plus several other search engines
Snap	Inktomi

LookSmart: www.looksmart.com/

Open Directory Project: dmoz.org/

Snap: www.snap.com/

Yahoo!: www.yahoo.com/

Yahoo!: an example of a Web directory

Browsing Yahoo!

The health category within Yahoo! features alongside other general-interest categories such as computers and the Internet, entertainment, recreation and sports, science, etc. Yahoo! may be browsed, with each successive link followed through the hierarchical structure until the required listing is discovered or the search is curtailed. For example, to explore the prevalent viewpoint with regard to the medicinal use of marijuana, it was possible to start from the top of the Yahoo! directory hierarchy and navigate with six clicks before reaching the appropriate Yahoo! category (Health > Pharmacy > Drugs and Medications > Specific Drugs and Medications > Marijuana > Medicinal). However, none of the links led to research-based information. As with search engines, the collection of links seemed more likely to be of interest to the general information seeker than the health professional.

Searching Yahoo!

Yahoo! offers a search option which usefully complements the hierarchical browsing approach. Using the Yahoo! search option and typing *zinc gluconate* retrieved just one entry listed in three different Yahoo! categories (see Figure 12.1). Up to seven clicks would otherwise have been required to reach the same entry by browsing the hierarchical structure.

Figure 12.1 Yahoo! site matches: example of Yahoo! search output

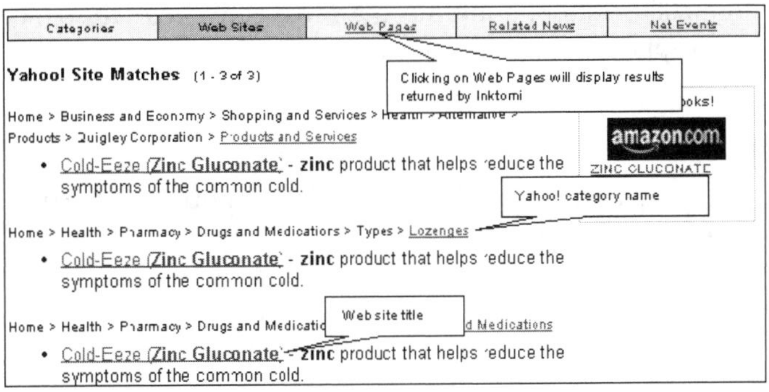

Both the Web site titles and the Yahoo! category name results are hyperlinked. Selecting a category of interest by clicking on the hypertext link may lead to groups of similar results. For example, selecting the category Health > Pharmacy > Drugs and Medications > Types > Lozenges will reveal additional companies specialising in zinc lozenges (Figure 12.2).

Figure 12.2 Yahoo! category search: search results retrieved by browsing the Yahoo! category names

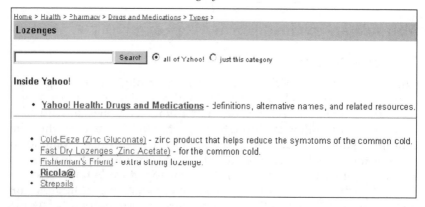

Yahoo!: a Web directory with a search engine attached

A link below the Yahoo! results invites the searcher to *'Go To Web Page Matches'*. Clicking on this link reveals the results of running the search against Inktomi. Predictably, Inktomi provides large numbers of hits, even for very specific queries. A search for *"zinc gluconate"* returned 2,166 matches when Inktomi was interrogated via Yahoo!. Yahoo! displays the search results 20 matches at a time. Retrievability is comparable to HotBot, which as a search engine also uses Inktomi data, though Yahoo! supplies less information: for example, HotBot offers consecutive numbering of hits (which provides contextual information so that a searcher knows how many matches there are to view at any time) and the date the page was last visited by the Inktomi robot.

In late June 2000, Yahoo! announced a prospective switch to Google as the prime supplier of Web search results.

Other Web directories

LookSmart, Snap and Open Directory are other popular Web directories and operate in very similar ways.

LookSmart

LookSmart provides over 170,000 hierarchically organised categories and incorporates in the region of 1.8 million Web listings.[3] As with Yahoo!, the health and fitness category is just one general interest subject area covered, alongside automotive, hobbies and interests and shopping and services. As with Yahoo!, LookSmart categories may be browsed. For example, the following sequence of links will lead to entries for the common cold within seven clicks from the top of the hierarchy: Personal > Health > Conditions / Illnesses > Conditions A-Z > Conditions C > Conditions Com-Con > Common Cold.

This results in several matches, most of which link to commercial organisations' Web pages and provide information targeted at the consumer (see Figure 12.3).

Figure 12.3 Browsing the hierarchy of LookSmart categories

Health	You are here: Conditions & Illnesses A-Z	
Guides & Directories	Brain/Nervous System	Conditions A
Conditions/Illnesses >	Bone, Skin & Muscle	Conditions B
Diet & Nutrition	Cancer	Conditions C
Drugs & Medicines	Digestive & Endocrine	Conditions D
Family & Community	Disabilities	Conditions E
Fitness & Exercise	Eye/Ear/Nose/Throat	Conditions F
For Professionals	Genetic Disorders	Conditions G-H
Hospitals & Services	Heart, Lung & Blood	Conditions I-L
Natural Therapies	Immune & Infectious	Conditions M-O
Public Health	Liver/Kidney/Bladder	Conditions P-Q
Reference & News	Mental Health	Conditions R
Sexual Health	Reproductive Health	Conditions S
Weight Management	Conditions A-Z >	Conditions T-Z

By browsing LookSmart for information on Fluoxetine (Prozac), relevant links may be found under either drug name. As with Yahoo!, listings may be placed under multiple category headings (e.g. see the PharmInfoNet entry for Prozac – Depression and Suicide in Figures 12.4 and 12.5). In addition, many LookSmart entries may originate from a small selection of resources, such as RxList, The Internet Drug Index.

Figure 12.4 LookSmart listings for Fluoxetine

Fluoxetine or Prozac	New! <u>Submit a Site</u>

<u>Fluoxetine (Prozac) - PSYweb</u>
> Offers advice on living with this serotonin-specific drug used to treat depression. Lists side effects, proper dosage, and cautions

Fluoxetine - Pharm InfoNet
> Scroll down to Prozac to find information regarding this antidepressant with Q&As, links to journal articles, and press releases.

<u>Fluoxetine - RxList</u>
> Factsheet on antidepressant used in the treatment of depression and bulimia includes both clinical and patient information.

<u>Prozac - Depression and Suicide</u>
> PharmInfoNet article from February 1000 discusses the effects of Prozac like drugs on the incidence of suicide.

Figure 12.5 LookSmart listings for Prozac

Prozac or Fluoxetine	New! <u>Submit a Site</u>

<u>Estronaut - Salpingtis</u> New!
> Salpingitis is listed as one of the rare side effects of taking the antidepressant drug Prozac. View other side effects that are unique to women.

<u>Prozac - Depression and Suicide</u>
> PharmInfoNet article from February 1999 discusses the effects of Prozac-like drugs on the incidence of suicide.

<u>Prozac - Fluoxetine for PMS</u>
> Medical Sciences Bulletin reports on a study of the use of Fluoxetine in premenstrual syndrome to improve symptoms of depression and anxiety.

Occasionally, long pages of listings are returned while browsing through a topic category within LookSmart. In order to search through the page for occurrences of the search terms, it is possible to use the browser's Edit / Find option instead of scrolling through the page in the hope of identifying the relevant matches.

As well as browsing, LookSmart also allows searching of its database of listings. LookSmart also passes search queries to Inktomi. The results are returned with the LookSmart listings hits displayed first, followed by matches from the Inktomi search.

> The Internet Drug Index: www.rxlist.com/

Snap

Snap looks and behaves similarly to Yahoo! and LookSmart, returning matches from category names as well as the titles of listings and brief one-line descriptions. However, its coverage is smaller.[4] As with LookSmart,

Snap entries may originate from a small selection of resources, for example, a search for *donepezil* retrieved links to the Virtual Drug Store, and also to RxList, the Internet Drug Index, with entries from the same drug indexes appearing for other drug listings within Snap.

As with Yahoo! and LookSmart, results from Inktomi appear after Snap's own listings. It is also possible to query the Inktomi database directly from Snap's advanced search page.

> Virtual Drug Store: www.virtualdrugstore.com/

Open Directory Project

More recently, the Open Directory Project (ODP) was released, which relies on volunteer editors for its entries. At the time of writing, ODP claimed to cover over 1.8 million sites in over 280,000 categories, and is reminiscent of the Yahoo! hierarchical style of presentation. Searches are not extended by default to search engines external to ODP, even when no matching hits are returned for a query; however, the option is offered to try the search on AltaVista, Google, GoTo or Yahoo!. A free use license exists for the Open Directory Data, making it a popular choice as an additional service provided by a range of search engines.

Web directory search features

Typically, a Web directory will provide the search features supported by its associated Web search engine via an Advanced Search option. However, this is not always the case. Key search features that are more commonly supported include the +- notation and phrase matching. Support for wildcard matching and Boolean operators, especially in combination with other features, e.g. in nested queries or phrase searching, can sometimes vary.

Table 12.2 summarises the range of search features that are supported by the Web directories. As with search and metasearch engines, Web directory help pages provide the most reliable and up-to-date information on which search features are supported.[5, 6, 7]

Table 12.2: Search features supported by Web directories

	Yahoo!	LookSmart	Snap	Open Directory
+-	Yes	Yes	Yes	Yes
Phrase matching (using double quotation marks)	Yes	Yes	Yes	Yes
Wildcard matching	Yes	Yes	Yes	Yes
Boolean	AND, OR via Advanced Search	No	AND, OR, (AND) NOT (select Boolean phrase option in Power search)	AND, OR, ANDNOT

Understanding the results from a Web directory search

Web directories search their own and associated Web search engine contents in a similar fashion. A Yahoo! search, for example, targets:

- Yahoo! category names,
- Web site titles and brief one-line descriptions as listed in the Yahoo! directory, and
- content from individual Web pages as indexed by an associated Web index or search engine (Inktomi or Google)

Results are presented in that order.

Matches are returned from Web directories in ranked order, first from their own databases, then from the associated Web search engines. Yahoo! returns results from its own database in ranked order, which may be influenced by a number of factors:[5]

- multiple word matches: the greater the number of search words matched, the higher the rank,
- exact word matches: exact word matches are ranked higher than approximate matches,
- location of matches: a match in the category name or title of a site is ranked higher than a match in the descriptions or the URL, and
- generality of category: matching categories that are listed higher up in the Yahoo! hierarchy are ranked higher than specific categories listed deeper within the hierarchy.

Search engines that also display directory links

Search engines are also increasingly providing links to directories of their own or enhancing their results lists with listings provided by Web directories. LookSmart is the most popular directory to be used in this way, as both HotBot and AltaVista provide links to its directory listings:

- Open Directory powers the HotBot Directory.

- Google goes further, by applying its PageRank technology to rank the Open Directory sites according to their popularity (number and importance of sites that link to them).

- The AltaVista Directory combines both LookSmart and the Open Directory, to produce possibly the largest Web directory, covering over 2 million unique sites.

AltaVista: www.altavista.com/

Google: www.google.com/

HotBot: www.hotbot.com/

Review sites

Concern about the quality of information generally available on the Web gave rise early on to review sites, which have attempted to assign ratings (percentage scores or stars, for example) to denote the relative quality of sites. Quality criteria are usually poorly described, and the ratings have been criticised as inappropriate for health and medicine.[8, 9] Like Web directories, review sites select material primarily for its appeal to consumers and not for its applicability to professional education, research or practice.

Review sites are more restricted in their coverage than Web directories. This is partly due to the incorporation of sometimes lengthy reviews about a site or service. Although these are usually far more extensive than the one-line entries used by the Web directories, they are often written in an entirely light-hearted fashion.

Magellan Internet Guide: an example of a review site

A small selection of sites can be browsed from the Health category, which is one of 18 categories that Magellan addresses, alongside homes, horoscopes and lifestyle. Browsing the hierarchical structure in search of Infectious Diseases (Home > Health > Diseases & Conditions > Infectious Diseases) revealed three Recommended Web Sites. Not all sites in Magellan are reviewed and, in this case, Bugs in the news! was one of only two recommended sites that were accompanied by a review. Although a four-star rating system was originally deployed,[9] Magellan now simply distinguishes between Recommended Web Sites (awarded a single star), and More Sites (no star).

Bugs in the news!: falcon.cc.ukans.edu/~jbrown/bugs.html

Magellan Internet Guide: magellan.excite.com/

References

1. P\S\L Consulting Group. Physician Internet usage: a global survey. Executive Summary. 1998 Aug.

2. Yahoo! How-to: a message from [Yahoo!'s] founders. Available from: http://howto.yahoo.com/message/

3. LookSmart. Looksmart gains momentum as category search leader: three of top 10 Web sites utilize Looksmart's directory [press release]. San Francisco, CA; 1999 Feb 9. Available from: http://www.looksmart.com/aboutus/pressroom/pr/pr99-02-09b.html

4. Search Engine Watch. Directory sizes. Available from: http://www.searchenginewatch.com/reports/directories.html

5. Yahoo! How-to. Available from: http://howto.yahoo.com/

6. LookSmart. Help. Available from: http://www.looksmart.com/aboutus/user/

7. Snap. Search with Snap. Available from: http://www.snap.com/main/help/item/0,11,home-6736,00.html

8. Jadad AR, Gagliardi A. Rating health information on the Internet: navigating to knowledge or to Babel? *JAMA* 1998 Feb 25; **279**(8): 611-614. Available from: http://www.ama-assn.org/sci-pubs/journals/archive/jama/vol_279/no_8/jrv71042.htm

9. McNab A, Anagnostelis B, Cooke A. Never mind the quality, check the badge-width. *Ariadne* 1997 May;(9). Available from: http://www.ariadne.ac.uk/issue9/quality-ratings/

Chapter 13

Health and medical Web search engines

A major advantage of search engines is that they allow full text searching, so that potentially every word of a Web page is indexed and so may be searched. Medical World Search and MedHunt offer two different approaches to search engine retrieval on the Web with a health and medical subject focus. These are discussed in this chapter.

Medical World Search: filtering queries submitted to generic Web search engines

Medical World Search employs a filter of terms that originate from the Unified Medical Language System (UMLS) produced by the US National Library of Medicine (NLM).[1] The UMLS Metathesaurus is a database of information on concepts that appear in one or more of a number of different controlled vocabularies and classifications used in the field of biomedicine. The 1999 Metathesaurus contained 1,358,891 different concept names from more than 50 vocabularies and classifications, matched to 626,893 concepts and included the French, German, Italian, Portuguese, Russian (transliterated), and Spanish translations of NLM's Medical Subject Headings (MeSH).

Medical World Search allows search queries to be submitted to a range of generic Web search engines, which include AltaVista (Advanced Search), HotBot, Infoseek and WebCrawler. By first passing queries through the filter of the UMLS, which includes mainly technical terminology, many searches may return more focused results. For example, a query for *mad cow disease* is translated to *("encephalopathy bovine spongiform" OR "mad cow disease" OR "bse")* before it is submitted to a selected Web search engine (see Figure 13.1). As a result, hits that contain informal use of a term may be outweighed by documents that use more formal terminology.

Figure 13.1 Medical World Search: a query for mad cow disease

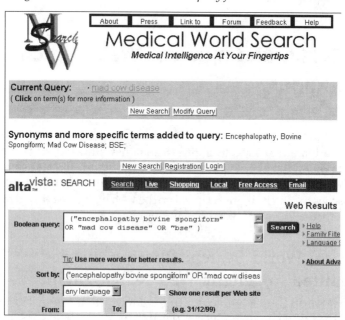

If a search phrase is recognised as a thesaurus term, it is possible that several synonyms may be added to the query automatically, which may have the effect of broadening the search. For example, a query for *esophageal reflux* is submitted to AltaVista as *("gastroesophageal reflux" OR "esophageal reflux" OR "cardioesophageal relaxation gastroesophageal reflux" OR "gastro-esophageal reflux" OR "gastro-oesophageal reflux" OR "gastroesophageal reflux disease").*

If a search phrase is not recognised as a thesaurus term, its constituent terms are simply submitted unmodified directly to the target search engine, with a Boolean OR operator separating them. For example, when *oesophageal reflux* is entered, no further terms are added to the query, which is submitted as *oesophageal OR reflux*. This emphasises the need to check how search phrases are interpreted, especially since British spellings may not be recognised.

Medical World Search does not support phrase searching using double quotation marks.

Medical World Search: www.mwsearch.com/

Boolean searching and result ranking using Medical World Search

Medical World Search allows Boolean queries to be created and modified, albeit only once a search has been submitted to a target source. Clicking on the Boolean Query button, which is displayed once a search has been conducted, takes the searcher to a page that allows alternative Boolean operators to be selected. Consequently, the default Boolean OR operator can be replaced by AND, NOT or NEAR, although such operators may not be supported by the target sources (e.g. HotBot does not support the NEAR operator).

For example, a search for *alveolar microlithiasis* resulted in 92,332 hits when first submitted to AltaVista via Medical World Search; a modified search for *alveolar AND microlithiasis* resulted in 16 hits. By contrast, a search for *alveolar NEAR microlithiasis* resulted in 98 hits and a phrase search for *"alveolar microlithiasis"* submitted directly to AltaVista produced 95 hits. Indeed, care needs to be exercised in accepting the automatic translation of search terms as implemented by any system and Medical World Search is no exception. Direct submission to AltaVista of the above Boolean queries for *alveolar microlithiasis* gave different results, and the discrepancies can possibly be explained as follows.

Medical World Search submits searches to AltaVista as Advanced Search Boolean queries, but the same search terms, including Boolean operators, are submitted as ranking terms as well (i.e. they are also submitted to AltaVista's 'Sort by' query box, even though Boolean operators are not supported by this type of query). For example, a search for *esophageal reflux* returned 24,940 matching hits when submitted to AltaVista via Medical World Search. By comparison, only 1,749 pages were returned when *esophageal reflux* was submitted directly to AltaVista as an Advanced Search Boolean query alone. A comparable result could be achieved if the suggested ranking terms submitted to AltaVista by Medical World Search were eliminated from the 'Sort by' query box and the query resubmitted.

The drawback of excluding any ranking terms from the search query is that irrelevant pages may be returned in preference to more relevant ones, since AltaVista applies relevance ranking only if ranking terms are used. An alternative option would be to edit the suggested ranking terms, once a search query has been generated, always bearing in mind that AltaVista imposes a limit on the number of hits returned when ranking terms are employed (see Chapter 10 on search engines).

Using Medical World Search to emulate an explosion MeSH search

Generic search engines generally support no features that allow searching for synonyms, related terms, or subordinate concepts because they can only cope with retrieval based on 'string matching'.[2] For example, a search for *"urinary tract infection*"* submitted directly to AltaVista Advanced Search retrieved 25,808 hits, but specific infections were not included comprehensively in the results. Consequently, although pyuria is a urinary tract infection, only about half the number of pages that mentioned the word were picked up by a search for *"urinary tract infection*"*.

Medical World Search queries that involve MeSH headings with narrower terms result in an implicit MeSH 'explosion' search, by adding terms that are more specific (displayed below a candidate search term in the MeSH tree). For example, navigating the MeSH tree for *urinary tract infections* reveals specific infections (namely, bacteriuria, pyuria and Schistosomiasis haematobia). In addition to identifying possible synonyms, then, Medical World Search offers another way of broadening a search strategy, by employing related narrower terms. Submitting a search for *urinary tract infections* to AltaVista via Medical World Search produced the following query, which returned 154,100 hits:

("urinary tract infections" OR "urinary tract infectious disease" OR "uti" OR "renal abscess" OR "schistosomiasis haematobia" OR "pyelonephritis" OR "pyuria" OR "bacteriuria" OR "cystitis" OR "renal abscess" OR "pyuria" OR "cystitis interstitial" OR "acute cystitis" OR "trigonitis" OR "cystitis chronic interstitial" OR "other chronic cystitis" OR "renal abscess")

Similarly, a query for *polycystic kidney* submitted to Medical World Search generated a search that included the following synonyms and more specific terms: *Kidney, Polycystic; Kidney, Polycystic, Autosomal Dominant; Kidney, Polycystic, Autosomal Recessive*. In this instance, however, employing the order in which MeSH presents words in the subject headings (kidney, polycystic) may cause important pages to be missed. For example, the above query for *polycystic kidney* resulted in only a small proportion of possible pages being retrieved. However, it is simple to edit the word order of terms and resubmit a query direct at the target search source. In this case, inverting word order to natural word order (polycystic kidney) caused many times more the number of hits to be retrieved (4,678 compared to just 108). See Figure 13.2.

Figure 13.2 Medical World Search: a search for polycystic kidney

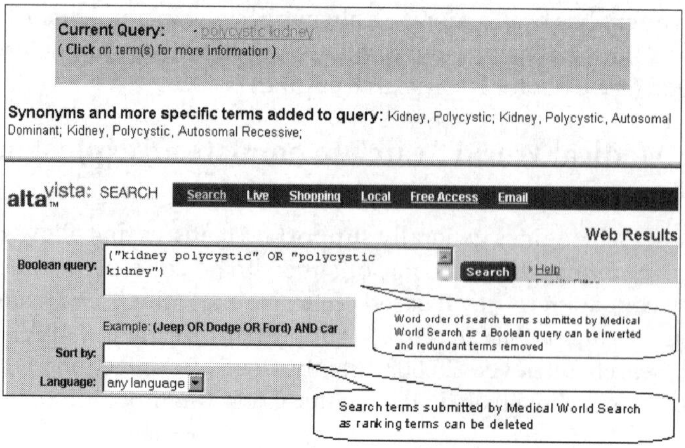

Medical World Search also allows a default explosion search to be over-ridden once a search has been conducted. Clicking on the 'Tune Explosion' button causes the chosen thesaurus term to be displayed; clicking on the hypertext link for the candidate thesaurus term reveals the position of the term in the MeSH tree. If none of the more specific terms are required, it is possible to uncheck the candidate thesaurus term and repeat the search. For example, a search for *food allergy* would map to the MeSH heading *food hypersensitivity* and by default would also include the synonym *food allergy* and the more specific term *milk hypersensitivity*. Unchecking *food hypersensitivity* would result in a search for the term itself and its synonym *food allergy*, but not the more specific term *milk hypersensitivity*. See Figure 13.3.

Figure 13.3 Medical World Search: a default explosion search may be overridden

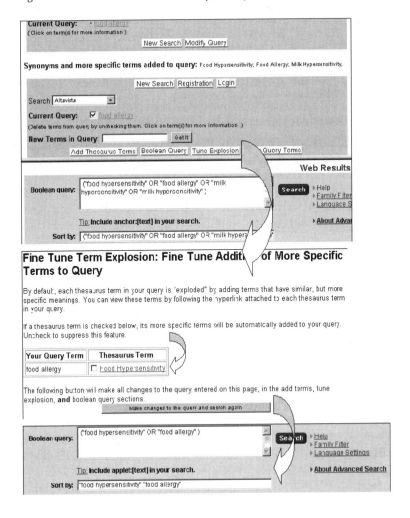

Optimising Medical World Search generated queries

As indicated above, for topics in an established area that are described by mature terminology Medical World Search may provide a useful means of focusing a search in such a way as to avoid informal terms. It also allows broadening a search by the inclusion of synonyms and related terms. However, care needs to be taken when relying on the automatic translation and expansion features offered by Medical World Search by:

- checking that useful search terms are not omitted (e.g. by incorporating additional word spellings if these are not included),

- correcting errors of submission to target search sources (e.g. eliminating Boolean operators when these are submitted as AltaVista ranking terms),

- optimising search terms submitted to target search sources (e.g. by rearranging the order of words submitted, for example by preferring natural order rather than inverse order of words; e.g. by being selective about terms submitted as AltaVista ranking terms), and

- manipulating the search query in any other appropriate way directly at the target search source.

Additional sources accessible via Medical World Search

In addition to providing a filter for the submission of queries to generic search engines, Medical World Search also allows filtered queries to be submitted to major sites that are recognised as containing high quality clinically relevant information, and also to PubMed. This facility is discussed in greater detail below (see 'Searching the full text of selected resources' later in this chapter, and also Chapter 15).

PubMed: www.ncbi.nlm.nih.gov/PubMed/

MedHunt: a health and medical Web search engine

The Health On the Net Foundation (HON) operates MedHunt, a search engine with a health and medical focus. Like generic Web search engines, MedHunt uses a robot, called MARVIN (Multi-Agent Retrieval Vagabond on Information Networks). MARVIN trawls the Web visiting health and medical pages and creates a searchable index. Unlike generic search engines, MARVIN selects only documents that are relevant to healthcare and medicine. Document relevance is computed according to a formula that takes into consideration the number of words from a medical dictionary that are found in the document, as well as their associated weights. Eight languages have so far been included (French, English, Spanish,

Portuguese, Italian, Danish, German and Dutch), a thesaurus of 20,000 medical terms has been built and the medical terms in each language have been associated to concepts.[3] The selected documents are indexed word by word and stored in a database (described as 'Auto-Indexed') that may be queried through MedHunt. A MedHunt search returns results from this Auto-Indexed database, as well as an "HONoured" database, which is compiled separately by HON staff (see Chapter 14).

MedHunt: www.hon.ch/MedHunt/

MedHunt advanced search

MedHunt advanced search allows search terms to be specified as phrases (adjacent words, e.g. *infection* control*) or synonyms (assuming an implied Boolean OR operator, e.g. *hospital [OR] nosocomial*). Figure 13.4 shows how a search may be conducted using MedHunt for guidelines on hospital infection control.

Figure 13.4 MedHunt advanced search

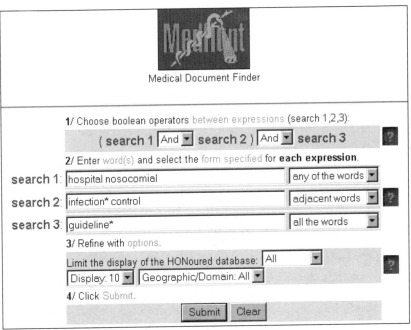

Figure 13.5 MedHunt results display

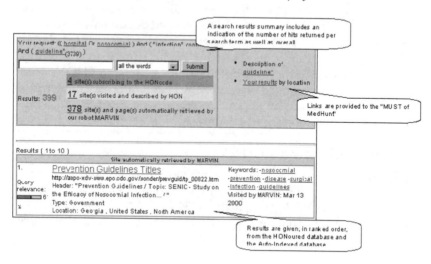

Results returned by MedHunt are displayed in three parts (see Figure 13.5):

- a search results summary including an indication of the number of hits returned per search term as well as overall,
- links to the "MUST of MedHunt" (see below), and
- results in ranked order from the HONoured database, and from the Auto-Indexed database.

A query relevance score is assigned to each hit returned. The score is calculated taking account of the location of a search term in pages retrieved (title, URL, text, meta description, etc.). For example, pages that contain a search term in the title will attract a higher score compared to those where the term is present in the body of the page. It is possible, therefore, that a score given to an Auto-Indexed site will be higher than a score assigned to an HONoured site. To make the reading of the results easier, MedHunt associates an image with the score of the page. MedHunt's results display also provides additional information (for example, keywords, hypertext links to the source, as well as description metadata where available) that is intended to help the user assess the value of a page.

When a search is conducted, MedHunt offers a number of options for further result analysis (the 'MUST of MedHunt'):

- Topics related to a request: a list is offered of the medical terms that occur most frequently in the returned documents. For example, a search for *urinary tract infections* returned the twenty most commonly occurring terms, including pyuria and bacteriuria. Clicking on one of the terms causes a new search to be generated.

- MeSH descriptions: available when a query term matches a MeSH term. For example, a search for *melioidosis* generated the prompt to see a description of *"melioidosis"*. When this was selected, the MeSH description for *melioidosis* was displayed, along with the option to display the MeSH tree (by clicking on the highlighted term).

- Results by location: sorts the results of a search by domain, continent and country (as well as states for USA sites).

- Translation: where a term exists in the multilingual dictionary employed by MedHunt, it is possible to view a translation in the languages covered. For example, a translation for bacteriuria was offered in all eight languages (English, Danish, German, Spanish, French, Italian, Dutch and Portuguese). Clicking on *bacteriurie* generated a search for pages that contained the French language term.

- Spell checker: if a query returns no results, MedHunt proposes dictionary terms that have a similar spelling. Spell checking is performed on the health and medical terms included in the MedHunt dictionary. For example, a search for *melloidosis* returned zero hits, but MedHunt suggested a variety of possible alternatives; among those was *melioidosis*, and it was simple to click on the term with the correct spelling in order to initiate a search.

MedHunt Advanced Search:
www.hon.ch/MedHunt/AdvSearch.html

Browsing the MeSH trees using MedHunt

HON offers a facility for browsing the MeSH trees. If the MeSH heading is known for a particular term, it is possible to search for this directly, to display the definition of the term, to view broader and narrower terms as appropriate, and to select to search for a MeSH heading directly within PubMed (see Figure 13.6). Narrower terms will not be automatically included in a search query, i.e. MedHunt will not automatically invoke an explosion search, so a search on *Burkholderia Infections* would not include *melioidosis* resources in the retrieved results.

Figure 13.6. Browsing the MeSH trees using MedHunt

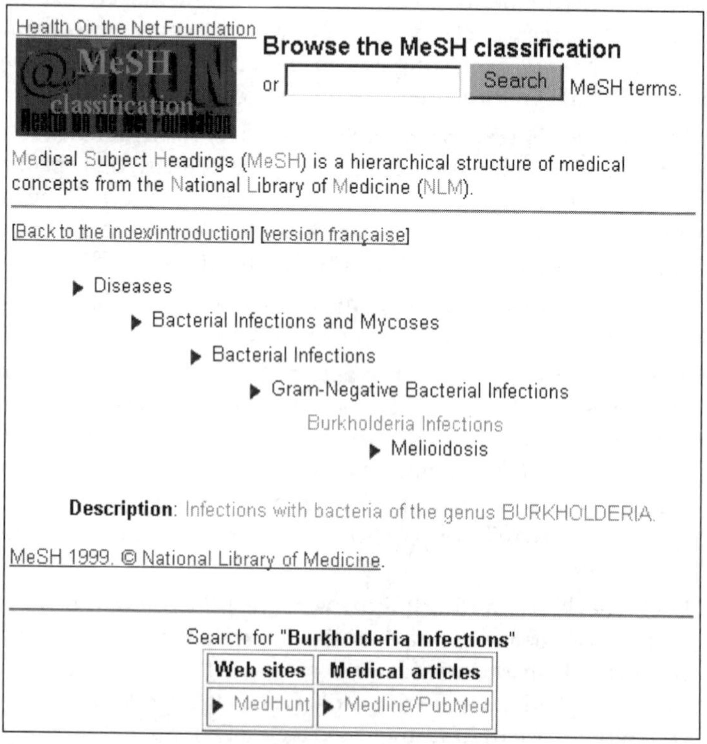

Health On the Net Foundation		

Browse the MeSH classification

or [   ] Search MeSH terms.

Medical Subject Headings (MeSH) is a hierarchical structure of medical concepts from the National Library of Medicine (NLM).

[Back to the index/introduction] [version française]

▶ Diseases
   ▶ Bacterial Infections and Mycoses
      ▶ Bacterial Infections
         ▶ Gram-Negative Bacterial Infections
            Burkholderia Infections
               ▶ Melioidosis

Description: Infections with bacteria of the genus BURKHOLDERIA.

MeSH 1999. © National Library of Medicine.

Search for "**Burkholderia Infections**"

Web sites	Medical articles
▶ MedHunt	▶ Medline/PubMed

HON Browse the MeSH classification: www.hon.ch / MeSH /

Additional sources accessible via Health on the Net

In addition to the Auto-Indexed database, MedHunt also interrogates the HONoured database, the HON information gateway to selected resources, which is discussed in the next chapter.

HON additionally operates BioHunt which specialises in retrieving molecular biology sources. MARVIN is employed to construct this index, too, using a dictionary of 3,000 specialist terms.

Further services from HON are referred to under Hybrid information gateways in the next chapter. MedHunt as an interface to PubMed is discussed in Chapter 15.

BioHunt: www.expasy.ch / BioHunt /

Health and medical Web search engines: tools for greater relevance?

Both Medical World Search and MedHunt offer full text searches of the Web via search engines with a medical focus. Medical World Search achieves this indirectly, by submitting queries that are filtered for medical terminology to existing generic search engines, whereas MedHunt queries HON's own Auto-Indexed database that is compiled directly by MARVIN, the MedHunt robot. They therefore allow quite specific querying, in common with the generic search engines.

Retrieval from either service is potentially more relevant, compared to that from querying generic Web search engines, due to their terminologically defined subject focus. However, in common with generic Web search engines, Medical World Search (when submitting queries to generic Web search engines) and MedHunt (when querying the HON Auto-Indexed database) both lead to the retrieval of information that has not been evaluated in any way. Results from both sources are ranked according to relevance scores. Nonetheless, MedHunt Help takes care to clarify that 'the score does not indicate the value (in a medical view) of a page', but only the relation between a query and the words in a page: 'So, for a same page, two different requests will give two different scores'.[4] While automated methods can rank Web pages according to the frequency of occurrence of query terms, they are not in a position to establish the scope, provenance or validity of a resource. Therefore, an element of human assessment is necessary, and that is at the root of creating the gateways to pre-evaluated information discussed in the following chapter.

References

1. National Library of Medicine. Fact Sheet: Unified Medical Language System. Available from: http://www.nlm.nih.gov/pubs/factsheets/umls.html

2. Krabshuis J. Endoscopy information online: can endoscopists close the gap between what is known and what they do? *Endoscopy* 1997; **29**:871-882.

3. Baujard O, Baujard V, Aurel S, Boyer C, Appel RD. MARVIN, multi-agent softbot to retrieve multilingual medical information on the Web. *Medical Informatics* 1998; **23**(3):187-191.

4. MedHunt. Help – Score. Available from: http://www.hon.ch/MedHunt/Help/score.html

Chapter 14

Health and medical information gateways

The need to assess the quality of Web-based information is probably greater in health and medicine than in any other field of knowledge, particularly if information from the Internet is to inform professional education, research or clinical practice. Information gateways have been developed by health and medical practitioners and information professionals with the aim of bringing together selected resources based on criteria that address the needs of a professional audience. In a recent survey, a number of such health and medical information gateways were compared according to a range of criteria.[1] Declared best overall in terms of content were Medical Matrix and OMNI (Organising Medical Networked Information), as well as healthfinder for consumer health information. In assessing content, the most significant criteria for comparison were that the sites in question:

- clearly identified their target audience,
- defined their purpose and how they intended to achieve it (usually with some sort of collection development policy),
- indicated both an intent to regularly review links and content, and appeared to do this, and
- clearly separated the informational content of the site from any advertising or commercial content.

The resources included in such services are usually derived from the publicly accessible Internet, i.e. pages that have generally not been subject to peer review prior to publication or appraised for their appropriateness to clinical practice. However, what distinguishes health information gateways from Web search engines is the prior evaluation of information.

Common features are:

- they provide a gateway to resources: descriptions, brief or extended, are given to help the information seeker assess the likely usefulness of a resource prior to viewing it directly,
- only evaluated resources are included in the gateways: subject-relevant evaluation criteria are usually explicit and publicly disclosed, and

- links are made at the level of a resource, rather than individual Web pages: information gateways do not generally index all the words of all the pages of the resources to which they provide links.

---

healthfinder: www.healthfinder.gov/

Medical Matrix: www.medmatrix.org/

OMNI: omni.ac.uk/

OMNI: an example of an information gateway

Through a process of evaluation, description, indexing and classification, OMNI provides a gateway to high quality information resources on the Internet. OMNI places an emphasis on UK-based information, as well as high quality international resources. The evaluation of resources concentrates on relevance and appropriateness of content rather than presentational features (see the OMNI guidelines for resource evaluation). Indicatively, a search for *gastroesophageal reflux* retrieves a selection of resources, including a quantitative systematic review, a CME module and a practice guideline. A search for common diseases produces links to patient information from a range of providers. For example, a search for *influenza* returned a collection of patient resources from sources such as the Health Education Board for Scotland, the American Academy of Family Physicians, the Loyola University Health System, the State of Maryland Department of Health and Mental Hygiene, the American Lung Association, and also the Ridgeway Surgery, a UK general practice.

OMNI includes in the region of 5,000 resource descriptions that can at times be extensive, and these are indexed using MeSH headings. A search in OMNI will target all the available information created by OMNI about a resource. The availability of the MeSH indexing allows specific retrieval also through browsing (see below).

In addition to the databases that OMNI creates and maintains, access is also supported to resources that are provided by a range of contributors. These include: DerWeb (Dental Education Resources), NHCON (Nursing and Healthcare Resources on the Net) and CTI Biology. Originally a project funded under the UK Higher Education electronic libraries programme (eLib), OMNI is now a part of the BIOME service, which offers broader coverage and addresses a wider, cross-sectoral audience.

BIOME: biome.ac.uk/

CTI Biology: www.liv.ac.uk/ctibiol/

DerWeb: www.derweb.ac.uk/

eLib Programme: www.ukoln.ac.uk/services/elib/

NHCON - Nursing and Healthcare Resources on the Net: www.shef.ac.uk/~nhcon/

OMNI guidelines for resource evaluation: omni.ac.uk/agec/evalguid.html

OMNI search options

OMNI offers a range of search and browse features. In addition to the default simple search, OMNI also supports advanced searching, which allows the constituent databases to be selected and a variety of options to be set, including case sensitivity, stemming and the facility to display titles only. Field specific searching is also possible (e.g. restricting a search to words in the title of a resource). Boolean and phrase searching are both supported.

For example, a search for (*food or nutrition) and (allergy or hypersensitivity*) produced eleven matches when a simple OMNI search was conducted. The same number of matches was retrieved when the default advanced search options were set, but additional matches were retrieved when additional databases were selected.

OMNI allows limited fielded searching. Publication types are entered as keywords and can be retrieved by restricting a search to the keywords field. For example, systematic reviews are indexed by OMNI with the publication type 'review, literature'. Systematic reviews of treatments for prostate cancer might be sought by entering the query *prostate and keywords=review literature*. Similarly, clinical practice guidelines are indexed with the publication type *practice guideline*. Clinical practice guidelines relating to infection control might be sought by entering the query *infection and keywords=practice guideline*. Patient information can be retrieved specifically by searching for *keywords=patient education*.

Using MeSH headings to search or browse for a topic

All OMNI records are indexed with MeSH headings. The option to browse the index to MeSH headings is consequently one of the most useful of OMNI's browse features, with relationships among MeSH headings derived from the National Library of Medicine's UMLS metathesaurus. It is possible to select a term in an alphabetical sequence and identify other relevant terms that may be alphabetically collocated. For example, looking up *influenza* in the alphabetical listings reveals an additional potentially useful term: *influenza vaccine*. Following through the link from *influenza* leads to a list of other related available terms, for which OMNI holds records, for example *bronchitis, common cold, pharyngitis, rhinitis, sinusitis*, etc.

It is also possible to explore broader and narrower headings. For example, selecting *insomnia* from the alphabetical listing displays the broader term *sleep disorders* and the related term *somnambulism*, with links directly through to those records that are indexed using the suggested related terms. Clicking on the link to *sleep disorders* would generate additional records of possible interest.

The facility to search directly for MeSH headings is also supported. For example, a search for *influenza* retrieved both *influenza* and *influenza vaccine* as possible search terms, and selecting to search both simultaneously led to wider retrieval.

Searching for a topic using thesaurus terms allows some mapping to preferred MeSH headings if a non-MeSH term is entered. For example, a query for *"mad cow disease"* mapped to *Encephalopathy, Bovine Spongiform*, and a search on the latter (preferred MeSH heading) could then be initiated. A search for *bse* similarly translated to *Encephalopathy, Bovine Spongiform*. A search for this would result in greater specificity of retrieval than the search term *bse* alone (which can potentially be expanded to Breast Self Examination as well as Bovine Spongiform Encephalopathy).

OMNI's thesaurus search supports the equivalent of a MeSH heading explosion search as well as the selection of multiple MeSH headings. For example, a search for *prion* mapped to the MeSH headings *Prion Diseases* and *Prions*, for which OMNI had records catalogued. The tree for *Prion Diseases* included the more specific *Creutzfeld-Jacob Syndrome* and *Encephalopathy, Bovine Spongiform*. A search could be initiated to include *Prion Diseases* and the more specific terms, i.e. to reproduce the equivalent of a MeSH heading explosion search, by clicking in the check box alongside the *Prion Diseases* MeSH tree. Multiple MeSH headings can also be selected, so this search could be expanded to include the additional term *Prions* by clicking additionally in the check box alongside the *Prions* MeSH tree. See Figure 14.1.

Alternatively, MeSH headings can be selected individually. Consecutive as well as non-consecutive lines of headings can be selected by holding down the Control key (PC) or the Command key (Mac) while left-clicking with the mouse on each required heading. For example, a more focused search could be conducted by selecting just the two terms *Prion Diseases* and *Creutzfeld-Jacob Syndrome*, which would restrict hits to just the human diseases.

> *Figure 14.1 OMNI: a query for* prion *is mapped to the MeSH headings* Prion Diseases *and* Prions, *for which OMNI has records catalogued*

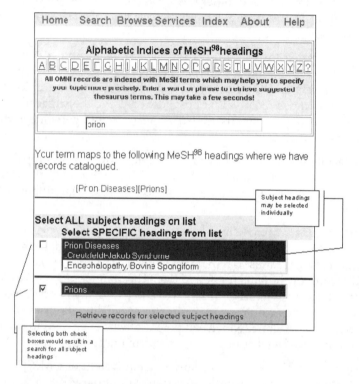

While viewing OMNI resource descriptions, it is possible to click on a keyword of interest (generally a MeSH heading or publication type) and to initiate a lateral search. This will generate a direct search on that keyword alone, but will not allow browsing of broader or narrower terms. For example, several records were retrieved by a search for *oestrogen replacement therapy*. In addition to *Estrogen Replacement Therapy*, the MeSH heading *Menopause* was also assigned to the records. Clicking on the Keyword hypertext link for *Menopause* caused a new search to be initiated, which generated additional records. See Figure 14.2.

Figure 14.2 OMNI lateral searching: clicking on the Keyword hypertext link initiates a new search for Menopause

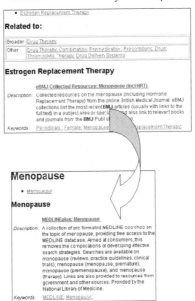

OMNI Index to MeSH headings: omni.ac.uk / umls /

OMNI Thesaurus: omni.ac.uk / search / thesaurus /

Medical Matrix

An initiative of the American Medical Informatics Association (AMIA), Medical Matrix is devoted to posting, annotating and continuously updating 'full content, unrestricted access, Internet clinical medicine resources' and is targeted primarily at US physicians and healthworkers.[2] A ranking system is employed by which one to five stars are assigned to each resource. An editorial board, comprising members of AMIA's Internet Working Group, reviews resource evaluations.[3]

Medical Matrix offers an easy to browse arrangement of resources by broad specialty area, as well as by disease. Resources are further categorised by type within each broad topic area, which can aid fast retrieval. For example, resources on infectious diseases are subdivided into the following categories: searches, news, full text / multimedia, abstracts, textbooks, major sites / home pages, practice guidelines / FAQs, cases, images path / clinical, CME, patient education, directories, educational materials, classifieds, forums. Brief annotations are given for each resource.

Medical Matrix also offers Clinical Searches, an array of database sources that may be interrogated in succession for specific topics or types of information. For example, four databases are recommended for AIDS related information. Although the direct submission of search queries is often not allowed, the Clinical Searches page provides a useful reminder of sources to search in addition to Medical Matrix.

Also available from Medical Matrix is a Search Hub page, which brings together a more varied selection of search services, ranging from sources of drug information through to generic Web search engines such as AltaVista.

Medical Matrix: www.medmatrix.org/

Medical Matrix Clinical Searches: www.medmatrix.org/info/search.asp

Medical Matrix Search Hub: www.medmatrix.org/info/searchhub.asp

---

CliniWeb

CliniWeb focuses on biomedical information on the Web that could be used in healthcare education and practice. Information is organised using MeSH, including the Anatomy, Diseases and Chemical and Drugs MeSH trees. CliniWeb values information from peer-reviewed journals more highly than other sources of information, and health sciences universities and government agencies are also valued highly.[4]

Although CliniWeb aims to index information at the level of individual pages on the Web, links are often made to resources within a site. In the region of 10,000 resources are included in CliniWeb. All of these are indexed using MeSH headings but no further information is given about a resource other than its title.

CliniWeb offers both browsing and searching of MeSH terms. Searching is possible in English, French, German, Portuguese and Spanish, although the resources included in CliniWeb are all English-language. Direct links are also provided from the MeSH terms to PubMed, and these are commonly the only links available.

CliniWeb International: www.ohsu.edu/cliniweb/

Medline*plus*

Produced by the US National Library of Medicine (NLM), Medline*plus* aims to provide a selective list of authoritative Web pages on health, with an emphasis on information that is available from NLM and the National Institutes of Health (NIH). Selection criteria include quality, authority and accuracy of content, educational rather than commercial purpose, availability and maintenance of the Web page, and special features such as accessibility to persons with disabilities.[5] The information covered includes sources on health topics, dictionaries and glossaries, links to major associations, publications and news sources, as well as directories. No annotations are provided, but the resources are organised into subcategories for ease of retrieval. For example, ten resources about measles were subdivided into the following categories: general / overviews, children, organisations, prevention / screening, specific conditions / aspects, statistics, and pictures / diagrams. Spanish language material is also specifically signposted. Medline*plus* allows browsing of health topics alphabetically or by broad category and also supports searching. Links are provided to PubMed for recent research articles.

Medline*plus*: www.nlm.nih.gov / medlineplus /

The Karolinska Institute Library

The Karolinska Institute Library offers extensive lists of links (though no annotations) of resources in health and medicine. Disease links are indexed using MeSH headings and can be browsed or searched.

Karolinska Institute Library: www.mic.ki.se / Diseases /

MedWebPlus

Like the Karolinska Institute Library, MedWebPlus also provides links to a wide range of resources. Short annotations sometimes accompany the links and details of online periodicals can be quite extensive.

MedWebPlus: www.medwebplus.com /

Searching the full text of selected resources: HON MedHunt and Medical World Search

The gateways mentioned so far provide varied amounts of descriptive information about a resource. Some may offer links alone to selected resources with little or no additional annotation (e.g. the Karolinska

Institute Library, Medline*plus* and CliniWeb), whereas other gateways may offer brief annotations (e.g. Medical Matrix) or full and informative descriptions (e.g. OMNI). When searches are submitted to gateways, it is the descriptive information provided by the gateways that is searched. Consequently, the less information a gateway provides about a resource, the more likely it is that potentially useful resources may be missed.

HON's MedHunt and Medical World Search offer their own gateways to pre-selected resources, in addition to their search engines. However, because both services provide partial or complete access to the full text of the selected resources, they are able to offer comparatively more information and consequently potentially greater retrieval.

HON MedHunt: HONoured database

In addition to its Auto-indexed database, HON's MedHunt also interrogates a directory, called the HONoured database. This is created by the Health On the Net staff who select, describe and index resources and allocate them to several categories. Although MedHunt interrogates both databases simultaneously, it is possible to view the HONoured results separately (they are displayed first). Searches of the HONoured database target not only words in the title, description and keywords, but also a wide range of medical terms that are selected from the full text of the original resource.

MedHunt: www.hon.ch/MedHunt/

Medical World Search Major Sites

Medical World Search Major Sites is a database of selected medical resources, which is compiled to include resources that match a range of selection criteria.[6] According to these, resources that are included in Medical World Search contain information that is deemed to be useful for medical professionals in clinical practice, although high quality information that is useful for patients has also been included. Information that has been peer-reviewed is viewed as particularly valuable. Additionally, resources are included if the information is well maintained and highly accurate, and if the information provider is considered reputable. Some of the resources are chosen because they are listed in major medical sites that match the Medical World Search selection criteria, and these include Medical Matrix and CliniWeb.

However, Medical World Search captures and indexes the full content of the target sites instead of providing just a link or an annotation for each resource, and as a result covers in the region of 100,000 Web pages. It is consequently the full content of a resource that is searchable via Medical

World Search's Major Sites, rather than a description of its content. The search queries supported can therefore be more specific, and retrieval is likewise potentially greater.

Medical World Search Major Sites: www.mwsearch.com/

Hybrid information gateways

It is becoming increasingly difficult to distinguish between the different functions supported by any one service. Originally individual services provided access to the resources that they alone compiled. However, it is now more common that additional sources are offered, some of which may not be the product of the host, but the result of collaborative agreements or links to third party services. As a result, hybrid services that query a range of original and sometimes heterogeneous target sources are now in abundance.

For example, linking to PubMed is increasingly popular as an additional supplementary source of high quality information. Different services vary in the manner in which they interpret queries prior to submission to PubMed. Access to the medical literature, including searching databases such as PubMed, is discussed in detail in the following chapter, where differences such as these are explored in greater detail.

Some gateways that compile their own descriptions of resources will also cross-search other resources. For example, as mentioned earlier, OMNI provides access to a range of resources from collaborating partners, which can be simultaneously cross-searched with the OMNI databases. Far greater coverage of pre-evaluated sources can be provided by such an approach.

Medical World Search compiles its own database of resources, but also incorporates resources from other sites. Medical World Search Major Sites therefore in essence provides a cross-searching facility for those sources that are included. Medical World Search also allows searches to be submitted to PubMed, as well as a selection of search engines (AltaVista, HotBot, Infoseek, Webcrawler). Queries to these sources need to be submitted in sequence to each separate source.

Health On the Net's MedHunt offers the option to submit a single search to a range of pre-selected resources, some of which are created and maintained by HON but with other sources being compiled by a robot (MARVIN). In 1999 HON launched a new service, HONselect, which adds PubMed references, news via Individual.com and images (still and moving) to the retrieval from MedHunt (see Figure 14.3). HONselect also allows MeSH tree browsing.

Figure 14.3 HONselect: a search for tendinitis retrieves Web resources from HON databases, medical images, medical news for muscular diseases and links to PubMed

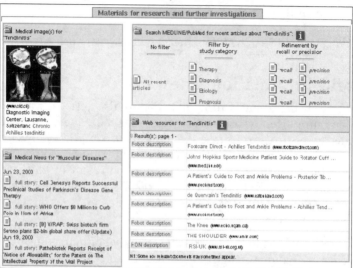

This is a development that is likely to become more significant over time. As different types of resources are brought together and possibly even become cross-searchable from a single source, there is the potential for higher and lower quality material to be presented simultaneously without adequate signposting. Users of such resources will need to be increasingly discriminating in their information use.

HONselect: www.hon.ch/HONselect/

HONselect MeSH browsing:
www.hon.ch/HONselect/Browse.html

Individual.com: www.individual.com/

Other health and medical information gateways

Several compilations exist that bring together potentially useful directories and search tools in health and medicine. A number are listed by Medical Matrix. OMNI also lists a selection of such tools on a Launchpad page, providing a search form wherever possible so that each one can be searched directly from the page.

Medical Matrix guide to Internet guides: www.medmatrix.org/
_SPages/Medical_Internet_Guides.asp#Directories

OMNI Launchpad: omni.ac.uk/other-search/

Specialist sources of health and medical information

Regardless of how effectively a gateway may cover key resources in a field, the sheer range of potentially useful information on the Web means that individual specialist sources, which may contain high quality information, may remain undetected. This highlights the need for increased awareness by the information seeker of the breadth of sources available and knowledge of how and when these may be most usefully tapped. The following provides an indication of sources of specialist types of health and medical information.

Given the breadth of health and medicine, specialty-specific directories of resources, or resource lists, have been produced by a wide range of compiling editors. In orthopaedics, for example, Orthogate brings together the efforts of the orthopaedics community worldwide by identifying and organising information resources that are deemed by practitioners to be of relevance. Myles Clough, one of Orthogate's Chief Content Editors, asserts that 'orthopaedic surgery now leads all medical fields in the development of a comprehensive gateway resource, Orthogate'.[7] Orthogate contains Orthopaedic Web Links (OWL), a searchable and browsable database of over 3,000 links to orthopaedic Web resources.

Many similar sites have now appeared, sometimes compiled by scientific societies or professional associations. A selective compilation of these is provided by the Hardin MetaDirectory of Internet Health Sources (Hardin MD), so named because it aims to be a 'directory of directories'. Arranged broadly by specialty, and then by size of directory, it can be a useful first port of call for those wishing to acquaint themselves with the range of resources available. For example, looking up nursing will point the searcher to a list of large, medium or small lists of nursing related resources on the Internet.

The Hardin MD determines selection and rank order of resource lists primarily by their connection rates. As a result, although Hardin MD suggests that the independent lists selected for inclusion are those that are most frequently cited by the people in the field,[8] only those that are regularly accessible by Hardin MD are included.

Different specialty headings link to several subdivisions of established health and medical directories,[9] so the Hardin MD offers one way of sequentially browsing through the specialty sections of some of the gateways mentioned above, for example the Karolinska Institute Library and Medline*plus*, as well as MedWebPlus.

Other specialist sources of health and medical information are discussed elsewhere in this book, and include gateways to evidence-based information (Chapter 3); accessing information on diseases, conditions and disease outbreaks (Chapter 4); health and medical news sources (Chapter 9); finding atlases and images (Chapter 2) etc.

Hardin MD: www.lib.uiowa.edu/hardin/md/

Orthogate: www.orthogate.org/

Orthopaedic Web Links: owl.orthgate.org/

Health and medical gateways: tools for higher quality information

Health and medical information gateways are becoming increasingly popular owing to the unwieldy retrieval and low quality of hits from generic search tools. However, the trawl for high quality information on the Internet can be a long and time-consuming one. Resources have proliferated and no single service offers a comprehensive one-stop approach. There is therefore a heightened need to be aware of the wide range of tools available and care is required to ensure that sources are appropriately selected. Audience level, quality of evaluation or appraisal and extent of coverage are some of the criteria by which health and medical Web search tools may be assessed.

Any Web-based search for health and medical information on the Internet will not be complete without reference to the peer-reviewed research literature. This includes bibliographic databases such as Medline, as well as the full text of journal articles, most of which are not available for free on the Web, and the content of which cannot be searched systematically via the search tools mentioned so far. The following chapters aim to illustrate the power of the Internet in bringing together high quality, peer-reviewed information resources such as these, and to highlight ways in which this information may be accessed.

References

1.   Anderson PF, Allee N, Chung J, Westra B. Comparison of health information megasites. Available from: http:// www.lib.umich.edu/megasite/

2.	Medical Matrix. About Medical Matrix. Available from: http://www.medmatrix.org/info/about.asp

3.	Medical Matrix. Peer review and editorial board. Available from: http://www.medmatrix.org/info/edboard.asp

4.	CliniWeb. About CliniWeb International. Available from: http://www.ohsu.edu/cliniweb/about.html

5.	Medline*plus*. Selection guidelines. Available from: http://www.nlm.nih.gov/medlineplus/criteria.html

6.	Medical World Search. Selection of sites. Available from: http://www.mwsearch.com/selection_of_sites.html

7.	Clough M. A guide to orthopaedic information on the Internet. *He@lth Information on the Internet* 1999 Feb; (7):8-9. Available from: http://www.wellcome.ac.uk/en/images/hioti4_pdf_694.pdf or http://www.wellcome.ac.uk/en/1/homlibinfacthiiarc7gid.html

8.	Hardin MetaDirectory. About Hardin MD. Available from: http://www.lib.uiowa.edu/hardin/md/about.html

9.	Hardin MetaDirectory. Comprehensive health and medical index sites. Available from: http://www.lib.uiowa.edu/hardin/md/idx.html

Chapter 15

Searching the medical literature

It has been suggested that the best sources of health and medical information on the Internet for both research and clinical practice are the online versions of established medical literature sources: bibliographic databases such as Medline, and electronic journals available in full text online.[1-3] However, the published medical research literature cannot generally be retrieved via generic Web search tools, and even gateways to evaluated sources of health and medical information may include material that has not been peer reviewed prior to appearing on the Web. This chapter focuses on searching the traditional sources of peer reviewed medical literature.

Conventional bibliographic databases contain references or citations to full text documents, commonly of the published literature. Such databases have traditionally provided the main route to accessing the peer reviewed health and medical journal literature. Originally available as indexes and abstracts in a printed format, and available back to the previous century, databases such as these are clearly well established – whether or not a journal is indexed in one of these can be taken as an indicator of its quality.

Publishers have made bibliographic databases available through commercial online database hosts since the mid-1960s, covering all manner of subject specialisms. Databanks detailing scientific information in the fields of chemistry, physics and molecular biology in particular, also blossomed alongside these through the same or specialist online hosts. Databases and databanks are now often available through the Internet, targeting the occasional searcher with user-friendly Web interfaces. The databases usually provide access to proprietary information, and subscription is still required to access such resources, reflecting the cost and added value involved in acquiring, processing, compiling and quality assuring the information made available in this way.

There are many reasons why searching such sources directly is essential:

- bibliographic databases may contain in the order of 10 million records each;

- databanks may contain thousands, millions or billions of discrete data on chemical elements, or molecular and gene sequence information. It is estimated that over 2 million bases are deposited into GenBank every day;[4] and

- the content available through bibliographic databases and databanks is not generally searchable or retrievable via Web search engines.

Several of the databases mentioned below feature in the collections of individual institutions or professional organisations. Consortia and national strategies for access to electronic resources also often incorporate resources such as these. For example, provision is made for their inclusion in the national collection portfolio for UK Higher Education (HE) and collaborating sectors. As a result, UK HE users are able to access several databases from a range of national data centres[5] and a list is maintained of health and medicine related databases that are available.[6] Some may become available also via the National electronic Library for Health (NeLH). Elsewhere, institutional subscriptions are usually required to enable access to these databases, or they can be accessed via traditional commercial online database host services (see below).

> National electronic Library for Health (NeLH):
> www.nelh.nhs.uk/

General bibliographic databases

Numerous databases may be of interest to health and medical professionals. From social science to economics and education, Web-based database services are increasingly becoming available, which provide novel interfaces to established or new databases. Most are available only on subscription, via commercial online database host services. However, some may be available for free, partially or in their entirety. An example is ERIC, one of the largest databases of information about education. Updated monthly, the database provides access to document and journal citations going back to 1966. Full text ERIC Digests can also be accessed for free.

More commonly, only partial access is granted for free to bibliographic databases. For example, the ProQuest Digital Dissertations service provides Web access to the most recent three months of Dissertation Abstracts for free, while institutional subscribers alone have access to the entire database. Electronic versions of the full dissertations are available to download for a fee in several formats.

The Web of Science from the Institute for Scientific Information (ISI) is a collection of databases in the fields of the sciences, the social sciences and the arts and humanities. Data are included from around 7,500 international journals. The popularity of the Web of Science owes much to the inclusion of cited references with each record. As well as allowing subject-based searching, each database also supports the facility to search by cited references (to find references citing a known document), and so research can be followed forward in time. The Science Citation Index database allows multidisciplinary searching of the scientific literature, including most medical specialties. The Social Sciences Citation Index database covers subjects such as public health, psychology and psychiatry. Multiple links may be provided internally between references and their citations, as well as externally to the original published literature, gene sequence data and patents, which make it possible to explore conceptual as well as practical relationships in the published research literature.[7] Prior subscription is required in order to access most journals online.

Access to the Web of Science requires subscription and is available to UK HE users via the Manchester Information and Associated Services (MIMAS). The ISI citation databases are also searchable via commercial online database hosts (see below). Also available from ISI (and to the UK HE community via MIMAS) is the Index to Scientific and Technical Proceedings (ISTP), a multidisciplinary database of conference papers.

> ERIC: askeric.org/Eric/
>
> ERIC Digests: www.ed.gov/databases/ERIC_Digests/index/
>
> ISI Cited Reference Searching: An Introduction: www.isinet.com/training/tutorials/citedreference/
>
> ISI Web of Science and Index to Scientific and Technical Proceedings (ISTP) via MIMAS: wos.mimas.ac.uk/
>
> MIMAS: www.mimas.ac.uk/
>
> ProQuest Digital Dissertations: wwwlib.umi.com/dissertations/

General health and medical bibliographic databases

Several databases aim to index the published literature within health and medicine specifically, among which Medline, produced by the US National Library of Medicine (NLM), has long been regarded as central. Later in this chapter, we focus on the free Medline services available via the Web. In addition, however, several other high quality databases exist.

EMBASE is a European database produced by Elsevier Science in the Netherlands, with coverage complementary to Medline in the areas of European literature and drug and toxicology related information. It includes data from 3,500 biomedical journals. The importance of EMBASE in complementing Medline for drug and therapy related research in particular has been widely documented.[8–11] EMBASE is not available for free, although it may be available to individual users for no fee due to institutional subscriptions or membership of professional organisations. For example, in the UK, membership of the British Medical Association (BMA) entitles users to register for free access to the BMA Library's Medline Plus service, which provides access to EMBASE as well as Medline.

Several nursing databases are available. The International Nursing Index is partially incorporated within Medline itself, and widely used also is the Cumulative Index to Nursing and Allied Health Literature (CINAHL). Like EMBASE, CINAHL is available only via subscription. In the UK, the British Nursing Index provides coverage of the UK nursing literature from 1994 onwards.

BIOSIS Previews is the electronic version of the printed Biological Abstracts and Biological Abstracts/RRM (Reports, Reviews, Meetings), and indexes the research literature in the biological sciences, including aspects of medical research. In addition to the journal literature, this database also provides in depth coverage of the meetings literature, reviews, research reports, books and monographs. By the end of 2000, the BIOSIS Previews database is likely to include around 12.5 million records dating from 1985.[12] BIOSIS is available via several proprietary interfaces and is not available free of charge.

BIOSIS: www.biosis.org/

British Nursing Index: www.bni.org.uk/

CINAHL: www.cinahl.com/

EMBASE: www.elsevier.nl/inca/publications/store/5/2/3/3/2/8/

Medline Plus, BMA Library: ovid.bma.org.uk/

Specialist health and medical bibliographic databases

Owing to the need for focused retrieval of information in clinical practice, databases abound that offer coverage of the research literature by specialty (e.g. PsycINFO), disease (e.g. CancerNet) or age group (e.g. AgeLine). These are usually available only via a subscription or pay-as-you-go schemes through commercial online hosts. Catalogues of database suppliers and directories of online hosts give up-to-date information about available databases and current charges (see section on commercial online database hosts below).

CancerNet from the US National Cancer Institute (NCI) provides free access to its files of the CANCERLIT and Physician Data Query (PDQ) databases, as well as a range of other resources for consumers and practitioners. PDQ and the CANCERLIT Topic Searches (monthly special topic searches for about 90 topics, along with recent monthly editions) are also available via several mirror sites. For example, CancerWEB at the Gray Laboratory Cancer Research Trust offers a UK mirror site.

It is not uncommon for a database to be made available via several services, each supplying their own search interface. For example, AgeLine is available via the following database distributors, all of which charge a fee:

- Cambridge Scientific Abstracts,
- The Dialog Corporation,
- HealthGate Data Corporation,
- Ovid Technologies, and
- SilverPlatter Information.

It is also not uncommon for subsets of established databases to be made available instead of the full databases. For example, the American Psychological Association produces PsycINFO with subsets, including ClinPSYC. At the time of writing, under a special arrangement, registered users of Doctors.net in the UK received free access to ClinPSYC, but not the whole of PsycINFO.

AgeLine: research.aarp.org/ageline/

Cambridge Scientific Abstracts: www.csa.com/

CANCERLIT: cancernet.nci.nih.gov/cancerlit.html

CANCERLIT Topic Searches: cancernet.nci.nih.gov/canlit/canlit.htm

CancerNet: cancernet.nci.nih.gov/

CancerNet: CancerWEB UK mirror: www.graylab.ac.uk/cancernet.html

ClinPSYC: www.apa.org/psycinfo/clinpsyc.html

Dialog Corporation: www.dialog.com/

Doctors.net: www.doctors.net.uk/

HealthGate Data Corporation: www.healthgate.com/

Ovid Technologies: www.ovid.com/

PDQ: cancernet.nci.nih.gov/pdq.html

PsycINFO: www.apa.org/psycinfo/

SilverPlatter Information: www.silverplatter.com/

Databases from the US National Library of Medicine (NLM)

The NLM allows databases to be accessed for free via two different services: PubMed (which is discussed separately below) and Internet Grateful Med (IGM). TOXNET and LocatorPlus also provide access to clusters of databases.

IGM allows the following Medline and related databases to be searched:

- Medline: citations in the fields of clinical and preclinical medicine from over 4,000 journals;

- OLDMedline: 771,287 citations originally printed in the 1960–1965 Cumulated Index Medicus;

- PREMedline: basic citation information prior to indexing for Medline. Citations are added daily until indexing data is added; the records are added weekly to Medline once complete; and

- SDILINE: citations from the most recent complete month in Medline.

IGM Medline supports searching for subject, author name and title word. Up to three concepts may be searched using AND or OR Boolean operators. IGM offers a 'Find MeSH/Meta Terms' feature, which suggests MeSH and UMLS search terms for inclusion in a search. For example, a default search for *esophageal reflux* is translated as *"gastroesophageal reflux"[MeSH Terms] OR esophageal reflux[Text Word]*. Entering *esophageal reflux* and selecting the 'Find MeSH/Meta Terms' option leads to additional terms being displayed in an IGM Metathesaurus Browser Screen. Searches can also be further analysed for ambiguous synonyms of search qualifiers. Limit options are available for publication types and languages (a selective range of options for these is presented via pull-down menus), as well as study group (human or animal subjects), gender, age groups, journal sub-sets and year range. Details of the search may be displayed. Full citation and related articles can be displayed for each citation retrieved. It is possible to download up to 1,000 records at a time, and different start records can be specified, so that an entire range of records can be downloaded if more than 1,000 have been retrieved. The amount of detail to be downloaded can be specified as three different options are offered (short, long without MeSH, long with MeSH). Two download formats are available: either IGM or tagged MEDLARS, the latter of which is appropriate for subsequent importing of references into reference management applications. Because IGM uses the PubMed search engine, a search can be copied and pasted from PubMed to be run using the IGM interface (for example, to overcome the PubMed 5,000 records download limit).

Additional databases can be accessed via IGM and the searcher is presented with search screens specific to the database in question. IGM transfers as much of a previous search strategy to the new search screen as possible.

AIDS related databases include:

- AIDSLINE: citations to AIDS related literature covering research, clinical aspects and health policy issues, derived from Medline, HealthSTAR, and BIOETHICSLINE as well as other sources;
- AIDSDRUGS: chemical and biological agents evaluated in the AIDS clinical trials covered in the companion AIDSTRIALS database; and
- AIDSTRIALS: completed as well as ongoing clinical trials of substances tested for use against AIDS, HIV infection, and AIDS-related opportunistic diseases.

Health services related databases include:

- HealthSTAR: clinical and non-clinical aspects of healthcare delivery, international in scope; and
- HSRPROJ: health services research projects including health technology assessment and the development and use of clinical practice guidelines.

Other databases include:

- BIOETHICSLINE: ethical, legal and public policy issues surrounding healthcare and biomedical research;
- ChemID: a dictionary of over 344,000 compounds of biomedical interest;
- HISTLINE (HISTory of medicine onLINE): literature about the history of health related professions, sciences, specialties, individuals, institutions, drugs, and diseases worldwide;
- POPLINE: family planning, population law and policy and primary healthcare; international in scope, including maternal/child health in developing countries;

- SPACELINE: space life sciences research literature, a joint venture by the NLM and the National Aeronautics and Space Administration (NASA); and
- TOXLINE: toxicological, pharmacological, biochemical and physiological effects of drugs and other chemicals.

TOXNET Online from NLM's Specialized Information Services Division, provides access to a cluster of databases in addition to TOXLINE, in the fields of toxicology, hazardous chemicals and related areas. The TOXNET databases are of many different types and are briefly described below.

Toxicology literature (scientific studies, reports, and other bibliographic material):

- TOXLINE (see above);
- DART / ETIC / ETICBACK (from the Developmental and Reproductive Toxicology and Environmental Teratology Information Center): literature on developmental and reproductive toxicology involving biological, chemical, and physical agents; and
- EMIC and EMICBACK (Environmental Mutagen Information Center): references to chemical, biological, and physical agents that have been tested for genotoxic activity. Produced by the Oak Ridge National Laboratory in co-operation with the NLM.

Toxicology data (factual information on toxicity and other hazards of chemicals):

- CCRIS (Chemical Carcinogenesis Research Information System): carcinogenicity, mutagenicity, tumour promotion and tumour inhibition data provided by the US National Cancer Institute (NCI);
- GENE-TOX (GENetic TOXicology), from the US Environmental Protection Agency (EPA): factual peer reviewed information about chemicals tested for mutagenicity;
- HSDB (Hazardous Substances Data Bank): factual peer reviewed information on hazardous chemicals, including human and animal toxicity, environmental fate, safety and handling; and
- IRIS (Integrated Risk Information System): data about potentially toxic chemicals, chemical-specific health risk and regulatory information prepared by the US EPA, with a special reference to human health risk assessment and a focus on hazard identification and dose-response assessment. Toxic risk data undergo scientific review.

Chemical information (nomenclature, identification, structures):

- ChemIDplus: chemical synonyms, structures, regulatory list information and links to other databases;

- HSDB Structures: 2D structural information on the HSDB chemicals; and
- NCI-3D: 2D and 3D information compiled by the NCI.

Toxic release information:

- TRI (Toxic chemical Release Inventory): data submitted by industrial facilities around the US to the EPA.

Finally, LocatorPlus from the NLM gives access to:

- AVLINE: citations about audiovisual and computer based educational materials;
- CATLINE: bibliographic data for all catalogued titles in the NLM collection, from the fifteenth century to the present;
- DIRLINE: directory of resources providing information services primarily in the US, with some coverage of international organisations; and
- SERLINE: bibliographic records for all serials catalogued for the NLM collection and all serial titles indexed for Medline and HealthSTAR.

LocatorPlus provides links to online journals from many records and these links are displayed when the detailed view is selected, along with title abbreviations, ISSN, publisher information and details of the abstracting and indexing services that index the journal.

Internet Grateful Med: igm.nlm.nih.gov/

LocatorPlus: www.nlm.nih.gov/locatorplus/

TOXNET Online: toxnet.nlm.nih.gov/ or sis.nlm.nih.gov/

Free Internet Medline services

Medline is produced by the NLM as the database equivalent of Index Medicus and in part also the Index to Dental Literature and International Nursing Index. Covering all aspects of health and medicine, Medline remains one of the most authoritative indexes to the published medical journal literature, containing references to articles published in around 4,000 biomedical journals.

Although access to Medline via the Web had been provided via the Internet for a number of years, free or for a fee, prior registration or subscription had usually been required. Since June 1997, however, the NLM has been offering free access to the database directly via the Web, targeting consumers and health professionals alike[13] and no prior registration or subscription is required. As well as Internet Grateful Med (IGM), the NLM offers an interface to Medline via PubMed. This section focuses on PubMed and some of the features that healthcare professionals and researchers may find particularly attractive.

Medline is also available through several other Web-based services – see for instance OMNI's Medline Resource Centre for reviews and other information about Medline and other databases available via the Internet. Evaluations of different versions of Medline are also available from Medical Matrix. Care should be exercised when a service is selected for use, as on occasion comprehensive searching can be hampered – guides to criteria for selecting different versions of Medline are available.[14, 15]

Medical Matrix Medline: www.medmatrix.org/_Spages/medline.asp

NLM Medline: www.nlm.nih.gov/databases/medline.html

OMNI Medline Resource Centre: omni.ac.uk/medline/

PubMed: www.ncbi.nlm.nih.gov/PubMed/

PubMed

The PubMed service was developed by the US National Center for Biotechnology Information (NCBI) of the NLM (see Figures 15.1, 15.2). Medline bibliographic records are integrated in PubMed with data from a range of NCBI products, including gene sequence databases and databases associated with taxonomy and molecular modelling (see Figure 15.3). PubMed also has links to a number of external resources, including Online Mendelian Inheritance in Man (OMIM), a continuously updated full text source of human genes and genetic disorders information. For example, searching PubMed for references relating to *screening for cystic fibrosis*, retrieves a number of records; those referred to from the extensive OMIM bibliographies will carry a link to the full text of the appropriate OMIM chapters, and vice versa. A textbook is now also linked from PubMed.[16] Clicking on Books when viewing an article abstract in PubMed causes links to the textbook to be generated from relevant terms in Medline abstracts.

In addition to Medline's 10 million records, PubMed also includes records from HealthSTAR and PREMedline (see above). PREMedline, updated daily, provides basic citation details and abstracts before indexing information is assigned. PubMed also includes citations supplied each day electronically by individual publishers, prior to or at the time of publication; journals that may be only partially indexed by Medline may consequently be indexed in their entirety in PubMed. By incorporating these records PubMed, like IGM Medline, is more comprehensive than other versions of Medline as well as consistently up-to-date.

Increasingly, databases include full text availability information or direct links to the electronic full text of documents. The PubMed retrieval system has been developed in collaboration with biomedical journal publishers with the aim of linking PubMed records directly to the full text of individual journal articles at the publishers' own Web sites. This wealth of links from PubMed makes it a popular database for searching. A new LinkOut feature now makes it possible to display several different links to the full text of individual articles known to PubMed, over and above those supplied by the original publishers (see Figure 15.4). Ever greater numbers of electronic journals are potentially accessible from PubMed. However, most publishers continue to require some form of authorisation so that access is not immediately possible without prior subscription. For example, Academic Press has linked a significant number of journals and their individual articles to PubMed but only subscribers can access the full text of the individual articles.

Searching PubMed

Detailed discussion of how to conduct searches using databases such as Medline is beyond the scope of this chapter. Clearly, however, the quality of searches depends on the effective use of available search features and

Figure 15.1 PubMed: search terms are entered in the query box. Additional search options are available from the Features bar beneath the query box

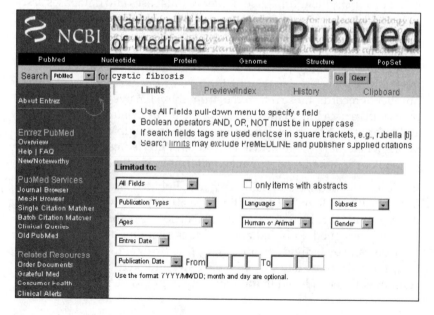

Figure 15.2 PubMed. Both MeSH and Text Words are searched. Click on the Details button to display the original user query and how PubMed translates it

Figure 15.3 PubMed. Supporting increased cross-linking between scientific resources and the bibliographic literature

Tables 15.1 to 15.5 therefore summarise key search features as offered by PubMed. PubMed offers a single search interface, which can be expanded to support most search features.

For simple searches, PubMed can offer an important means of searching the medical literature directly from the desktop. Comprehensive searches, or those that involve the use of a large number of terms (e.g. in support of systematic reviews), or searches that produce large sets of references, all of which needs to be downloaded, may not be as straightforward to con-

Figure 15.4 PubMed. Extract of external links offered by LinkOut. LinkOut provides links to a range of resources external to PubMed, including the full text at publisher sites, Medlineplus, and Online Mendelian Inheritance in Man (OMIM)

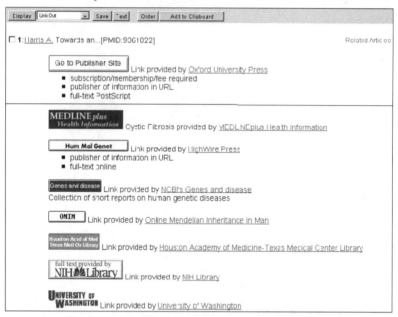

Table 15.1: General search features. Free text search features are generally supported, e.g. truncation, phrase searching, etc.

PubMed features	Notes and comments
Different fields can be browsed or searched, e.g. author, title	Use the Index to select a field to browse Use the Limits feature to select a field to search
The Index allows browsing of terms in a field index	To select multiple terms, hold down the Control (PC) or Command key (Mac), and click on each individual required term
Field-specific searching is possible using the Limits feature	A full range of fields may be selected using the All Fields pull-down menu. Only one field at a time may be selected to search

PubMed features	Notes and comments
Search terms may be truncated using the asterisk (*)	PubMed uses only the first 150 variations of a truncated term. Truncation turns off automatic term mapping and also the automatic explosion of a MeSH term. Often search queries with truncated words retrieve fewer citations than when truncation is not used
Phrases are parsed automatically, as PubMed consults a phrase index and groups terms into logical phrases. In order to force PubMed to search a term as a phrase, place search phrases in double quotes ("term1 term2")	If a phrase is entered without double quotes and there is no match within the phrase index, then the individual terms are combined (ANDed) together and searched in All Fields. Automatic phrase parsing may be avoided by entering each term separated by the Boolean operator AND, e.g. *sore AND throat*
Boolean operators (AND, OR, NOT) are supported. Word adjacency and proximity are not supported	Upper case (AND, OR, NOT) must be used when specifying Boolean operators
A search may be refined using the Limits feature. The following limits are available: publication type, ages, Entrez date, publication date, items with abstracts, languages, human vs. animal, subsets, gender	The Publication Types and Languages pull-down menus contain a list of frequently searched publication types and languages respectively. Limiting by most of the available limits will restrict retrieval to Medline records by default
Separate search statements are created and can subsequently be combined	The History feature can be used to combine search statements, or to combine search sets with new terms, using Boolean operators. To combine searches use # before search set numbers, e.g. *#1 AND #2; #3 AND asthma*
Nested queries are supported, allowing complex search statements to be constructed	Parentheses can be used to specify the order in which PubMed should process a search statement
The History feature summarises the search strategy developed within a session. The maximum number of queries held in History is 100. Once the maximum number is reached, PubMed will remove the oldest search from the History to add the most current search	It is possible to display the results from previous sets without re-executing a search statement by selecting the appropriate Results link. The Search History is lost after one hour of inactivity, or if the Web browser is closed
Searches may be constructed using field tags and Boolean operators	Longer strategies may be created in a text editor outside of PubMed and then copied / pasted into the query box or Details window
PubMed Clinical Queries offers built-in research methodology filters for therapy, diagnosis, aetiology and prognosis queries	Clinical Queries may be refined for sensitivity (will locate the majority of high-quality articles but will also generate many less relevant records) and specificity (for greater precision, will locate fewer records but the majority of these will be relevant)

Table 15.2: Thesaurus searching. Two different ways of searching MeSH headings are supported by PubMed: search queries may be entered at the default query box or via the NCBI MeSH Browser. An alternative MeSH browser, which contains supplementary concept records, is also available.

PubMed features	Notes and comments
A. Entering search terms at the default PubMed query box	
A MeSH heading search may be entered directly at the default PubMed query box. Automatic term mapping is supported	Terms are matched against a MeSH translation table
If a match is found in the MeSH translation table, the term is searched both as MeSH and as a Text Word	A Text Word search is not enriched in any way, i.e. the search term is queried as entered originally
MeSH, major MeSH and subheading terms may be searched specifically using the Limits option. Select the MeSH Terms, MeSH Major Topic or Subheading option from the All Fields pull-down menu to select the field to search	A Text Word search is not conducted when a MeSH, major MeSH or subheading search is conducted using the Limits option
MeSH terms searched using a 'MeSH Terms' or 'MeSH Major Topic' Limits search are automatically exploded and all subheadings included	To turn off the automatic explosion feature, use the search syntax [field:noexp] e.g. *asthma [mh:noexp],* or *asthma [majr:noexp]*
Subheadings searched using a Subheading Limits search are automatically exploded and are searched as "free-floating" subheadings. Families of subheading explosions are displayed within PubMed Help	To turn off the automatic subheading explosion feature, use the search syntax [sh:noexp], e.g. *therapy [sh:noexp]*
MeSH Terms, MeSH Major Topics and Subheadings may be browsed using the Index. Select the MeSH Terms, MeSH Major Topic or Subheading option from the Index pull-down menu to browse terms alphabetically. A citation count is provided for each term	To select multiple terms, hold down the Control key (PC) or the Command key (Mac), and click on each individual required term
Separate search statements are created and can subsequently be combined	The History feature can be used to combine search statements, or to combine search sets with new terms, using Boolean operators. To combine searches use # before search set numbers, e.g. *#1 AND #2; #3 AND asthma*
Nested queries are supported, allowing complex search statements to be constructed	Parentheses can be used to specify the order in which PubMed should process a search statement
PubMed features	**Notes and comments**
B. Using the MeSH Browser	
Automatic mapping to MeSH is supported	Mapping to MeSH headings using the MeSH Browser may be less comprehensive than that achieved using the default PubMed query box as the MeSH heading search is not accompanied by a Text Word search

The MeSH Browser allows scope notes to be displayed and MeSH trees to be navigated	A single MeSH heading at a time may be selected to browse and search
MeSH explosion searching, restricting to MeSH major focus and applying subheadings are supported features	A Detailed display allows several subheadings to be chosen, the search to be restricted to Major topic headings, and automatic explosion to be turned off
Automatic subheading explosions are supported. Families of Subheading Explosions are displayed within PubMed Help	To turn off the automatic subheading explosion feature, use the search syntax [sh:noexp], e.g. *therapy [sh:noexp]*. In a search where both heading and subheading may be exploded, it is possible to turn off the automatic explosion feature for both, using the search syntax [mh:noexp], e.g. *asthma/therapy [mh:noexp]*

Table 15.3: Displaying references, search strategies and related articles

PubMed features	Notes and comments
Several display options are available, including Summary, Brief, Abstract, Citation and Medline	The tagged Medline format can be used to save references to disc for later importing into reference management software (see Table 15.5 below)
PubMed displays references in Entrez Date order, i.e. in reverse order of addition of the references to the database	When Related Articles are displayed, these are ranked in order of relevance (see below)
The number of references displayed per page can be set by clicking on the Show pull-down menu and selecting an appropriate number, to a maximum of 500 items. Clicking the Display button will cause PubMed to redisplay the citations according to the new selection	To have all of the citations displayed on a single page, select a number higher than the total number of search results. Conversely, waiting time can be reduced by reducing the number of citations per page
Click on the Text button to display references as plain text for any of the available Display formats	Use the browser's Back button to return to the PubMed results
Click on the Details button to display the current PubMed query in a window, which may be amended	As well as the original query, the Details window also displays the number of results and all translations of search terms. Clicking on the Results link displays the references directly
Details of a session's search strategy can be displayed by selecting the History feature. PubMed uses cookies to maintain a search history	The search history can be cleared by clicking on the Clear History button and is automatically cleared after an hour of inactivity, or if the Web browser is closed. It is not possible to clear individual search statements

PubMed features	Notes and comments
The Clipboard is used to collect citations selected from one or more searches, using the "Add to Clipboard" button. Multiple references can be selected from several pages of results before clicking on Add to Clipboard. References can be added to the Clipboard from different searches. Up to 500 items can be added to the Clipboard. PubMed uses cookies to add selections to the Clipboard	Clicking on the Add to Clipboard button without previously having selected any references causes all references in a set up to 500 to be added to the Clipboard. Individual items can be removed from the Clipboard by clicking the check box next to each required reference and clicking the Remove from Clipboard button. Clicking the Remove from Clipboard button without checking any checkboxes causes all items to be removed from the Clipboard. The contents of the Clipboard are lost after one hour of inactivity, or if the Web browser is closed
PubMed displays a related set of articles for single articles (by clicking on Related Articles to the right of the selected citation) or for several selected articles (by selecting the Related Articles Display format). Articles in the Clipboard, which may originate from several searches, may also be displayed using the Related Articles Display format	Related Articles are pre-computed and are created by comparing words from the title, abstract, and MeSH terms. Citations are displayed in rank order. Limits are not in effect when a Related Articles link is selected
Although Limits are not in effect when a Related Articles link is selected, it is possible to refine the list of Related Articles using the History Feature. The search number assigned to this can be used in a new search and the desired limit applied	Related Articles are ranked in order of relevance. Refining a set of Related Articles may remove citations that are most relevant

Table 15.4: Linking to full text articles and other resources

PubMed features	Notes and comments
PubMed provides links to sources of full text articles via both Publisher-supplied links and a LinkOut feature. LinkOut may provide additional options if the publisher's link does not supply a link to full text (see Figure 15.3)	Prior subscription or some other type of fee is usually required to access the full text of articles from most journals
Publishers who supply their data to PubMed electronically usually include a link back to the journal site with each citation	Publisher-supplied links are displayed in the Abstract and Citation formats
Links to sources outside of PubMed are provided by LinkOut. When search results are viewed in the Brief, Abstract or Citation formats, a LinkOut link may be displayed to the right of some citations	LinkOut may display multiple links to different sources of full text articles, including Publisher-supplied links. LinkOut also allows individual references to be linked to several other sources external to PubMed, e.g. sequence databases, OMIM, etc

PubMed features	Notes and comments
The LinkOut option is also available from the Display pull-down menu	PubMed will process only the first 500 items with links when the Display pull-down menu is used to select the LinkOut option
In collaboration with book publishers, NCBI is adapting textbooks for the Web and linking them to PubMed, so that unfamiliar concepts found in search results may be explored further. Books links are additional to LinkOut links	The Books link redisplays a selected abstract, in which key phrases are presented as hypertext links. Clicking on a hypertext link produces a list of book pages in which the phrase is found. Further navigation within selected sections is also possible. Books links are displayed from the Brief, Abstract and Citation Display options

Table 15.5: Output: printing and saving references and search strategies

PubMed features	Notes and comments
Citations may be printed only one page at a time. The display and print limit is 500 items per page	Citations may be displayed as Text to strip the sidebar menu and toolbars prior to printing
It is possible to increase the number of documents displayed per page to accommodate large retrievals by clicking on the Show pull-down menu and selecting a higher number, to a maximum of 500 items	To display all citations on a single page, select a number higher than the total number of search results. Click on the Display button to display results in the required format before printing
Records can be printed or saved selectively from one or more searches using PubMed's Clipboard. The Clipboard can contain a maximum of 500 items	Within the Clipboard, first display the citations in the required format before printing or saving
Records can be downloaded to disc. The maximum number of items that can be saved is 5,000	To save a set of search results as a text file to disc, first select the required Display format and display a page of search results
Sets of over 5,000 references must be refined or records saved selectively	Limiting a search query by publication date may reduce the number of references retrieved to a manageable level
Records can be downloaded to disc in Medline format, employing a two-character tagged field format	Records saved in Medline format may be imported into reference management software
Search strategies may be saved. Clicking on the URL button displayed beneath the PubMed Details window generates a URL that can be saved as a bookmark or favorite for later re-execution of the same search	Searches that were created using a search statement number in History (e.g. #1 OR #2), should not be saved using the URL feature as the search statements represented by these numbers are lost when History is deleted

duct. For these, more enhanced interfaces to the Medline database, typically provided by locally networked versions, may be preferred.

NLM MeSH browser: www.nlm.nih.gov/mesh/99Mbrowser.html

PubMed Clinical queries: www.ncbi.nlm.nih.gov/PubMed/clinical.html

PubMed help: www.ncbi.nlm.nih.gov/entrez/query/static/help/pmhelp.html

PubMed MeSH browser: www.ncbi.nlm.nih.gov/entrez/meshbrowser.cgi

---

PubMed incorporated within third-party resources

Increasingly, health and medical resources provide targeted links through to PubMed. For example, references cited at the end of electronic articles offer cross-links to full PubMed citations (including abstracts, where available). myMedline allows journals to be selected by specialty before searches are submitted to PubMed.

Educational resources are now also making direct links into PubMed as a key additional source of information. An example is the Dermatology Online Atlas (DOIA), which allows users to submit a search directly to PubMed on any topic selected from an alphabetical list. For example, selecting *hemangioma* from the alphabetical list generates a Links tab, which displays related patient information as well as allowing a search to be submitted directly to PubMed, albeit restricted to major MeSH headings.

Health and medical Web search tools are becoming increasingly hybrid in nature, as discussed in the previous chapter, and PubMed is a key additional source that complements information retrieval from a range of gateways. For example, using either MedHunt or HONselect from HON, it is possible to choose to submit a search to PubMed. In addition, HONselect also allows predefined Clinical Queries to be submitted and offers the option to refine the search by sensitivity or specificity.

However, several sources may result in restricted retrieval from PubMed due to the manner in which they pre-format a search query. For example:

- CliniWeb provides direct links from the MeSH terms in its browsable lists to PubMed, and sometimes these are the only links available. A PubMed search conducted as a result of selecting one of these links is restricted to major MeSH headings, human subjects and English language articles, with a one-year limit applied.

- Medical World Search also offers the possibility of submitting searches to PubMed. Although its submission of searches to other third-party sources, e.g. generic search engines, often results in enriched searches, the same is not always the case with search queries submitted to PubMed. For example, a search query for *esophageal reflux* that would normally be submitted as (*"gastroesophageal reflux" OR "esophageal reflux" OR "cardioesophageal relaxation gastroesophageal reflux" OR "gastro-esophageal reflux" OR "gastro-oesophageal reflux" OR "gastroesophageal reflux disease"*) to AltaVista was submitted simply as *"gastroesophageal reflux"[MESH]* to PubMed. In other words, the search phrase was not submitted as a text word search and none of the synonyms were included in the search query, thus possibly reducing relevant retrieval. Conversely, a search for *alveolar microlithiasis*, which is not a MeSH heading, resulted in the query *(alveolar[All Fields] OR microlithiasis[All Fields])*, which caused an unmanageably large number of records to be retrieved (43,094). In contrast, the same search submitted directly to PubMed generated the following search query instead: *(alveolar[All Fields] AND microlithiasis[All Fields])*, which resulted in the retrieval of a more focused set of matching references (199 at the time of writing).

Consequently, relying on third-party submission may not always be the optimal way to retrieve PubMed references. Submitting queries to PubMed directly often gives more comprehensive or more focused retrieval, and therefore more control, allowing further addition of terms to a query and further modification.

CliniWeb International: www.ohsu.edu / cliniweb /

Dermatology Online Atlas (DOIA): dermis.net / bilddb / index_e.htm

HON: www.hon.ch /

HONselect: www.hon.ch / HONselect /

MedHunt: www.hon.ch / MedHunt /

Medical World Search: www.mwsearch.com /

myMedline: www.mymedline.com / medline /

Database proliferation on the Web: the invisible Web

Any search for *tuberculosis prevention* programmes is likely to retrieve resources provided by the US Centers for Disease Control and Prevention (CDC), as well as other key specialist organisations in the field. Sites such as the CDC can provide a wealth of insight on specific conditions for the healthcare professional and also the health consumer. In particular, highly specialist resources may be made available in the form of searchable databases, for example via the CDC Prevention News Update, Funding, and Educational Materials Databases.

However, the content of Web databases such as these can usually be accessed only by visiting each database in turn and completing each search form separately. Their content cannot be tapped directly via ordinary Web search engines such as AltaVista or Google, so databases such as these are sometimes referred to as the 'invisible' or 'hidden' Web. Consequently, valuable information may be missed if such resources are not included in a search and it is advisable to consider searching several of the invisible Web databases that cover a particular topic area. Indeed, it has been estimated that:

> While only two-thirds of all information on the Internet is invisible to traditional search engines, over 90% of the content relevant to the healthcare industry is found in invisible Web resources.[17]

New in 1999 was a US government research publications service developed by Northern Light, usgovsearch, which provides a comprehensive collection of millions of Web pages from US government and military sites. Both simple and power search options are available. Because of the breadth of coverage and specialisation, cross-agency retrieval using this service can sometimes be impressive.

A number of services attempt to identify searchable databases of this kind, and gateways like those referred to in the previous chapter can be most useful in highlighting their existence. For example, OMNI indexes databases with several terms, so selecting to Search for Thesaurus Terms and submitting a search for *databases* reveals the three terms for which OMNI records exist:

> *Databases, Bibliographic*
> > *MEDLINE*
> *Databases, Factual*

It is possible to retrieve all three together by left clicking the mouse, dragging the cursor over the three lines and clicking on the button to Retrieve records for selected subject headings.

Medical Matrix brings several searchable sources together on a single Clinical Searches page. Wherever possible, a search may be submitted direct to a source from a search box on this page. Very often, however, sources do not allow direct searching from a third party page, so must be visited individually. For example, a search for *kaposi* could not be submitted directly to any of the four databases selected be Medical Matrix under the category AIDS; the search query would need to be submitted to each source separately. Nonetheless, the page provides a useful reminder of sources to search in addition to Medical Matrix.

Another useful search page offered by Medical Matrix is Search Hub: from here, searches may be submitted to one out of a number of possible search sources, ranging from drug information through to Web search engines such as AltaVista.

Proprietary directories of resources of this type are also becoming increasingly more commonplace, and a charge is often imposed for access to compilations of such premium data. For example, CiteLine Professional, which is available via subscription, releases its directory of Web-based databases via updates of its proprietary client software.

CiteLine Professional pre-screens and organises Web sites of value to healthcare industry professionals, and claims to provide access to more than 90 million pages that are usually invisible to ordinary Web search engines. CiteLine editors have compiled a list of more than 2,000 'invisible Web' databases. Although each of the source databases provides its own search form for free online, which would otherwise need to be searched separately, CiteLine Professional provides a single interface for cross-database searching wherever this is permitted.

CDC: www.cdc.gov/

CDC. National Prevention Information Network. Educational Materials Database: www.cdcnpin.org/db/public/ematmain.htm

CDC. National Prevention Information Network. Funding Database: www.cdcnpin.org/db/public/fundmain.htm

CDC. National Prevention Information Network. Prevention News Update Database: www.cdcnpin.org/db/public/dnmain.htm

CiteLine Professional: Free trial and demo available from www.citeline.com/screen_2_pro.html

Medical Matrix Clinical Searches: www.medmatrix.org/info/search.asp

Medical Matrix Search Hub: www.medmatrix.org/info/searchhub.asp

Northern Light usgovsearch: usgovsearch.northernlight.com/publibaccess/

> OMNI Thesaurus:
> omni.ac.uk/search/thesaurus/

Commercial online database hosts

Despite the availability of several databases for free via the Web, access to commercial online database hosts may still be essential, particularly if comprehensive searches are required. For example, searches in support of systematic reviews would need access to multiple database sources, which may overlap substantially. Online database hosts may offer facilities for simultaneous cross-file searching and de-duplication of references from different databases. Where there is a requirement for access to the latest research, or to geographically disparate research sources, this may also necessitate access to online database hosts, which offer a much wider range of databases to search. In addition, such hosts also offer mature search interfaces, which are robust and can accommodate complex search strategy development. Although in past decades they required knowledge of esoteric command languages, the same scientific, technical and medical online database hosts now offer easier to use Web-based interfaces with helpful guiding features.

Several Web-based gateways to databases are available, such as HealthGate, which advertise the availability of a range of databases. Most databases and databanks that are accessible through such services usually require prior subscription and charges can vary significantly, depending on the database and the service provider. For example, HealthGate includes AgeLine, CINAHL, EMBASE and PsycINFO. Although charges are not levied for the display of titles alone, fees were charged at the time of writing for each detailed citation as follows:

- AgeLine: $0.50
- CINAHL: $1.50
- EMBASE: $2.00
- PsycINFO: $0.75

Charges such as these are typical also of traditional online database hosts, such as DataStar, Dialog, Deutches Institut fur Medizinische Dokumentation und Information (DIMDI), Ovid Online and STN International. In addition, however, traditional hosts usually charge online connect time fees and variable display, print and save charges for data downloaded, and may charge individual database access fees. Further charges, such as an annual account maintenance fee or charges for the delivery of up-to-date database search guides, are also not uncommon.

The Dialog Corporation provides access to hundreds of databases via three constituent hosts: DataStar, Dialog and Profound. Dialog provides information about DataStar datasheets, Dialog bluesheets and Profound databases, as well as multiple cross-host subject specific tables of databases.

DIMDI provides access to approximately 80 biomedical and related databases. DIMDI does not charge for connect time, but other search-related charges are levied, depending on the database. DIMDI's free grips-WebSearch allows several databases to be cross-searched. These include some key databases from the NLM as well as CANCERLIT from the NCI, but also some European databases: Euroethics, Gerolit, Medikat and Russmed Articles. De-duplication across the retrieved references is possible, and several other search features are supported (e.g. thesaurus explosion searching). References may be sorted and output in HTML, or in a text format for subsequent incorporation into a bibliographic reference software package.

Ovid Online provides access to a similar number of health and medical databases via its Web interface.

STN International (the Scientific and Technical Information Network) provides access to more than 200 databases in science and technology. STN on the Web allows chemical structure searching and full STN command functionality.

Several of the above online hosts and other information providers feature trials of their products. For example, each month Ovid features a different database that allows potential customers to assess the functionality of the Ovid Web interface in real time. SilverPlatter also provides a free data-base of the month feature via its MedXtra service.

DataStar datasheets: ds.datastarweb.com/ds/products/datastar/ds.htm

DataStarWeb: www.datastarweb.com/

Dialog bluesheets: library.dialog.com/bluesheets/

Dialog Corporation: Authoritative content: www.dialog.com/info/content/

DialogWeb: www.dialog.com/

DIMDI: www.dimdi.de/homeeng.htm

DIMDI Alphabetical list of databases: www.dimdi.de/engl/hoste/dbkurze.html

DIMDI's free grips-WebSearch: gripsdb.dimdi.de/

HealthGate research tools: www.healthgate.com/res/

Ovid Database of the month: www.ovid.com/demo/dotm/

Ovid Online: gateway.ovid.com/

Ovid Online database catalog: www.ovid.com/products/databases/

SilverPlatter MedXtra: medicine.silverplatter.com/

STN database summary sheets: www.cas.org/ONLINE/DBSS/dbsslist.html

STN Databases in science, technology, patents and business: www.fiz-karlsruhe.de/onlin_db.html

STN International: www.fiz-karlsruhe.de/

STN on the Web: stnweb.fiz-karlsruhe.de/

Managing database searching on the Web

Effective literature searching

Although it is beyond the scope of this chapter to discuss effective database search strategy development, several sources are available on the Internet that might be helpful in this regard. To begin with, the skill of formulating answerable clinical questions has been identified as key to evidence-based decision making.[18] It is also an essential first step in the process of search strategy development.[19] Articles in medical journals attempt to introduce key search concepts for busy clinicians,[20, 21] and database search systems offer extensive context-sensitive help.

Numerous guides and tutorials for searching databases are available on the Web. For example, an interactive tutorial is available from Duke University Medical Center Library that aims to introduce users to searching Medline using the Ovid Web interface. JEFFLINE at Thomas Jefferson University makes available several tutorials, which once again utilise the Ovid Web interface. The National Library of Medicine offers PubMed and IGM training manuals.

Guides also abound that aim to introduce users to sources of effectiveness literature, including the New Zealand Health Technology

Assessment (NZHTA) search protocol, itself influenced by a protocol developed by ScHARR. An article in the journal *Evidence-Based Medicine* provides a critique of a variety of sources for finding answers to well-built questions.[22] SUMSearch applies a particular model for effective literature searching across heterogeneous sources and is discussed elsewhere in this book.

Handbooks and manuals are also available to help users identify reports of high quality studies for inclusion in systematic reviews. For example, the UK NHS Centre for Reviews and Dissemination (CRD) makes available a guide to finding studies for systematic reviews and the Cochrane Collaboration provides a Reviewers' Handbook.

The Canadian Centres for Health Evidence.net maintain a collection of resources on strategies for searching the health literature, most of which are based on the *ACP Journal Club* 'how to harness Medline…' series of articles.[23–28]

Centres for Health Evidence.net (CHE.net) Principles: how to: www.cche.net/principles/howto_all.asp

Cochrane Reviewers' Handbook: www.cochrane.org/cochrane/hbook.htm

JEFFLINE Evidence-based medicine information: jeffline.tju.edu/Education/courses/informatics/activities/ebm_info.html

JEFFLINE Medline searching strategies: jeffline.tju.edu/Education/courses/informatics/activities/med_search.html

JEFFLINE Searching basics: jeffline.tju.edu/Education/courses/informatics/activities/basics.html

New Zealand Health Technology Assessment Search protocol: nzhta.chmeds.ac.nz/nzhtainfo/protocol.htm

NHS CRD Finding studies for systematic reviews: a basic checklist for researchers: www.york.ac.uk/inst/crd/revs.htm

Ovid tutorial, Duke University Medical Center Library: www.mc.duke.edu/mclibrary/respub/guides/ovidtut/

PubMed and Internet Grateful Med training manuals: www.nlm.nih.gov/pubs/web_based.html

ScHARR Seeking the evidence protocol: www.shef.ac.uk/~scharr/
ir/proto.html

SUMSearch: sumsearch.uthscsa.edu/

Research methodology filters

Research methodology filters are predefined search strategies that aim to assist
the searcher in retrieving high quality research papers. Better known are the
search filters for therapy, diagnosis, aetiology and prognosis type clinical queries, defined as a result of work by Haynes *et al.*.[29] PubMed incorporates these
in its Clinical Queries search options and allows the focus of the search to be
adjusted for sensitivity or precision (see Figure 15.5). For example, a therapy
search for *cystic fibrosis*, adjusted for 'sensitivity', generates a search for:

*(cystic fibrosis) AND (randomized controlled trial [PTYP] OR drug therapy
[SH] OR therapeutic use [SH:NOEXP] OR random* [WORD])*

A similar search, adjusted for 'specificity', generates a search for:

(cystic fibrosis) AND ((double [WORD] AND blind [WORD]) OR placebo
[WORD])*

Figure 15.5 PubMed. Clinical queries using research methodology filters

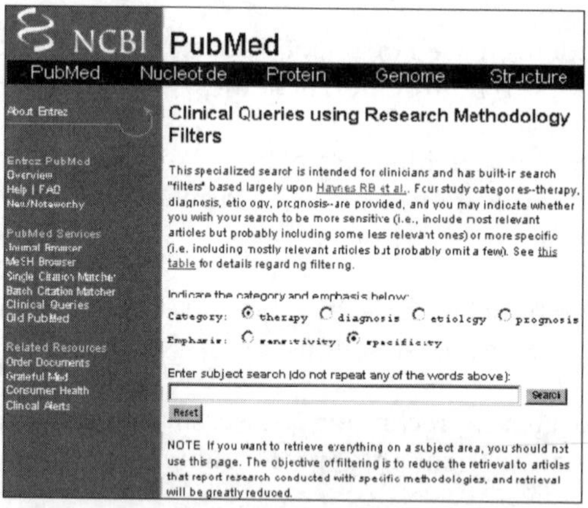

The NHS CRD includes several such filters in its guide to finding studies
for systematic reviews. These include a suite of search strategies validated by the NHS CRD for finding reports of systematic reviews and
meta-analyses in Medline or CINAHL (mainly Ovid), which are provided
for varying levels of sensitivity and precision. Additionally, CRD Report
No. 6 includes recommended search strategies and suggested databases
for extending the scope of searching for reports of economic evaluations.[30]

The Cochrane Collaboration has produced an optimally sensitive search strategy for finding reports of randomised controlled trials in Medline. This is documented in the Cochrane Reviewers' Handbook: Appendix 5c. Reports of randomised controlled trials identified by these methods from Medline are now regularly added to the Cochrane Controlled Trials Register (available as a database within the Cochrane Library) and are also being added from EMBASE.

The Sociedad Argentina de Pediatría provides predefined filters from a Spanish-language page, from which searches may be launched with PubMed for therapy, aetiology and diagnosis type clinical queries. In addition, predefined search strategies may be submitted directly to PubMed for randomised controlled trials (using a translation of the Cochrane Collaboration optimally sensitive search strategy), and also for systematic reviews.

Libraries worldwide provide their own links to research methodology search filters. These include:

- a search filters page from the Institute of Health Sciences (IHS) Library, University of Oxford, with predefined search strategies available for direct downloading and use with either Ovid or SilverPlatter Medline, and including the filters used by PubMed. In addition to those, the page also provides guidelines, treatment outcomes and evidence-based healthcare methodological filters that were developed from several sources for use with Ovid or SilverPlatter Medline. The filters from this site are intended also to work with HealthSTAR;

- evidence-based filters for Ovid CINAHL searches from the Edward G Miner Library, University of Rochester Medical Center;

- Expertsearch (evidence-based filters for Ovid Medline), also from the Edward G Miner Library, University of Rochester Medical Center; and

- evidence-based search strategies for SilverPlatter Medline from the Levy Library, Mount Sinai School of Medicine.

Cochrane Reviewers' Handbook optimal search strategy for RCTs: www.cochrane.dk/cochrane/handbook/ cchb99APPENDIX_5C_OPTIMAL_SEARCH_STRAT.htm#b7e137b3

EBM search strategies for SilverPlatter Medline: www.mssm.edu/ library/ebm/spsea.html

Evidence-based filters for Ovid CINAHL: www.urmc.rochester.edu/Miner/Educ/ebnfilt.htm

Expertsearch: evidence-based filters for Ovid Medline: www.urmc.rochester.edu/Miner/Educ/Expertsearch.html

IHS Library filters: www.ihs.ox.ac.uk/library/filters.html

NHS CRD Finding studies for systematic reviews: a basic checklist for researchers: www.york.ac.uk/inst/crd/revs.htm

NHS CRD Search strategies to identify reviews and meta-analyses in Medline and CINAHL: www.york.ac.uk/inst/crd/search.htm

PubMed. Clinical queries using research methodology filters: www.ncbi.nlm.nih.gov/PubMed/clinical.html

Sociedad Argentina de Pediatría, Filtros Metodológicos para la búsqueda en Medline: www.sap.org.ar/medline/filtros.htm

Database alerting and current awareness services

Automated alerting or current awareness services are available to help users keep up-to-date with a subject of interest. Once a search profile has been set up, alerting services ensure that references to new articles dealing with a subject, mostly with abstracts, are sent regularly by email (the frequency of updating depends on the alerting service used).

Complex search queries are more likely to be supported by locally networked database systems or commercial online hosts. For example, Ovid Web supports AutoAlert searches, i.e. saved searches that run automatically each time a database is updated. AutoAlert profiles retrieve newly-added documents on a topic, which are then emailed to the user. There is a charge for such services if supplied by commercial online hosts.

Both PubMed and IGM offer the opportunity to save Medline search strategies for later reuse by saving a search strategy as a URL. Saved search strategies can be created for fifteen different databases using IGM. Once a URL for a saved strategy has been constructed, it can be saved in a Web page or as a bookmark or favorite, so the search can be recalled and re-executed as required. However, in such instances, the onus is on the user to remember to rerun a search at required intervals.

NLM. Entrez PubMed FAQs: www.ncbi.nlm.nih.gov/ entrez/query/static/faq.html#savesearch

NLM. Entrez PubMed Help: www.ncbi.nlm.nih.gov/ entrez/query/static/help/ pmhelp.html#SavingaSearchStrategy

NLM. Save a search strategy by constructing an IGM URL:
igm.nlm.nih.gov/splash/IGM_url.html

Automatic alerting services for Medline and related databases

Increasingly, free Medline alerting services are appearing, most of which submit queries to PubMed and initiate regular email delivery of new search results. Several such services are now available, offering varying flexibility in the search and delivery options.

MedFetch allows registered users to create and refine a search using PubMed, to save the search and have it automatically resubmitted on a weekly or monthly basis to PubMed. Up to five searches can be stored and up to 20 hits per search are returned. Alternatively, E-Med, from the Medline Workbench, allows daily automatic updating from PubMed. Up to two keywords are encouraged per account, although multiple accounts are allowed.

JournAlert, from Doctors.net, allows registered users to save search strategies and select the frequency of updates, which may be daily.

Infotrieve maintains personalised profiles. As the bibliographic databases hosted on Infotrieve's site are updated, queries are checked against the updates and results are sent by email. Infotrieve allows SDI/Alerts to be set up for any combination of the databases it hosts, which include AIDSLINE, CANCERLIT, Medline and TOXLINE. Infotrieve Medline updates are weekly.

PubCrawler from Dublin, Ireland, is an article alerting service that searches more widely, so that update searches are submitted to both PubMed and GenBank. This makes it possible to monitor new DNA sequences in GenBank, although searches are conducted on the annotation text of GenBank entries rather than the sequence data itself. PubCrawler applies no limit on the number of searches that can be saved and conducted. Searches can be set to run daily, if required. The results page maintains access to older results so as to allow users to catch up on missed sets. PubCrawler can be complemented by several services that perform BLAST searches against DNA and protein databases:

- Munich Information Center for Protein Sequences (MIPS) Alert creates queries for the ATLAS program – a multi-database information retrieval program designed to access several sequence databases. New database entries for protein sequences of interest are emailed weekly;

- Swiss-Shop from Expasy provides weekly alerts for new protein sequences that are added to the SWISS-PROT database; and
- the Sequence Alerting System, provided by the Bork group at the Biocomputing Unit at EMBL, conducts daily searches for homologues of sequences.

EMBL Sequence Alerting System: www.bork.embl-heidelberg.de/Alerting/

E-Med: www.cshl.org/medline/

Infotrieve: www.infotrieve.com/

JournAlert: www.doctors.net.uk/

MedFetch: www.medfetch.com/

Munich Information Center for Protein Sequences (MIPS) Alert: vms.mips.biochem.mpg.de/mips/programs/alert.html

PubCrawler: www.gen.tcd.ie/pubcrawler/

Swiss-Shop: www.expasy.ch/swiss-shop/

Managing references using personal bibliographic database applications

Many bibliographic databases referred to in this chapter allow selected references to be marked and downloaded to disc. Researchers are often keen to import references into personal bibliographic management software for many reasons, including their ability to:

- import and store references from disparate database sources;
- de-duplicate references imported from a variety of database sources;
- impose an element of standardisation by offering global author, keyword and journal indexes;
- support retrieval of references according to specific fields (e.g. by authors' names, by journal title);
- support output of the references in a variety of journal styles ;
- monitor the acquisition of the full text of a journal article or to link directly to an article online;
- conduct simple searches of remote databases directly from within the software itself, especially if complex search features are not required (e.g. explosion searching); and

- post configurable databases of journal articles to the Web.

Suitable tagged formats need to be sought when downloading records from any database. For example, PubMed allows downloading of records in a tagged Medline format, ready for downloading to reference management applications, but this option needs to be selected specifically. Although usually references will be acquired from bibliographic databases, some journals are also encouraging direct download of citations from the journal site itself. For example, *Pediatrics* offers tips for downloading references directly from the journal in a tagged format.[31]

The main reference management products include EndNote, Papyrus, ProCite and Reference Manager. Details of these and other packages, and comparisons between them, are maintained by several sites, including the UK Online User Group (UKOLUG). ISI ResearchSoft owns several of these popular reference management packages and maintains relevant information on its Web site. Deals negotiated with consortia or institutional site licences often lead to significant price reductions. In the UK Higher Education sector, the Combined Higher Education Software Team (CHEST) often maintains sector-wide consortial software deals.

Capture files allow data downloaded from a wide range of databases to be imported into reference management applications. Similarly, journal citation format files are also available, and allow data from within reference management applications to be exported to a list of references or a bibliography in a variety of journal citation styles. Up-to-date links to such files are made available over the Web by ResearchSoft.

CHEST: www.chest.ac.uk/

ISI ResearchSoft: www.researchsoft.com/

ISI ResearchSoft. EndNote Support and Services:
www.researchsoft.com/en/help/ENsupport.htm

ISI ResearchSoft. ProCite Technical Support:
www.researchsoft.com/pc/PCsupport.html

ISI ResearchSoft. Reference Manager Technical Support:
www.researchsoft.com/rm/RMsupport.html

UKOLUG. Links: bibliographic software: www.ukolug.org.uk/
links/biblio.htm

Looking up journal information: finding journal abbreviations

Standardisation of journal titles and abbreviations used in reference management databases is important, if output is to be consistent. Journal titles and abbreviations can be verified from several sources. For example, the NLM publishes Journal Title Lists: the List of Serials Indexed for Online Users, which is designed to provide complete bibliographic information on serials cited in three NLM databases: Medline (including the backfiles), AIDSLINE, and HealthSTAR.

Additional sources include NLM's LocatorPlus and PubMed's Journal Browser. For example, PubMed's Journal Browser can be used to search for specific journals. The Journal Browser (available from PubMed's sidebar) allows journals to be looked up by title or by the Medline journal abbreviation. The Journal Browser will display a listing of possible matches along with the full journal title, ISSN and Medline abbreviation.

LocatorPlus: www.nlm.nih.gov/locatorplus/

NLM Journal Title Lists: www.nlm.nih.gov/tsd/serials/lsiou.html

PubMed: Journal Browser: www.ncbi.nlm.nih.gov/entrez/jrbrowser.cgi

---

Searching using personal bibliographic management packages: Z39.50 targets for biomedical databases

Bibliographic databases that support the Z39.50 standard[32] can be searched directly using the search interface of personal reference management applications. The results of such searches can then be imported directly, so it is unnecessary to download the data to a file and then import the data separately into the reference management package. Several directories of databases supporting Z39.50 are available, including those compiled by the US Library of Congress and UK Office for Library Networking (UKOLN). ISI ResearchSoft also provides a comprehensive list of connection files for use with EndNote.

ISI ResearchSoft EndNote 3 connection files: www.researchsoft.com/en/help/Enconnections.htm; also available from www.endnote.com/ENz3950.htm

Library of Congress. Z39.50 Maintenance Agency Home Page: lcweb.loc.gov/z3950/agency/

UKOLN Directory of Z39.50 targets in the UK: www.ukoln.ac.uk/dlis/zdir/

References

1. Hersh WR, Gorman PN, Sacherek LS. Applicability and quality of information for answering clinical questions on the Web. *JAMA* 1998 Oct 21; **280**(15):1307-1308.

2. Krabshuis J. Endoscopy information online: can endoscopists close the gap between what is known and what they do? *Endoscopy* 1997; **29**:871-882.

3. Nogler M, Wimmer C, Mayr E, Ofner D. The efficacy of using search engines in procuring information about orthopaedic foot and ankle problems from the World Wide Web. *Foot & Ankle International* 1999; **20**(5):322-325.

4. Baxevanis AD. The Molecular Biology Database Collection: an online compilation of relevant database resources. *Nucleic Acids Research* 2000; **28**(1):1-7. Available from: http://www.oup.co.uk/nar/Volume_28/Issue_01/html/gkd115_gml.html

5. JISC (Joint Information Systems Committee). Committee on Electronic Information (CEI) - Content Working Group. An integrated information environment for Higher Education: developing the Distributed, National Electronic Resource (DNER). Available from: http://www.jisc.ac.uk/cei/dner_colpol.html

6. JISC(Joint Information Systems Committee). Current content collection: health studies. Available from: http://www.jisc.ac.uk/collections/health.html

7. Atkins H. The ISI Web of Science: links and electronic journals. *D-Lib Magazine* 1999 Sep; **5**(9). Available from: http://www.dlib.org/dlib/september99/atkins/09atkins.html or http://mirrored.ukoln.ac.uk/lis-journals/dlib/dlib/dlib/september99/atkins/09atkins.html for UK or European users.

8. Hallam E, Plaice C. An evaluation of EMBASE within the NHS: findings of the Database Access Project working partnership to extend the knowledge base of healthcare. *Health Libraries Review* 1999 Sep; **16**(3):192-203.

9. Woods D, Trewheellar K. Medline and Embase complement each other in literature searches [letter]. *BMJ* 1998 Apr 11; **316**(7138):1166. Available from: http://www.bmj.com/cgi/content/full/316/7138/1166

10. Burnham J, Shearer B. Comparison of CINAHL, EMBASE, and Medline databases for the nurse researcher. *Medical Reference Services Quarterly* 1993; **12**(3):46-57.

11.   Biarez O, Sarrut B, Doreau CG, Etienne J. Comparison and evaluation of nine bibliographic databases concerning adverse drug reactions. *DICP* 1991 Oct; **25**(10):1062-1065.

12.   BIOSIS Previews: the world's most comprehensive reference database in the life sciences. Available from: http://www.biosis.org/htmls/products_services/previews.html

13.   NLM. Press release: free Medline. Vice President launches free access to world's largest source of published medical information on World Wide Web: consumers and health professionals worldwide to have fingertip access to cutting-edge research. Bethesda, MD. 1997 Jun 26. Available from: http://www.nlm.nih.gov/press_releases/free_medline.html

14.   Anagnostelis B, Cooke A. Evaluation criteria for different versions of the same database: a comparison of Medline services available via the World Wide Web. In: Online Information 97 Conference Proceedings; Online Information 97: the 21st International Online Information Meeting; 1997 Dec 9-11; London, UK. London; 1997. Available from: http://omni.ac.uk/agec/iolim97/

15.   Detmer WM. Medline on the Web: ten questions to ask when evaluating a Web based service. Available from: http://www.med.virginia.edu/~wmd4n/medline.html

16.   Alberts B, Bray D, Lewis J, Raff M, Roberts K, Watson JD. Molecular Biology of the Cell, 3rd ed. Garland Publishing Inc; 1994.

17.   CiteLine Professional. CiteLine tutorial: searching the invisible Web. Downloadable from http://www.citeline.com/client/citeline/3.0/tutorial.html

18.   Richardson WS, Wilson MC, Nishikawa J, Hayward RS. The well-built clinical question: a key to evidence-based decisions. *ACP Journal Club* 1995 Nov-Dec;**123**(3):A12-A13. Available from: http://www.cche.net/principles/education_all.asp

19.   Palmer J, Lusher A, Snowball R. Searching for the evidence. *Genitourinary Medicine* 1997 Feb; **73**(1):70-72.

20.   Greenhalgh T. How to read a paper: the Medline database. *BMJ* 1997 Jul 19;**315**(7101):180-183. Available from: http://www.bmj.com/cgi/content/full/315/7101/180

21.   Lowe HJ, Barnett GO. Understanding and using the medical subject headings (MeSH) vocabulary to perform literature searches. *JAMA* 1994 Apr 13; **271**(14):1103-1108.

22. McKibbon KA, Richardson WS, Walker-Dilks C. Finding answers to well-built questions. *Evidence-Based Medicine* 1999 Nov-Dec; 4(6):164.

23. McKibbon KA, Walker-Dilks CJ. Beyond ACP Journal Club: how to harness Medline to solve clinical problems. *ACP Journal Club*. 1994 Mar-Apr; **120** Suppl 2:A10-A12.

24. McKibbon KA, Walker-Dilks CJ. Beyond ACP Journal Club: how to harness Medline for therapy problems. *ACP Journal Club*. 1994 Jul-Aug; **121** Suppl 1:A10-A12. Document based on this *ACP Journal Club* article available from: http://www.cche.net/principles/howto_therapy.asp

25. McKibbon KA, Walker-Dilks CJ. Beyond ACP Journal Club: how to harness Medline for diagnostic problems. *ACP Journal Club*. 1994 Sep-Oct;**121** Suppl 2:A10-A12. Document based on this *ACP Journal Club* article available from: http://www.cche.net/principles/howto_diagnosis.asp

26. Walker-Dilks CJ, McKibbon KA, Haynes RB. Beyond ACP Journal Club: how to harness Medline for etiology problems. *ACP Journal Club*. 1994 Nov-Dec; **121**(3):A10-A11. Document based on this *ACP Journal Club* article available from: http://www.cche.net/principles/howto_harm.asp

27. McKibbon KA, Walker-Dilks C, Haynes RB, Wilczynski N. Beyond ACP Journal Club: how to harness Medline for prognosis problems. *ACP Journal Club*. 1995 Jul-Aug;**123**(1):A12-A14. Document based on this *ACP Journal Club* article available from: http://www.cche.net/principles/howto_prognosis.asp

28. McKibbon KA, Walker-Dilks CF, Wilczynski NL, Haynes RB. Beyond ACP Journal Club: how to harness Medline for review articles. *ACP Journal Club*. 1996 May-Jun; **124**(3):A12-A13. Document based on this *ACP Journal Club* article available from: http://www.cche.net/principles/howto_overview.asp

29. Haynes RB, Wilczynski N, McKibbon KA, Walker CJ, Sinclair JC. Developing optimal search strategies for detecting clinically sound studies in MEDLINE. *Journal of the Medical Informatics Association* 1994 Nov-Dec; **1**(6):447-458.

30. NHS CRD. CDR Report 6. Making cost-effectiveness information accessible: the NHS Economic Evaluation Database Project. CRD guidance for reporting critical summaries of economic evaluations. Available from: http://www.york.ac.uk/inst/crd/report6.doc

31. Tips for better Web browsing: download to citation manager. *Pediatrics*. Available from: http://www.pediatrics.org/tips/download.dtl

32. Library of Congress. Z39.50 Maintenance Agency Home Page. Available from: http://lcweb.loc.gov/z3950/agency/

Chapter 16

Electronic journals and full text journal articles on the Web

Scientific, technical and medical research has for many centuries been published in journals, and peer review has become synonymous with this traditional pattern of journal publication. Although it has come under sustained criticism and its shortcomings have been discussed widely,[1] nonetheless peer review continues to be valued by both researchers and practitioners as providing a quality filter for the recording of ongoing research findings:

> Peer review is a quality-control and certification filter necessitated by the vast scale of learned research today. Without it, no one would know where to start reading in the welter of new work reported every day, nor what was worth reading, and believing, and trying to build one's own research upon.[2]

> Peer review, albeit improved, will survive the electronic age, since few readers, especially those in clinical practice, are clambering for more (and less refined) information.[3]

As with databases and databanks, the full text of journals is fast becoming available directly over the Internet. This chapter considers the range of features offered by electronic journals, describes tools that may be used to find electronic journals and individual articles and outlines recent developments in the publication of preprints in biomedicine.

Electronic journals: accessibility issues

The content accessible through electronic journals is not generally retrievable by searching generic Web search engines. Indeed, a search using several search engines for full text articles from the *BMJ*, one of the few journals that makes its full content available without the need for registration, login or prior subscription, reveals how few *BMJ* articles can be retrieved at all in this way.

Electronic journals have mainly come on-stream since the mid-1990s, with few years of the full text available at present online. In many cases, research conducted in previous decades will be of interest. Exceptionally, JSTOR, a not-for-profit organisation set up in the US by the Andrew W

Mellon Foundation, and supported in the UK by Higher Education's JISC (the Joint Information Systems Committee), provides centralised storage and archiving of important journals back in time.[4] The *BMJ* is due to inaugurate the JSTOR medical collection, with the aim that all published issues of the *BMJ* will be digitised and made available online from 1840 to 1993, after which time the *BMJ* is already available online.[5]

Most electronic journals require prior subscription. Where no fees are levied, at the very least, a journal site will generally require prior login and there are very few exceptions to this. For example, it is possible to access online the full text of *Morbidity and Mortality Weekly Report* well in advance of the print issues being received by a local library. Access to this title remains free to all, although the trend overall is for free access to be curtailed following brief trials.

More commonly, journals make available for free only instructions to authors and table of contents information - sometimes with abstracts of published articles. While some publishers are making online access free with print subscriptions, it is more common to find that joint print and online subscriptions are pegged at significant levels over the print only subscription. Typical examples include the *Journal of Biological Chemistry* and *Science*, both of which charge significantly more than the cost of the print subscription for institution–wide access to the electronic version.

In pursuit of this pricing policy, publishers may erect other barriers to access, such as restriction of access by IP number, limiting use of an electronic journal to the workplace or place of study alone. For example, access to the *Biochemical Journal - online* is restricted to institutional subscribers by employing this approach.

Electronic journals appear in a variety of formats. For example, many journals make their electronic content available in PDF format (portable document format), in addition to HTML. The PDF format is popular for printing, as it maintains the recognisable layout of the printed journal page. In order to view and print out articles in PDF format, it is essential that a copy of the Adobe Acrobat Reader [6] has been installed. This is freely available to download from the Web, and most journals do not require special software, other than the Web browser of choice.

Biochemical Journal - online: www.biochemj.org/

BMJ: www.bmj.com/

Journal of Biological Chemistry: www.jbc.org/

Morbidity and Mortality Weekly Report: www.cdc.gov/mmwr/

Science: www.sciencemag.org/

Journal features

A range of features is generally available for accessing and handling information with the electronic version of journals. The *BMJ* offers several options, such as displaying an article in PDF format, sending an electronic response, viewing electronic responses, finding related articles in the *BMJ* or PubMed, viewing the PubMed citation for an article, downloading bibliographic details of an article to a reference management application, searching for other articles by the author, and setting up an alert so as to be notified when new articles cite an article.

More importantly, however, the electronic version of a journal often contains at least as much as the print version, and many electronic journals are beginning to include material additional to that available in print. For example, the *BMJ* regularly publishes *news eXtra* as well as expanded methodology sections that are available only with the online version of the journal.

Like the *BMJ*, subscribers to the *Biochemical Journal – online* have access to the full text of articles, including tables and graphics. In addition, subscribers to either journal will find that inter-journal linking is available from the references section of the papers to other selected online journals.[7] HTML or SGML (Standard Generalized Markup Language) is increasingly being used to enhance linking internally, and also between online journals and bibliographic or other databases. Such a facility can significantly enhance the effectiveness of the literature search process, by providing seamless linking:

- within individual articles from the text to the appropriate references,
- between references and PubMed or other database citations, and
- between different journals directly.

Several systems now exist that enable inter-journal linking. HighWire Press and other publishers use the PubMed PubRef system,[8] ISI's Web of Science and others use proprietary linking systems, whereas Digital Object Identifiers offer another approach altogether.[9]

Other features to which users may be attracted include:

- convenient access from the desktop,
- articles available online in advance of the print copy,
- speedy delivery of full text articles as HTML files via the Web or PDF files for printing,
- hypertext links to abstracts in MEDLINE and other databases,
- hypertext links to relevant Web sites,

- hypertext links to gene sequence and other biological databases via PubMed,
- hypertext links from article references to related abstracts in PubMed,
- search facility enabling the rapid location of information within a journal or across collaborating titles,
- access to fully searchable archives of papers (though these can sometimes be limited),
- email current awareness service giving advance notice of papers to be published, and
- email links to authors.

The electronic publishing medium potentially has several advantages over print for authors as well, such as

- quick turnaround time from submission to appearance on the Web,
- no page limit,
- inclusion of full colour images and additional material, e.g. picture, sound or movie files, and
- no limit on additional media.

Indeed, increasingly, electronic publishing makes it possible for a number of media to be available with a journal article, so that supplemental data such as videos, images and experimental procedures are becoming available online. For example, *Anesthesiology* features several video presentations that enhance published articles (see for example an article by Chelly *et al.*)[10] and *Protein Science* makes available online kinemages ('kinetic images') - scientific illustrations presented as interactive computer displays.[11]

Anesthesiology: www.anesthesiology.org/

Protein Science: www.proteinscience.org/

Electronic-only journals: quality issues

Several concerns had originally been raised about the quality of electronic-only journals. In particular, Lundberg, then editor of *JAMA*, issued the reminder that 'in medical information quality of content will continue to be king for the benefit of all of us as patients'.[12]

Rennie, in discussing measures of quality,[13] listed three indicators that have been used successfully in assessing the quality of medical journals in the print environment: library lists (whether libraries subscribe to a journal), indexing (whether it is included in indexing and abstracting publications or bibliographic databases such as Medline) and citation (a journal's impact factor, as recorded in ISI's *Journal Citation Reports*). Similar measures have been suggested as being equally important in the electronic environment, such as whether or not a title is rigorously peer reviewed, the reputation of its editorial board, whether or not it is indexed by key abstracting and indexing publications, and its impact factor.

Indeed, as Harnad pointed out: 'prestige will continue to depend on the rigor of the peer review and the quality of the authors and submissions, not on the medium'.[14]

A number of electronic-only journals are now beginning to be indexed by authoritative indexing and abstracting services. For example, *Experimental Biology Online (EBO)* is a multimedia electronic journal. All papers are submitted and refereed by peer review electronically. The journal is published on the Web, although once or twice a year an archival printed issue is released, containing all papers published since the previous issue. A CD-ROM is issued annually containing the full annual contents of *EBO*, including multimedia features. *EBO*, like the *World Wide Web Journal of Biology*, is indexed in Biological Abstracts, whereas *Molecular Vision* is indexed also in MEDLINE, the Science Citation Index and Chemical Abstracts.

> *Experimental Biology Online (EBO)*: link.springer.de / link / service / journals / 00898 /
>
> *Molecular Vision*: molvis.org / molvis /
>
> *World Wide Web Journal of Biology*: epress.com / w3jbio /

Finding journals online

An increasing number of journals are becoming available online, and checking the online availability of journal titles can be time-consuming. Although there is no single comprehensive directory, the following resources may be useful:

- JournalSeek lists 8,500 science journal titles in several broad categories and presents especially good coverage of biochemistry and molecular biology. The directory provides abbreviated journal title, brief description, ISSN and an indication of whether the tables of contents, abstracts or full text are available for free online.
- MedWebPlus presents details for about 4,500 journal titles and can be easily searched. The directory gives extensive information about a journal: abbreviation, ISSN, start volume, publisher, frequency of

publication, where indexed, country and place of publication, and links through to PubMed for tables of contents and abstracts. MedWebPlus often indicates whether tables of contents, abstracts or full text are available online. It is possible also to browse journals in MedWebPlus by several specialties and topics.

- Also available is Science.komm, providing a handy breakdown of titles by specialty. Although this is one of the most comprehensive listings of medical journal titles online, no information is provided about journals other than a straight alphabetical listing of titles and a link through to each title's home page. Also, a search for a specific journal title does not result in direct retrieval: instead, the service points to a selection of subject areas that may include a listing of the journal sought.
- Medline journals with links to publisher Web sites are detailed in a listing provided by PubMed.
- HighWire Press maintains links to the top 500 science journals with rank determined by ISI citation frequency.
- Free medical journals, regardless of impact factor, are specifically brought together by FreeMedicalJournals.com and may be displayed by specialty or in alphabetical order. An alerting service is available.

In this fast-developing field, announcements of new resources are frequent. NewJour, the New Journal and Newsletter Announcement List for new serials on the Internet maintains archives, which include a useful alphabetical list by journal title or groups of journals for scanning of announcements.

FreeMedicalJournals.com: www.freemedicaljournals.com/

HighWire Press – Top 500 science journals:
highwire.stanford.edu/top/journals.dtl

JournalSeek: genamics.com/journals/

MedWebPlus Journals:
www.medwebplus.com/subject/Periodicals.html

MedWebPlus search: www.medwebplus.com/

Newjour: gort.ucsd.edu/newjour/NewJourWel.html

Newjour Archive: gort.ucsd.edu/newjour/

PubMed – MEDLINE journals: www.ncbi.nlm.nih.gov:80/entrez/ journals/loftext_noprov.html

Science.komm – Medical journals: www.sciencekomm.at/journals/ medicine/med-bio.html

Preprint servers

Papers have long been distributed by researchers prior to publication, albeit usually to small groups of close colleagues (sometimes described as the 'invisible college'). Presentations of papers and posters at conferences have also traditionally been important for the communication of new research findings. Electronic preprint archives took this a step further, opening up communication to a wider community. Notable has been the preprint archive at Los Alamos National Laboratory, where in 1991 Paul Ginsparg set up a system for receiving and storing preprints in the field of high energy physics. The archive is now funded by the US National Science Foundation and the US Department of Energy and provides a fully automated electronic archive and distribution system for research papers. arXiv.org, as it is now called, encourages the replacement of preprints with the final peer-reviewed version when this becomes available.

The Web now offers a highly effective medium for electronic preprint distribution. An eprint initiative by Stevan Harnad in the field of cognitive sciences is also under development and is modelled on arXiv.org. CogPrints aims to provide an electronic archive for papers in any area of psychology, neuroscience and linguistics and to provide a way for authors to archive pre-refereed preprints as well as refereed published reprints.

PubMed Central

Many have questioned whether this model may be extensible to medicine. However, following swift gestation of barely a year, a biomedical eprint server, PubMed Central, went live in January 2000 and was still under development at the time of writing.[15] Pursued by the US National Institutes of Health (NIH), the original proposal for PubMed Central caused significant discussion and feedback from researchers and publishers. As a result, PubMed Central is intended to 'archive, organize and distribute peer-reviewed reports from journals, as well as reports that have been screened but have not formally been peer-reviewed'.[15]

PubMed Central is to cover the life sciences in general. It will focus on the posting of peer-reviewed eprints, and peer-reviewed and screened material will be clearly distinguishable. Many of the non-peer-reviewed reports will be preprints deposited in PubMed Central, but also submitted to formal peer review. However, PubMed Central will not act as a clearinghouse for peer review or minimal vetting. Instead, the screening of non-peer-reviewed reports will be the responsibility of groups that are independent of the NIH.

Posting of peer-reviewed eprints will be at a time chosen by the rights owners, which may possibly be some time after publication in a journal. It is intended that participating journals and other organisations will submit research reports to PubMed Central and access will be free to individuals and that links will be given from PubMed Central to the publishers' Web sites. PubMed Central will be integrated with PubMed.

Several journals had agreed to participate at the end of January 2000:[16]

* *Canadian Medical Association Journal,*
* *Frontiers in Bioscience,*
* *Molecular Biology of the Cell* (content to be offered with 2 month delay),
* *PNAS: The Proceedings of the National Academy of Sciences* (content to be offered with 1 month delay), and
* 5 journals from the Current Science Group, in full and without delay.

Other biomedical eprint and preprint initiatives

Several initiatives are underway to complement PubMed. E-Biosci is set to launch a Europe-based eprint initiative for the scientific literature. Commercial publishers, in particular, who may not co-operate with PubMed Central, may agree to establish a full text searchable site with E-Biosci. E-Biosci might hold abstracts linked to the full text of articles and may be more complete than PubMed.[17]

In addition, a number of journal-specific initiatives have also been announced. The *BMJ* launched the ClinMed NetPrints eprint server in December 1999.[18] Papers are screened only for obvious flaws and the site displays a fairly prominent warning message that 'articles posted on this site have not yet been accepted for publication by a peer reviewed journal. They are presented here mainly for the benefit of fellow researchers'. The *BMJ* has agreed to transfer electronic versions of research articles to PubMed Central at the same time as they are made available on the *BMJ* Web site, so the full text of *BMJ* articles will be accessible from either PubMed Central or direct from the *BMJ* Web site. Related editorials, commentaries and rapid responses will be available only from the *BMJ* Web site itself, as will the PDF format of articles for printing.

ClinMed NetPrints provides a list of journals that will accept submissions that have appeared on preprint servers, as well as a list of journals that will not accept such submissions.[19]

The experimental *Lancet* Electronic Research Archive in international health and eprint server is a self-archive, owned by the authors. Access is unrestricted and content is intended to cover all issues of relevance to medicine in the developing world.

In addition, BioMedCentral from Current Science was also due to start during 2000. The new company is to provide peer review services for PubMed Central. Community of Science pursues a similar model.

In a separate initiative, twelve publishers, including Oxford University Press and Academic Press alongside Springer-Verlag, John Wiley and Sons, Macmillan Magazines and Elsevier Science among others, have joined together to develop an electronic linking service that is intended to serve as a fee-based alternative to PubMed Central. In this, 3 million articles initially will be interlinked so that researchers could be linked automatically from the online version of one journal to the article cited in another.[20, 21] The linking service would be free to licensed subscribers, or articles would be available for a fee.

---

arXiv.org e-print archive: xxx.lanl.gov/
Mirrored in the UK at: uk.arxiv.org/

BioMedCentral: www.biomedcentral.com/

CogPrints: cogprints.soton.ac.uk/

Community of Science (COS): www.cos.com/

NetPrints – Clinical Medicine & Health Research:
clinmed.netprints.org/

PubMed Central: pubmedcentral.nih.gov/

The Lancet Electronic Research Archive: www.thelancet.com/
newlancet/eprint/

Accessing tables of contents

Most journals that are available online now provide access to their tables of contents (TOCs), even if the full text may as yet be unavailable on the Web. Identifying a few favourite journals and bookmarking their TOCs pages can make it a very simple exercise to visit and revisit these on a regular basis.

WebMedLit conveniently brings together the current TOC pages for around 30 key medical journals, including the *BMJ, New England Journal of Medicine, JAMA, AIDS* and several *Archives* journals. WebMedLit allows registered users to personalise their use of the service by selecting subject areas and profile interests according to which electronic journal contents are delivered.

HUM-MOLGEN operates a similar service for bioscientists: the current TOCs are available for over 30 journals. These include *Cell, EMBO Journal, Genome Research* and the *Journal of Cell Biology*.

MD Digests provides clinical summaries from 5 key medical journals: *Annals of Internal Medicine, BMJ, JAMA, The Lancet* and the *New England Journal of Medicine*.

Similarly, journal publishers are increasingly making the TOCs and abstracts of journal articles available for searching for free. For example, Elsevier offers 'ContentsSearch' across more than 1,000 journals.

Increasingly, also, it is possible to search across several publishers' journal TOCs pages for broader retrieval. Journal aggregator services such as UK Higher Education's NESLI (the National Electronic Site Licence Initiative), Swetsnet*Navigator* and ingentaJournals, and document delivery services such as UnCover, may allow the cross-searching of TOCs across several publishers' journals.

Elsevier Science ContentsSearch: www.elsevier.nl/locate/ContentsSearch

HUM-MOLGEN: www.hum-molgen.de/journals/

ingentaJournals: www.bids.ac.uk/ or www.ingenta.com/

MD Digests: php2.silverplatter.com/physicians/digest.htm

National Electronic Site Licence Initiative (NESLI): www.nesli.ac.uk/

Swetsnet*Navigator*: www.swetsnetnavigator.com/

UnCover: uncweb.carl.org/

WebMedLit: www.webmedlit.com/

Journal TOC alerting and current awareness services

Increasingly, journal publishers are also making automatic alerting via email available, so that researchers and practitioners need not proactively seek out a page each time a new journal issue appears. For example, in common with most journal publishers with an online presence, Elsevier offers the Contents Direct service, by which electronic TOC notification is sent by email to those who register for the service. Where forthcoming issues' TOCs are provided, it is possible for researchers currently researching in a field to be notified of developments in advance of publication. For example, the *Annual Review of Biochemistry* planned TOCs for future volumes are generally available several months prior to publication.

UnCover Reveal and Reveal Alert provide table of contents as well as subject based current awareness search services. For an annual fee of $25.00 at the time of writing, TOCs from up to 50 titles may be delivered and up to 25 searches may be stored to be rerun against new UnCover content on a weekly basis.

Infotrieve Article Finder offers a free TOC alerting service for over 20,000 journals, which can be defined by subject or by journal title. An unlimited number of titles can be chosen. Email alerts are sent to users when new journal issues are added to the database.

Elsevier Science ContentsDirect: www.elsevier.nl/locate/ContentsDirect

Annual Review of Biochemistry – Planned tables of contents for future volumes: biochem.annualreviews.org/future.shtml

UnCover Reveal and Reveal Alert: uncweb.carl.org/reveal/

Infotrieve Article Finder: www.infotrieve.com/

Document delivery options

Increasingly journals are providing online pay-per-view options direct from the publishers' sites or via document delivery options. Journal aggregators may do the same for individual articles for which a subscription is not available. For example, where titles are not available for free (e.g. an institutional subscription is not in place), ingentaJournals quotes a price for online purchase of individual articles.

While many libraries, especially academic and professional libraries, operate comprehensive document delivery services, several sources for document acquisition are prepared to deliver direct to the individual researcher, albeit often at a significant fee.

Among these is UnCover, which allows document delivery from a wide range of journals. However, this may not be as fast as electronic individual article supply purchase direct from the publisher's site (where available) and may be just as expensive. The *BMJ* was an issue behind at the time the service was checked, which was marked given that access is available from the publisher's site several hours before the printed copy is available in any library.

UnCover offers Desktop Image Delivery from approximately 2,500 journal titles direct to the requester's personal computer. This may take less than an hour from the time an order is received and processed. Articles that may be delivered via this route are clearly marked in the UnCover database, as are the journal titles for which this service applies. Interestingly, UnCover displays the following disclaimer with every document processed: 'this article may be available in your library at no cost to you'. Indeed, on searching for articles from the *BMJ*, which is available for free to anyone on the Internet, desktop delivery for each article was charged at $17.50.

BioMedNet also operates a document delivery service for registered members, often at rates similar to those offered by UnCover, with a 17.5% VAT surcharge for European customers.

PubMed links straight through to a range of participating libraries internationally, which provide document delivery services at the click of the Order button, via a service called Loansome Doc.[22] The single UK library listed was the British Library, with standard pricing for single article delivery at around £9.[23]

Infotrieve offers document delivery from 65,000 journal titles. At $9.75 per article, in addition to any copyright royalty or purchase costs, its prices were not necessarily competitive. However, via Infotrieve's article finder it is possible to see which articles may be delivered within 24 hours. There is a $10.00 surcharge for rush service.

BioMedNet Library: journals.bmn.com/

PubMed: www.ncbi.nlm.nih.gov/PubMed/

Full text searching

Free searching across the full text of several journals simultaneously is now possible, for example via a Search Multiple Journals interface offered by the *BMJ*. Searching the full text of journal articles can retrieve far more than simply searching the titles and abstracts of the same articles. The benefits of this are summarised by the *BMJ*[24] and include the ability to retrieve articles:

- from a particular institution (if provided by a journal),
- that cite a paper written by a particular author,
- that refer to methods used, for example, the use of a special reagent or technique, or
- that report a particular research methodology.

Searching across the full text of many journals simultaneously can be rewarding when seeking very specific information, and indeed may open up options for retrieval that were otherwise available only through proprietary interfaces. For example, a quick search for the simple phrase *randomised controlled trial* in all journals in the category of medical research for the year 1999 resulted in 8980 matches. Repeating the same search by limiting the query to titles or abstracts of articles led to the retrieval of just 1175 matching references. The medical research category included 31 journals, all of high quality: *American Journal of Pathology, American Journal of Physiology – Gastrointestinal and Liver Physiology, Blood, BMJ, Gastroenterology, Gut, Hepatology, Journal of Clinical Investigation, Journal of Experimental Medicine, Proceedings of the National Academy of Sciences* and *Science*.

Although searches are possible back to 1965 (and a quick search for *secretin* did retrieve some references dating back to the 1980s), only abstracts were available for the earlier years. Also, even though the full text of articles may be searched, the full text may not be displayed unless a subscription is in place.

Along with the benefits of searchable full text of journal articles, there are also several drawbacks. The search options are of necessity rudimentary when searching across potentially heterogeneous sources. Perhaps most importantly, however, retrieval is hampered by the numerous references found that refer to the search term in passing only, making it necessary to sift through increased quantities of potentially less relevant or interesting content. For more established areas, the information overload this can bring about has been demonstrated conclusively by the enormous retrieval sets created by Web search engines. Fortunately there are well established alternatives, not least searching one or more bibliographic databases for words in titles, abstracts and keywords.

Full text searchable sites are likely to become more widespread, should developments such as PubMed Central and E-Biosci (see above) become further established.

BMJ Search multiple journals: www.bmj.com/searchall/

Instructions for authors / citing references

Instructions for authors submitting manuscripts for publications are now generally available for free on the Internet from publishers' sites. Several of these from journals in the health sciences have been brought together by the Mulford Library, Medical College of Ohio.[25]

Uniform requirements for manuscripts have been agreed among biomedical journal publishers representing over 500 journals.[26] The *Uniform Requirements* citation style (the Vancouver style) is based on an ANSI (American National Standards Institute) standard that was adapted by the US National Library of Medicine for its databases. Several links to other guides to citing electronic material are provided by UKOLUG[27] and IFLA (the International Federation of Library Associations and Institutions) also provides a selection of those on its Web site.[28]

In addition, several guides to citing electronic materials are available in print.[29, 30]

References

1. American Medical Association. International Congress on Peer Review in Biomedical Publication. Available from: http://www.ama-assn.org/public/peer/peerhome.htm

2. Harnad S. Free at last: the future of peer-reviewed journals. *D-Lib Magazine* 1999 Dec; **5**(12). Available from: http://www.dlib.org/dlib/december99/12harnad.html and mirrored in the UK at http://mirrored.ukoln.ac.uk/lis-journals/dlib/dlib/dlib/december99/12harnad.html

3. Fletcher RH, Fletcher SW. The future of medical journals in the western world. *Lancet* 1998 Oct 3; **352** Suppl 2:30-33. Available to subscribers from: http://www.thelancet.com/newlancet/any/supplements/vol352s2/body.article10.html

4. JSTOR. Available from: http://www.jstor.org/ and mirrored in the UK at http://www.jstor.ac.uk/

5. Delamothe T. BMJ to sign with PubMed Central, JSTOR, and WorldSpace. *BMJ* 2000 Jan 1; **320**(7226):8. Available from: http://www.bmj.com/cgi/content/full/320/7226/8

6. Adobe Systems Incorporated. Adobe Acrobat Reader. Available from: http://www.adobe.com/products/acrobat/readermain.html

7. *Biochemical Journal - online.* Interjournal linking. Available from: http://www.biochemj.org/bj/interjournal.htm

8. NCBI. NCBI bibliographic resources. Available from: http://www.ncbi.nlm.nih.gov/PubMed/bibres.html

9. Caplan P, Arms WY. Reference linking for journal articles. *D-Lib Magazine* 1999 Jul/Aug;5(7/8). Available from: http://www.dlib.org/dlib/july99/caplan/07caplan.html and mirrored in the UK at http://mirrored.ukoln.ac.uk/lis-journals/dlib/dlib/dlib/july99/caplan/07caplan.html

10. Chelly JE, Delaunay L. A new anterior approach to the sciatic nerve block. *Anesthesiology* 1999 Dec; 91(6):1655-1660.

11. *Protein Science*. Kinemages. Available from: http://www.proteinscience.org/Kinemage/

12. Lundberg GD. A Christmas fairy tale, *BMJ* 1996 Dec 21; **313**(7072):1612. Available from: http://www.bmj.com/cgi/content/full/313/7072/1612

13. Rennie D. The present state of medical journals. *Lancet* 1998 Oct 3;**352** Suppl 2:18-22. Available to subscribers from: http://www.thelancet.com/newlancet/any/supplements/vol352s2/body.article6.html

14. Scholarly journals at the crossroads: a subversive proposal for electronic publishing. An Internet discussion about scientific and scholarly journals and their future. XIV. Journal publishing systems and models. Available from: http://www.arl.org/scomm/subversive/sub14.html

15. PubMed Central: an NIH operated site for electronic distribution of life sciences research reports. Available from: http://www.nih.gov/welcome/director/pubmedcentral/pmc.html

16. PubMed Central. Update. Available from: http://pubmedcentral.nih.gov/pubmedcentral5.html

17. Butler D. All parties keen to press on with Europe-based science Website. *Nature* 2000 Jan 27; **403**:347-348.

18. Delamothe T, Smith R, Keeler MA, Sack J, Witscher B. Netprints: the next phase in the evolution of biomedical publishing. Will allow researchers to share their findings in full, for free, and fast. *BMJ* 1999 Dec 11;**319**(7224):1515-1516. Available from: http://www.bmj.com/cgi/content/full/319/7224/1515

19. ClinMed NetPrints. Clinical Medicine: journal policies. Available from: http://clinmed.netprints.org/misc/policies.shtml

20. Reuters. Scientific minds meet on the Net. 3.00 am 17 November 1999 PST. Available from: http://www.wired.com/news/reuters/0,1349,32592,00.html

21. Smaglik P. Fee vs. free in online research. *The Scientist* 1999 Dec 6; **13**(24):11. Available from: http://www.the-scientist.library.upenn.edu/yr1999/dec/smaglik_p11_991206.html

22. National Library of Medicine (NLM). Frequently asked questions. Getting articles and borrowing books. Available from: http://www.nlm.nih.gov/services/faqill.html

23. British Library Document Supply Centre. Articles Direct. Available from: http://www.bl.uk/services/bsds/dsc/artdir01.html

24. *BMJ*. Help with searching. Available from: http://www.bmj.com/help/search_help.dtl

25. Medical College of Ohio. Raymon H Mulford Library. Instructions to authors in the health sciences. Available from: http://www.mco.edu/lib/instr/libinsta.html

26. International Committee of Medical Journal Editors. Uniform requirements for manuscripts submitted to biomedical journals. Available from: http://www.icmje.org/

27. UK Online User Group. Links: bibliographic software. Guide to citing electronic resources. Available from: http://www.ukolug.org.uk/links/biblio.htm#gtc

28. IFLANET. Library & Information Science: citation guides for electronic documents. Available from: http://ifla.inist.fr/ifla/I/training/citation/citing.htm

29. Li X, Crane N. Electronic style: a guide to citing electronic information. Westport: Meckler; 1995.

30. Patrias K. National Library of Medicine recommended formats for bibliographic citation. Bethesda: National Library of Medicine; 1991.

Chapter 17

Searching the Internet strategically

According to the P\S\L Consulting Group, Yahoo! was the most frequently used search tool by health professionals (71%) in 1998, followed by AltaVista (58%).[1] This pattern prevailed in all regions of the world, with the exception of Europe where AltaVista appeared to be slightly more popular, and China where Yahoo! predominated. Popularity of search engines among professional searchers was found to differ from the above in an Internet 'search-off' – 45% of searchers used AltaVista, 20% HotBot, 14% Infoseek and 14% Excite.[2]

Search Engine Watch provides estimates of search engine popularity from Nielsen//NetRatings[3] and Media Metrix.[4] In 1998, Yahoo! was in the lead (40%), followed by Netscape, MSN and Excite (20–30%). From late 1999 onwards, this trend had changed very little, with Yahoo!'s popularity increasing even further, and Go replacing Excite in the most visited category.

All of the above tools are generic search engines or directories. For many users of healthcare and medical information via the Internet, these tools are often not the most appropriate, nor are they necessarily the most effective when attempting to access high quality information. The previous chapters have investigated how different types of Internet-based search tools work, and how they can be used to best effect. This chapter draws together comparisons between these different types of tools, highlighting their advantages and disadvantages. It also sets out information to enable searchers to plan a search, execute it with the right search tool, and understand the limitations of the results.

Words, pages, resources and sites

First, a brief introduction to the different elements that make up information resources available via the Internet. Discriminating use of different search tools hinges upon having a clear understanding of the difference between words, pages, resources and sites, as well as an appreciation of the mechanics of using the tools.

Each accessible page on the Web consists of a number of words. By page we mean a document or other object that is assigned a unique URL. It may be necessary to scroll down a number of screens to see a complete page, or a page may be short enough to be viewed within a single screen display. In addition, a single page may be a resource in its own right or it may be one of many pages that make up a resource. For example, one page may be a complete journal article or part of a multi-page document, such as a chapter from an electronic textbook. Some types of resources, such as a database or a journal, may have no directly accessible pages other than a 'home page'. From this entry point, some form of login or prior registration may be required before individual pages can be accessed. Some pages on the Web do not exist until a user requests them. The data making up the page is held in a database and the page is created 'on-the-fly', appearing in the user's browser and disappearing once the user has moved on. This type of page is transient, and may not be indexed by search engines.

A site might incorporate a number of resources. For example, the Canadian Medical Association (CMA) site links to a range of different types of resources, including:

- Ovid Search: Link to Electronic Resources (OSLER), a service for CMA members. This can be described as a distinct resource but one which also provides access to further resources, including Medline, AIDSLINE, CancerLit and HealthSTAR;
- clinical practice guidelines (CMA Infobase); and
- the *Canadian Medical Association Journal* (*CMAJ*).

The 1998 clinical practice guidelines for the management of diabetes in Canada[5] is a discrete resource consisting of ten pages in addition to the opening page. It is also part of a larger resource (*CMAJ*), since it was published as a supplement to *CMAJ*. The guidelines also appear as part of the CMA Infobase.

CMA: www.cma.ca/

CMAJ: www.cma.ca/cmaj/

CMA Infobase: www.cma.ca/cpgs/

Ovid Search: Link to Electronic Resources (OSLER): www.cma.ca/osler/

Indexability

Generic search tools often cannot capture the content of resources, such as those that are accessible from the CMA site. At the time of writing, the *CMAJ* offered free access to the full text of most articles. The 1998 clinical practice guidelines for the management of diabetes in Canada were available in HTML format and were therefore indexable by search engines.[5] However, they were also published by *CMAJ* in PDF format[6] – and the content of the document in PDF format was not captured by the search engines.

Were the CMA site to require prior registration or restrict access to the full text of the *CMAJ*, search engines would have no means of capturing the full text information. Web search engines are equally powerless at capturing the content of bibliographic and other databases, such as those provided by the OSLER service: their content is not directly publicly accessible as it is restricted to members only.

Granularity

The granularity at which information is captured and indexed additionally influences the choice of search tool and search strategy. Web search engines index at the word level and are therefore searched using word-based queries. This means that they cannot provide a browsable view of their contents. Directories, review sites and information gateways on the other hand do not capture all or even most words belonging to a page, but at most, the original title and URL. Review sites and information gateways will include reviews or descriptions that can be quite extensive – but the content of these will be under the editorial control of the service and will not be identical to the content of the original pages, resources or sites. Information gateways will often provide added value by assigning subject-based index terms to each resource description using, for example, Medical Subject Headings. The use of subject headings allows a structured approach to searching and can provide a functional outline for browsing.

Table 17.1: Words, pages, resources and sites: coverage by a range of Internet search tools and directories

	Words	Pages	Resources	Sites	Search strategy
Web search engines	Yes	Yes			Search on words, cannot browse
Web directories		Some	Yes	Yes	Search on title and one-line description, can browse (though usually not systematically)
Health and medical information gateways		Some	Yes	Some	Search on title and resource description, can browse (usually systematically), can often exploit hierarchical relationships between terms

Coverage of the Web by search engines

Many sources give the impression that search engines are capable of indexing the entire Web. For example, Microsoft offers a list of search engines, which includes two that are described as Full-Web – 'capable of searching every word on every page of the Web'.[7] Similarly, AltaVista has intimated that it indexes the entire Internet.[8]

In reality, no single search tool searches and indexes the entire Web. Lawrence and Giles estimated in December 1997 that a lower limit on the size of the 'publicly indexable' Web was 320 million pages.[9] The publicly indexable Web excluded pages typically not indexed by the major search engines e.g. pages behind search forms or requiring authorisation.[10] The same study found that coverage by any one engine is significantly limited, and that no single engine indexes more than about one third of publicly indexable Web pages. The researchers estimated that HotBot covered 34% of these, AltaVista 28%, Northern Light 20%, Excite 14%, Infoseek 10%, and Lycos 3%. Furthermore, according to Search Engine Watch, in February 1999, AltaVista indexed 47% of the Web, Northern Light 39% and Inktomi 34%. Excite, Lycos and Infoseek each indexed between 14% and 17%, assuming that there were 320 million indexable pages on the Web.[11]

According to Lawrence and Giles,[9] the combined content of the six engines examined in their study covered about 3.5 times as much of the Web as one engine alone, or twice the coverage of the largest engine. The implication is that individual search engines retrieve only a small proportion of documents potentially available via the Web.

Subsequent studies showed comparable findings,[12] although the publicly indexable Web size estimate at the time (February 1999) had risen to over 800 million pages. More recent estimates placed its size at over 1 billion pages. The relative size of search engines has also changed over time, and is likely to continue to change: at the end of June 2000, Google announced full coverage of 580 million pages and additional partial coverage of 500 million more, suddenly making it by far the largest Web search engine.

What is not covered by Web search engines

AltaVista's Chief Technical Officer at the time explained the problem of indexing the Web:

> The truth is that no search engine indexes the whole Web. The concept of 'the size of the Web' in itself is flawed, as there are many sites virtually infinite in size: dynamically generated documents, personalised news pages and shopping baskets us-

ing cookies, robot traps, scripts, the list goes on. Also unless one spends a lot of effort cleaning it up (we do), an index holds a lot of pages unlikely to ever be retrieved, like multiple copies of the same page and access logs. Size alone is a poor measure of usefulness.[13]

As mentioned above, pages or sites requiring prior login or other authentication, or pages that are in formats other than HTML, such as PDF, are not readily accessible to search engines. In addition, there are many other reasons why a Web page may not be indexed by a search engine:[10, 14]

- the software is unable to access the site during an indexing cycle: the server may be inaccessible because it is down or busy;
- the site employs the robots exclusion standard: a .txt file instructs spiders not to index the whole or part of the site;
- the site resides on an Intranet or is not linked to from anywhere else;
- the site imposes domain limitations;
- the page uses Javascript, frames or image maps;
- the page uses meta tags: some spiders do not index pages that use meta tags; or
- the page is hidden behind a search form.

The depth of coverage of search engines has also come under scrutiny. AltaVista was reported to be providing a sample from every Web site, but to be indexing the majority of the content of only the most frequently visited sites. Other search engines have been shown to adopt a similar approach.[15]

As a result, the following are not generally indexed by generic Web search engines:

- information held in databases (e.g. bibliographic databases);
- information held on pages that are password-controlled, that require prior authorisation, or that are subject to domain limitations (e.g. electronic journals); and
- information held behind firewalls (e.g. on intranets, or secure networks, such as the UK NHSnet).

These are often the sources that are potentially of the highest quality and of the greatest value when seeking information for healthcare and medicine. Such sources therefore need to be identified using tools other than search engines and searched separately.

Further limitations of search engines

In addition to poor coverage of the Web by search engines, several other limitations might also be noted. These include:

- poor relevance ranking caused by index spamming and other practices;
- little information returned with each hit by the search engines means that it can be difficult to determine the relevance of the pages that are returned; and
- a lack of standardisation across search engines in terms of search features.

Server downtime, temporary unavailability or network difficulties can result in inconsistencies in the numbers of hits returned.

The impact of such limitations means that using search engines to find health and medical information can be a slow and tedious process. In addition to the need to access multiple search engines, and the unknown numbers of potential hits that may go undetected, much effort must be expended in assessing the relevance and quality of each match returned. It may be necessary to access each page directly in order to assess its value, and it may be necessary to wait for each page to load before attempting to locate query terms in each page.

Furthermore, contrary to common belief, the Internet is not searched in real time or 'live'. Instead, the results pages that are returned following a search use information that is pre-stored in a search engine's index (AltaVista, for example, supports an index update rate of 28 days). The original page may no longer be available and therefore search engine results sometimes link to pages that exhibit error messages such as:

File Not Found
The requested URL ... was not found on this server.

HTTP Error 404
404 Not Found
The Web server cannot find the file or script you asked for.

In summary:

- the pages that are potentially indexable by Web search engines are only a subset of the information available via the Web, and an even smaller subset of the information available via the Internet as a whole;
- no Web search engine reaches all potentially indexable Web pages;
- much of the content of the best publicly accessible Web pages cannot be indexed by generic Web search engines; and

- as pages change content, this is not immediately reflected in the information indexed by search engines.

Limitations of metasearch engines

One of the implications of the above is that because individual search engines retrieve only a small proportion of documents potentially available via the Web, metasearch engines (discussed in Chapter 11) could provide a more comprehensive approach to searching because they combine the results from different tools. However, since metasearch engines are fuelled by search engines in their retrieval, they retain most of the limitations and are often subject to a few more.

Comprehensiveness of coverage remains impossible because:

- metasearch engines query only a subset of search engines. For example, none of the metasearch engines search Northern Light and few target Google;
- individual search engines are often unavailable to return hits within the maximum search time allotted by a metasearch engine; and
- ranking metasearch engines retrieve only a few hits (between ten and thirty) from each source search engine.

In addition:

- metasearch engines retrieve the same low grade quality of information as the source engines;
- ranking metasearch engines consolidate the results from individual search engines, removing duplicate hits and ranking according to their own algorithm. However, since some source search engines are likely to return hits with poor relevance, this will affect ranking effectiveness overall;
- queries submitted to a metasearch engine need to utilise only those features that are commonly recognised by all the source Web search engines otherwise they may be interpreted in an unpredictable manner;
- metasearch engines do not always submit queries appropriately to the source search engines and some metasearch engines may not report the precise query submitted; for example, Boolean expressions, especially those including the Boolean OR operator, are generally not translated correctly and may not be recognised by the source search engines;
- display features are usually reduced to a few common elements supported across a range of search engines – most results provide no indication of the length or currency of matching pages; and

- search results presented by metasearch engines can be inconsistent as they often rely on the results supplied by the faster-responding source search engines: resubmitting a search query may generate additional hits as individual search engines may contribute results that were unavailable first time round.

Search engines and directories compared

Table 17.2 summarises the key characteristics of Web search engines and directories, and outlines the types of query that each supports.

Table 17.2: Web search engines and directories compared

	Search engines	Directories (excluding associated search engines)
Size	Over 100 million pages	Hundreds of thousands of sites[11]
Granularity	Words, pages	Pages, resources, sites
Audience	General public	General public
Quality criteria for inclusion	None	None stated explicitly
General topic	With difficulty	Yes: browse
Specific topic	Yes	Yes: search / browse
Known Web site	Yes	Possibly: search
Words or phrase in a Web page	Yes	No

The sheer number of hits that are returned with any search using a general search engine might swamp users. Conversely a number of factors may limit the appeal of Web directories. These include the arbitrary and unpredictable structure of their organisation, and the relatively small number of sites covered compared with search engines (hundreds of thousands of Web sites rather than millions of pages).

Most Web directories will automatically submit a search query to an associated Web search engine. However, results may be limited compared with submitting a query directly to a search engine because search engines allow greater control over the outcome of a search and usually display more information about an item.

Web search engines and directories: quality issues

One of the problems associated with using search or metasearch engines is the low quality of the information. Material that is accessible via generic search engines has not been selected or evaluated according to any quality criteria prior to indexing.

Likewise, Web directories (discussed in Chapter 12) may impose no assessment of the value of resources prior to their inclusion. Instead, editorial control of the Web directories is often passive and listings of Web pages simply record those available. For example, the Yahoo! entry displayed in Figure 12.1 links to a company specialising in the sale of zinc gluconate lozenges, Quigley Corporation.[16] Cold-Eeze Studies, referred to under Product Information from the home page, listed no research more recent than 1996 at the time of writing.[17] A randomised controlled trial in 1998 and more recent reviews of the literature indicate that there is uncertainty about the effectiveness of zinc gluconate in treating the common cold, particularly in children (see for example two references by Macknin[18, 19]). None of this information was accessible from the Quigley Corporation pages and it was uncertain that any effort had been made to establish whether alternative views exist. This approach is not untypical of Web directories, and much of the information found using search engines and metasearch engines will be of the same unfiltered nature.

Furthermore, Web directories and review sites attempt to appeal to the general consumer rather than the health professional or researcher. As a result, 'accessible' information is usually preferred. However, much of the health and medical information that is most readily accessible via the Internet, i.e. via generic search tools, is of unclear and often undeclared provenance. It is often ephemeral in nature, it has not been subject to any form of peer review or editorial control, and most has not been assessed for its applicability to clinical practice.

Web search tools versus databases

While much information is currently available via the Web, little high quality information is accessible via the generic search tools. The medical research literature, for example, is locked inside databases and within journal sites, most of which require prior subscription or at least a login. Indeed, it has been estimated that:

> While only two-thirds of all information on the Internet is invisible to traditional search engines, over 90% of the content relevant to the healthcare industry is found in invisible Web resources.[20]

Hersh *et al.* also concluded that:

> The bulk of information on the World Wide Web, i.e. the 'HTML' pages, is of low applicability and poor quality for answering clinical questions. Users may be better off relying on online

versions of traditional information sources, e.g. medical literature and textbooks, an increasing number of which are available in World Wide Web format.[21]

Similarly, in an article reviewing the efficacy of using search engines in procuring information about orthopaedic foot and ankle problems from the Web, Nogler *et al.* suggest that specialised databases such as those available via Internet Grateful Med, continue to be the best source of peer-reviewed journal articles.[22]

Krabshuis, in an editorial reviewing the availability of endoscopy information on the Internet and via traditional sources, concludes that there is little published research available for free on the Internet.[23] He warns that often the information available via the Internet is out-of-date and recommends that users 'always ask ... how up-to-date' the information is, 'whether it is sponsored and why, whether it is peer-reviewed, and whether it represents promotion or advertising.'

Studies are beginning to demonstrate some of the areas of strength of Web search engines compared with traditional bibliographic databases. For example, the Web has been found to be useful for patient information, product information, teaching and training materials, and sometimes clinical practice guidelines.[23] However, in health and medicine, where peer review and the appraisal of information for research and clinical practice plays a significant role, it is hard to imagine that Web search engines will replace traditional bibliographic databases and peer reviewed journals as primary sources for research and clinical practice.

In September 1997, Dialog and Dow Jones Interactive conducted an Internet 'search-off' to compare the performance of traditional online databases and Web search engines. The search time using Web search engines was more than double that necessary for the same search conducted using a commercial online host.[24] The study also found that those interested in reproducing a search would probably have difficulty duplicating the results of an Internet search.

Furthermore, an estimate of the coverage of the databases provided by Dialog placed it at over 50 times the entire Web at the time: more than six billion pages of text contained in over 900 databases.[25] A similar array of content is available from several other conventional database host services, most of which provide Web-based search interfaces, but none of which make the content of their databases available via generic Web search engines.

Most importantly, however, the search-off found that commercial hosts provide information of uniformly higher quality than Web search engines. Searches conducted using Web search engines were more likely to return irrelevant hits.[24] In a report on the Internet search-off, Feldman concluded, 'traditional online services have been found to be predictable: providing high quality, authoritative, edited content and a wide coverage of most subjects'.[24] And elsewhere:

> The World Wide Web adds a new dimension and tool to finding information. Is it a substitute for traditional online sources? The Internet Search-Off proves that while it has great value, it does not replace the traditionals.'[26]

A paper by Coopers and Lybrand Consulting also concluded:

> The real problem is the quality of free information. Freely obtainable information on the Web lacks authority, completeness and depth... It is a fact that while the Internet represents a vast compendium of free data, often in disassociated factual bits, there is actually far more information available from commercial online database services that is complete, clean, well organized and of far greater value than that which may be skimmed from the Internet. The free information to be found on the Internet can and does act as a complement to the information available from commercial online database services, but is not a replacement for it.[27]

Health and medical search tools: accessing evaluated content

The role of gateways in providing access to material that has been identified, evaluated and described is discussed in Chapter 14, and the evaluation process is explained. However, one problem with information gateways is that resources that have not been catalogued cannot be retrieved. Indeed, the strongest criticism of information gateways is their inability to 'rate the entire Web'. The Web contained, according to Censorware, over 2 billion pages at the time of writing, over 48 million of which were estimated to have changed in the previous 24 hours, based on an estimate of the average lifespan of Web pages of 44 days. This is compared to, for example, 5,000 resources catalogued in the OMNI database.

Nonetheless, a searcher seeking clinically relevant documents might find a health and medical search tool to be more effective than a generic search engine. In particular, specialist health and medical search tools might be preferable when search terms or phrases occur frequently in the literature or are used colloquially. Conversely, a generic search engine may produce sufficiently clinically relevant results if a search term or phrase is unambiguous or is not used colloquially or is relatively uncommon.

Censorware: censorware.org/

Ten steps to searching strategically

The above discussions, as well as the preceding chapters in this section, highlight many of the benefits and limitations of using different categories of search tools. The Internet has become an increasingly complex information landscape and simply using any one tool to search for information is insufficient. It is important that users adopt a strategic approach to searching by considering, firstly, what it is that they are looking for, secondly, where to look for information, and thirdly, how they can use the available tools to best effect. We have attempted to define ten steps to adopting a strategic approach to searching – following these logical steps will ensure a structured and systematic approach to this process.

1. Identify which type of tool is the most appropriate to answer your question.

    It is possible to rank the different categories of tools discussed in this section in an approximate quality hierarchy:

    generic Web search engines < generic directories or review sites < health and medical search engines < health and medical gateways < traditional medical literature < critically appraised research literature

    For clinical application, it is likely that sources of effectiveness information would feature strongly.

    Ultimately, the choice to use a Web search engine is likely to be driven by the belief that the publicly accessible pages on the Web will offer information that is not retrieved more easily elsewhere. However, consider whether a traditional bibliographic database might be more appropriate, or a gateway to pre-evaluated Internet materials.

2. Select an appropriate tool within the category of tools.

    Search engines, for example, AltaVista, FAST Search, Google or Northern Light, all index a large portion of the Web, but you should consider using additional search engines as appropriate. If selecting a gateway, consider that OMNI is biased towards materials from the UK, whereas Medical Matrix is biased towards US-based resources. Selecting one tool within a particular category will offer only partial results but whether one or more tools is selected will depend upon the time available and the need for comprehensive retrieval.

3.   Generate an answerable question and analyse the search topic to decide on the key concepts to use as search terms (see for example article by Richardson[28]).

Think about the information that you are hoping to find, write down the question or query statement, and identify the key concepts within that question or statement – these are the concepts that you will be using to search for information.

4.   Think of synonyms or other term variations that describe each concept.

You need to consider:

- whether there are any singular or plural forms for the terms you have identified;

- whether there are any synonyms for the terms you have identified; and

- whether there are any alternative spellings (including misspellings) for the terms you have identified.

5.   Generate a search query that is appropriate to the type of tool you are using.

Be specific. Searching for *asthma* alone in a search engine will produce too many hits. You could use technical terminology that is less likely to have been used by lay Web page creators. However, this approach will miss pages that were created by health professionals with a lay audience in mind, so should be used with caution. Using rare or unusual words will cause pages that contain those to be retrieved first.

Do not be too specific. For example, a search for *pulmonary alveolar microlithiasis* using a gateway or even a search engine such as AltaVista results in few hits, while a search for *alveolar microlithiasis* produces more. Consider using synonyms, as mentioned above. A search for *alveolar microlithiasis or pulmonary microlithiasis or microlithiasis alveolaris* using AltaVista Advanced Search produced 97 hits, when a search for *alveolar microlithiasis* alone produced 78 and a search for *pulmonary microlithiasis* produced 9.

6.   Examine the help information for the tool that you are using to establish how to use that tool to best effect.

When you have decided where to search, which tool to use, and what your search terms are, you need to determine what options are available for searching. As you will have seen from the preceding chapters, each tool works slightly differently, each offers different search features, and many use a different syntax to denote a phrase, truncation, search fields or Boolean operators. It is therefore essential that you consult the available help information to ensure you know how to use each tool to best effect.

7. Create a search strategy in terms appropriate to the chosen tool.

    Once you have identified the possible terms and phrases that could be relevant to your search, you need to construct your search statement using the options that are available to you with each tool.

    Boolean operators: Use the OR operator to link together search terms that describe a single concept. Link different concepts together using the AND operator. Arrange the search terms in concept groups using parentheses where possible. Alternatively, if Boolean expressions are not supported, use +- notation to specify search terms that are required to be present (+) or absent (-). Double quotation marks are generally used to denote a phrase. Use other search features as appropriate (e.g. custom search folders, etc.).

8. Run the search!

9. Examine the hits and be iterative.

    This is especially important if you have only minimal knowledge of the topic. Match the search terms to the terminology of the subject experts. Reword the query to explore whether different phrasing will retrieve more relevant information. Examine your results and refine the search as necessary.

    If you find that you have too many results, you could try using more specific search terms, or restricting your search to find items where your terms appear in the title of documents alone, or using a more focused tool such as a gateway to pre-evaluated resources. If you have too few or no results, you could try using broader search terms, truncating terms, or using a tool that provides wider coverage such as a search engine or a metasearch engine.

    Table 17.3. summarises some of the features that help to narrow or widen a search.

Table 17.3: *Search features that help to narrow or widen a search*

	Narrows a search	Widens a search
+- notation	Yes	
Boolean AND, NOT	Yes	
Boolean OR		Yes
Proximity operators (eg NEAR)	Yes	
Phrase searching	Yes	
Capitalisation	Yes	
Truncation / wildcards		Yes
Word stemming		Yes
Fielded searching	Yes	

10. Evaluate the information you retrieve.

   For clinical queries, consider using a formal critical appraisal approach. Is the quality of information good enough? If not, should more reputable sources be sought?

   Last, but not least, reappraise your selection of search tool: depending on the type of query and the prevalence of search terms, it is possible that a different category of search tool may be selected.

References

1. P\S\L Consulting Group. Physician Internet usage: a global survey. Executive Summary. 1998 Aug.

2. Feldman S. The Internet search-off. *Searcher* 1998 Feb;**6**(2):28. Available from: http://www.infotoday.com/searcher/feb98/story1.htm

3. Search Engine Watch. Nielsen//NetRatings search engine ratings. Available from: http://www.searchenginewatch.com/reports/netratings.html

4. Search Engine Watch. Media Metrix search engine ratings. Available from: http://www.searchenginewatch.com/reports/mediametrix.html

5. Meltzer S, Leiter L, Daneman D, Gerstein HC, Lau D, Ludwig S, Yale JF, Zinman B, Lillie D. 1998 clinical practice guidelines for the management of diabetes in Canada. Canadian Diabetes Association. *Canadian Medical Association Journal* 1998;**159** Suppl 8:S1-29. Available from: http://www.cma.ca/cmaj/vol-159/issue-8/diabetescpg/

6. Meltzer S, Leiter L, Daneman D, Gerstein HC, Lau D, Ludwig S, Yale JF, Zinman B, Lillie D. 1998 clinical practice guidelines for the management of diabetes in Canada. Canadian Diabetes Association. *Canadian Medical Association Journal* 1998;**159** Suppl 8:S1-29. Available from: http://www.cma.ca/cmaj/vol-159/issue-8/diabetescpg/download.htm

7. Microsoft Corporation. Pick a search engine. Available from: http://home.microsoft.com/search/lobby/SearchSetup.htm

8. Digital's AltaVista search index grows to record heights [press release]. Maynard, Mass.; 1998 May 27. Available from: http://doc.altavista.com/company_info/press/pr052798.shtml

9. Lawrence S, Giles CL. Searching the World Wide Web. *Science* 1998 Apr 3;**280**(5360):98-100.

10. Lawrence S, Giles CL. How big is the Web? How much of the Web do the search engines index? How up-to-date are the search engines? Available from: http://www.neci.nj.nec.com/homepages/lawrence/websize.html

11. Search Engine Watch. Search engine sizes. Available from: http://www.searchenginewatch.com/reports/sizes.html

12. Lawrence S, Giles CL. Accessibility of information on the web. *Nature* 1999 Jul 8;**400**(6740):107-109.

13. Talkback to Jesse Berst: AltaVista CTO responds. *ZDNet* 1997 Apr 1. Available from: http://www5.zdnet.com/anchordesk/talkback/talkback_13066.html

14. Notess G. Search engine showdown. Strategy 3: Search engines for large searches. Available from: http://www.notess.com/search/strat/strat3.html

15. Brake D. Lost in cyberspace. *New Scientist Networld* 1997 Jun 28. Available from: http://www.newscientist.com/keysites/networld/lost.html

16. Quigley Corporation. Available from: http://www.quigleyco.com/

17. Quigley Corporation. Clinical studies: abstracts of published scientific articles. Available from: http://www.quigleyco.com/studies.htm

18. Macknin ML, Piedmonte M, Calendine C, Janosky J, Wald E. Zinc gluconate lozenges for treating the common cold in children: a randomized controlled trial. *JAMA* 1998 Jun 24; **279**(24):1962-1967.

19. Macknin ML. Zinc lozenges for the common cold. *Cleveland Clinical Journal of Medicine* 1999 Jan; **66**(1):27-32.

20. CiteLine Professional. CiteLine tutorial: searching the invisible Web. Downloadable from http://www.citeline.com/client/citeline/3.0/tutorial.html

21. Hersh WR, Gorman PN, Sacherek LS. Applicability and quality of information for answering clinical questions on the Web. *JAMA* 1998 Oct 21; **280**(15):1307-1308.

22. Nogler M, Wimmer C, Mayr E, Ofner D. The efficacy of using search engines in procuring information about orthopaedic foot and ankle problems from the World Wide Web. *Foot & Ankle International* 1999; **20**(5):322-325.

23. Krabshuis J. Endoscopy information online: can endoscopists close the gap between what is known and what they do? *Endoscopy* 1997; **29**:871-882.

24. Feldman S. The Internet search-off. *Searcher* 1998 Feb; **6**(2) :28. Available from: http://www.infotoday.com/searcher/feb98/story1.htm

25. Wagner, D. Message from the Chief Executive. *Chronolog* 1998 Jan/Feb. Available from: http://library.dialog.com/chron/1998/9801/message.html

26. Feldman S. Lessons from the Internet search-off. *The CyberSkeptic's Guide to Internet Research* 1998 May. Available from: http://www.bibliodata.com/skeptic/9805/lessons.html

27. Paris AL. The value of today's commercial online database services: a White Paper by Coopers & Lybrand Consulting. 1997 Nov. The Dialog Corporation: Quantum White Papers. Available from: http://library.dialog.com/quantum/wp/cooplybr.html

28. Richardson WS, Wilson MC, Nishikawa J, Hayward RS. The well-built clinical question: a key to evidence-based decisions. *ACP Journal Club* 1995 Nov-Dec;**123** (3) :A12-A13. Available also from: http://www.cche.net/principles/education_all.asp

Section 3

Communication

Electronic mail (email) communication is probably the most popular use of the Internet today, whether for one-to-one communication or for information exchange among groups. Both are potentially valuable to healthcare professionals in allowing near real time communication with colleagues,[1] and advantages include not only savings of time and expense, but also the ability to reach a far greater number of colleagues worldwide. Indeed, instances when rapid email communication has allowed timely interventions are widely reported.[2, 3] Although electronic communication, either directly between practitioners or via an online forum, cannot replace traditional sources of information, it is swiftly finding a role alongside person-to-person contact and attendance at scientific conferences as a valuable means of information exchange and the sharing of knowledge and experience.[3]

Furthermore, studies indicate that patients and health consumers are increasingly interested in engaging in electronic communications with their physicians and look to their own physicians to provide or recommend online sources of information.[4, 5] Other studies indicate that patients may find electronic consultations with anonymous medical experts less intimidating than personal conversations with their own physicians.[6] Patient groups are also able to actively engage in electronic communication, creating an important environment for exchange of experiences and information, providing support and a sense of community.

This section looks at tools for communicating via the Internet, including mailing lists and newsgroups, and considers some of the issues associated with their use for disseminating health and medical information.

Chapter 18

Using the Internet to communicate

Email

Email allows messages to be sent across the Internet for one-to-one or one-to-many communications. Although email messages are usually text-based, files can also be sent as an attachment that might include word-processed documents or graphics. In order to receive and send email messages, it is necessary to have an email account as well as access to the relevant software or a Web browser that includes email capabilities.

Many readers will already have access to email through their workplace. However, there are now a number of Internet services offering free access to an email account – see for example Yahoo! or HotMail. Doctors.net is a UK-based service for all doctors registered with the General Medical Council (GMC). All GMC registered doctors are eligible for a free email account, as well as access to a range of other services. These services have become increasingly popular in recent years, particularly as they enable an individual to have the same email address for life and to access their email from any computer connected to the Web.

Doctors.net: www.doctors.net.uk/

HotMail: www.hotmail.com/

Yahoo!: www.yahoo.com/

Finding email addresses

While the most popular use of the Internet today is for email communication, finding a person's email address is far from straightforward. Directories that exist are neither fully comprehensive nor are they up-to-date. An extensive list of directories is searchable via All-in-One while Inter-Links provides a search interface for a number of directories. However, simply interrogating a general search engine may produce better results, as might searching among the membership lists of mailing lists (discussed below). For example, Mailbase (also discussed below) has a directory of subscriber members.

It is essential to have some information about a person to begin to search for their email address - a surname and place of employment at the very minimum. If the place of employment is known it may be possible to locate the home page of their Web service where searchable directories of local information often can be found. In addition, email addresses are now being included for authors of articles indexed in Medline, EMBASE and other bibliographic databases, so a search for recently published articles in such databases can prove useful.

> All-in-One: www.allonesearch.com/all1user.html#People
>
> Inter-Links: www.nova.edu/Inter-Links/listserv.html
>
> Mailbase search for people: www.mailbase.ac.uk/search.html

Online communication fora

Online communication fora, such as mailing lists and newsgroups, provide a focus for participants who share a common interest in a particular discussion topic. Other types of fora are Internet Relay Chat (IRC) and Web-based fora, which are increasingly being used especially by health consumers and patients. Mailing lists and newsgroups share similar features in that email communication is involved. Software, usually referred to as an email or newsreader client, is required, or a Web browser with integrated email and newsreading features. Messages received from mailing lists are delivered to the subscriber's email address where they remain until cleared by the recipient. Conversely, newsgroup messages are stored remotely on a remote computer or server, and are simply read using the newsreader software when required by the user. IRC requires dedicated IRC software to be accessible, and involves the rapid exchange of brief lines of typed phrases among different people in near real time. Web fora are similar to newsgroups but users must visit a Web site in order to read or submit a message and access to a Web browser alone is required. These are discussed below.

Mailing lists

Mailing lists, also sometimes referred to as discussion lists, usually cover specific subject topics and can often support focused communication on a specific discipline or specialty. Messages can vary from topic-related debates and discussions, through news and announcements of meetings, to 'spams' (unsolicited mailings).

As mentioned, mailing lists require prior subscription. This is usually achieved by sending a joining message to the list server (see below). Frequently Asked Question (FAQ) files or welcome messages distributed to new subscribers usually outline the scope of lists, as well as providing instructions on how to post messages and unsubscribe. It is advisable to keep a copy of these details for future reference. Any communication submitted by a participant is transmitted directly to each member of the list concerned. Consequently, replying to a message received from a discussion list often means replying to the whole list. It is therefore considered good practice to 'lurk' on a list (i.e. remain a silent observer) for a while before starting to contribute.

Finding mailing lists on a topic

There are a number of directories of mailing lists. For example, Liszt is a directory of over 90,000 lists on almost every possible topic. Mailbase is the premier email discussion list service in the UK, providing access to thousands of mailing lists. Lists may be identified and selected by browsing through the alphabetical listings of their names or by searching the brief descriptions.

However, none of the directories is comprehensive and searching more than one may help to identify additional resources. For example, searching Liszt for *consumer health* results in a number of hits, including hltheduc - 'For all health educators, especially those using computers for professional and consumer education'. Repeating this search in Mailbase reveals an additional two lists (consumer-health-informatics and quality-consumer-health-info) not appearing in Liszt.

There are also various short guides to mailing lists on specific topics. For example, the ScHARR Web site, discussed in Chapter 3, includes a list of evidence-based health lists.

Liszt: www.liszt.com/

Mailbase: www.mailbase.ac.uk/

ScHARR list of evidence-based health lists: www.shef.ac.uk/~scharr/ir/email.html

---

Subscribing to a mailing list

Mailing lists are usually managed using software, or a 'list server', of which there are a number of types. Widely used applications include Listserv, Listproc and Majordomo. The list server handles any subscribing or unsubscribing requests automatically, and it is to the list server address that such requests are sent (not to the discussion list address). If a subscription or unsubscription request is sent to the discussion list address, it will be received by all list members and the request may not only cause annoyance, but it will not be processed.

Trying to join a list can be challenging because joining instructions and other commands may vary depending on the type of list.[7] However, directories of mailing lists can be used to identify a particular list and may offer further assistance. For example, Liszt gives helpful joining instructions specific to the individual mailing list of interest, as does Mailbase. OncoLink provides an automated email mailing list subscriber making it simple to join any cancer-related list.

> OncoLink cancer lists: cancer.med.upenn.edu/forms/listserv.html

Mailing list archives

Backdated mailing list messages are sometimes accessible through an archive. This may be via a list Web site or you may need to submit commands to the host list server. At present, however, there is no single global directory of archive information. Welcome messages, introductory information files and FAQ files are likely to include archive information. Alternatively, information about the existence of archives may be accessed through the available directories – Liszt often cites the location of Web archives of email discussion lists contained in its database. In addition, centralised archiving exists for some email lists – Mailbase provides a searchable archive.

At Mailbase, the archives of messages sent to Mailbase lists can be viewed one month at a time in order of four different variables: date, thread, subject and author. Displaying by thread allows replies to a message to be grouped and viewed together, even if they were separated in time by other messages. Mailbase also allows searching across a number of categories related to health and medicine – e.g. medicine and dentistry, subjects allied to medicine and biosciences. It is possible to choose a single category at a time or to specify individual Mailbase lists to cross-search. However, archives are usually not permanent – Mailbase archives messages for a year or two years in some cases.

Newsgroups

As mentioned earlier, no prior subscription is necessary to access the messages posted to newsgroups. Institutional or Internet service provider news servers receive newsgroup messages as a newsfeed and usually store current postings for a few days. To view messages, a newsreader or Web browser with newsreading capability is required – the user accesses their newsreader software to read any messages as and when required. Newsgroups exist on a variety of topics, not all of which will be accessible via every news server. In addition, because messages are not delivered to the individual's mailbox and because the messages are generally only stored for a short time, it is necessary to review newsgroups on a regular basis.

If your institution or Internet service provider does not receive a newsfeed or your news server is down, Yahoo! provides a Message Boards service. In addition, Deja News is particularly useful because it archives newsgroup postings continually and is generally up-to-date.

As with mailing lists, you should read the relevant FAQ file before contributing to a newsgroup - there is a collection of FAQ files at Oxford University.

Deja News: www.dejanews.com/

Oxford University newsgroup FAQ files: www.lib.ox.ac.uk/internet/news/

Yahoo! message boards: messages.yahoo.com/index.html

Finding newsgroups

Newsgroups are organised hierarchically into categories. Each category may include a number of sub-categories of groups. For example sci*, contains the sub-category, sci.med*, and the sub-sub-category, sci.med.aids. Some of the key categories of interest in health and biomedicine are alt.support*, bionet* and sci.med*. The Usenet Information Center provides a browsable, hierarchical list of groups. In addition, Liszt offers a directory of newsgroups. Deja News is primarily a newsgroup archive, rather than a directory, but it does operate an Interest Finder that pinpoints groups in which a topic has been popular in the past. For example, a search for *roaccutane* retrieved several likely groups, listed in order of confidence (see Figure 18.1).

Usenet Information Center: sunsite.unc.edu/usenet-i/hier-s/top.html

---

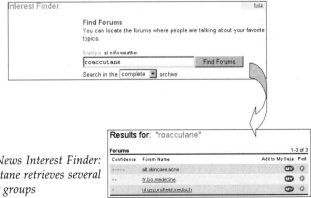

Figure 18.1 Deja News Interest Finder: a search for roaccutane retrieves several likely groups

Newsgroup archives

Extensive archives are now available that can be viewed and searched retrospectively. Newsgroup archives are searchable via Deja News, which archives more than three years' of newsgroup postings and covers over 80,000 groups. Additionally, some Web search engines such as AltaVista provide limited newsgroup archive search facilities.

Filtering the newsgroups

Keeping up-to-date with postings from more than a few newsgroups can be an onerous task because many groups attract a high volume of messages per day. Consequently services such as Deja News offer newsgroup current awareness services. These enable users to filter out inconsequential messages and see only those that fit a pre-defined personal profile.

Internet Relay Chat (IRC)

IRC services offer text-based fora for group discussion, providing channels of communication between different people dedicated to specific themes. An IRC client application, such as mIRC, is required to access an IRC channel which allows connection to the IRC servers.

OncoLink lists a number of electronic support groups for cancer patients and their carers, and OncoChat is a channel dedicated to 'support for cancer survivors, family, friends'. Liszt provides a directory of IRC channels, as does Yahoo!.

mIRC: www.mirc.co.uk or www.mirc.com/

OncoChat: www.oncochat.org/

OncoLink support groups: cancer.med.upenn.edu/psychosocial/support/

Yahoo! chat: chat.yahoo.com/

Web fora

Web fora are similar in function to newsgroups except that registered Web forum members submit postings via a Web interface. To read and submit messages, users must visit the Web site hosting the forum. A Web browser is therefore sufficient to access a forum.

Forum One maintains a directory of Web fora.

Forum One: www.forumone.com/

Multi-User Dimension (MUDs) and Multi-user dimension Object-Oriented (MOOs)

MUDs and MOOs have been developed with a biomedical subject focus. For example, the Weizmann Institute's BioMOO, which attempt to simulate the real life environment of laboratories and research centres, with layouts of familiar workplaces, including seminar rooms, libraries, etc.

BioMOO: bioinformatics.weizmann.ac.il/BioMOO/

Concerns about online communication

Many practitioners are concerned about the implications of providing medical advice online. Guidelines have been proposed by an American Medical Internet Association (AMIA) Task Force white paper for computer-based communications between physicians and patients within an established patient–physician relationship.[8] The paper addresses issues concerning both the effectiveness of the interaction between the clinician and the patient, and medico-legal and administrative issues. The need has been highlighted for additional guidelines to be developed to advise clinicians on how to handle unsolicited email requests from patients.[9] Commentators have suggested that services offering medical advice should be subject to a cyberlicence, issued by an independent international body, and that patients should be warned of the need to determine the credibility or qualification of cyberdocs on the Internet.[10]

Concerns have also been raised about the general quality of information that is exchanged in electronic fora, and the 'signal to noise' ratio is often deemed to be too low to make them useful to busy practitioners. As a result, practitioner-only communication fora are constantly being established. Due to the closed nature of such fora, directories are difficult to compile since information about them is more likely to be disseminated via discipline-specific channels of communication. Closed professional fora, or fora that are moderated (whereby the forum manager filters incoming messages), are likely to display a higher signal to noise ratio than that observed in openly accessible fora.[3]

Openly accessible fora attract a wide range of participants. Newcomers as well as experts in a domain may be present, and over time a forum develops its own ethos. The behaviours attached to communicating and using information on the Internet have been described as 'netiquette' and various guides are now available. 'The Net: User Guidelines and Netiquette' by Rinaldi provides a good introduction and includes a short introduction to 'emoticons', such as 'smileys'.[11] Guidelines for using discussion lists are available from the Mailbase site.

Although commonly used for everyday communication, to the extent that collaborators and co-authors need no longer meet face-to-face, email is not particularly secure, nor is it a suitable medium for the communication of confidential or sensitive information. In addition, word-processed documents may transmit viruses and it is advisable not to open files received by email without virus-checking them first.

References

1.   Hernandez-Borges A, Macias P, Torres A. Are mailing lists reliable sources of professional advice? *Medical Informatics* 1998; **23**(3):231-236.

2.   Kiley R. The Internet: a good-news story. *He@lth Information on the Internet* 1998 Aug;(4):1-2. Available from: http://www.wellcome.ac.uk/en/images/hioti4_pdf_694.pdf

3.   Hernandez-Borges AA, Pareras L G, Jimenez A. Comparative analysis of pediatric mailing lists on the Internet [electronic article]. *Pediatrics* 1997 Aug;**100**(2):e8. Available from: http://www.pediatrics.org/cgi/content/full/100/2/e8

4.   Ferguson T. Digital doctoring: opportunities and challenges in electronic patient-physician communication. *JAMA* 1998; **280**(15):1361-1362.

5.   Brown MS. Online communication gap between physicians and their cybersavvy patients. *Medicine on the Net* 1998; **4**(3):15-16.

6.   Borowitz SM, Wyatt JC. The origin, content, and workload of e-mail consultations. *JAMA* 1998; **280**(15):1321-1324.

7.   Milles, J. Discussion Lists: Mailing List Manager Commands. Available from: http://lawwww.cwru.edu/cwrulaw/faculty/milles/mailser.html

8.   Kane B, Sands DZ. for the American Medical Informatics Association Task Force to Develop Guidelines for Clinical Use of Electronic Mail and the World Wide Web. Guidelines for clinical use of electronic mail with patients [white paper]. *Journal of the American Medical Informatics Association* 1998; **5**(1):104-111. Available from: http://www.amia.org/pubs/jamia/v05n01/104.htm

9.   Eysenbach G, Diepgen TL. Responses to unsolicited patient e-mail requests for medical advice on the World Wide Web. *JAMA* 1998;**280**:1333-1335.

10.   Eysenbach G, Diepgen TL. Evaluation of cyberdocs [research letter]. *Lancet* 1998;**352**:1526. Available for subscribers from: http://www.thelancet.com/newlancet/sub/issues/vol352no9139/research1526.html

11.   Rinaldi A. The Net: user guidelines and netiquette. Available from: http://www.fau.edu/~rinaldi/net/

Section 4

Evaluation

The opening section of this book highlights the incredible array of useful health and medical information that is accessible via the Internet. Nonetheless, any casual user will soon discover that the quality of that information can be variable, generating genuine concerns. These relate particularly to information targeted at health consumers, but equally healthcare professionals may find themselves swamped by unmanageable amounts of information, most of which may be of unclear provenance and utility. Commentators have been vocal in drawing attention to issues of quality relating to the Internet. For example, Lundberg, then editor-in-chief of *JAMA*, warned at a Food and Drug Administration (FDA) meeting that the Internet 'has the potential of becoming the world's largest garbage dump of misinformation' and noted 'some believe that it is rapidly realizing that potential'.[1] This section examines both causes for concern in relation to Internet-based health and medical information and provides some suggestions for evaluation.

Reference

1. US Food and Drug Administration. FDA and the Internet: advertising and promotion of medical products. Available from: http://www.fda.gov/opacom/morechoices/transcript1096/fdainet7.html

Chapter 19

Evaluating the quality of information on the Internet

Causes for concern

A cartoon published in the New Yorker in 1993[1] is apposite: 'On the Internet, no one knows you're a dog', says one dog seated at a computer screen to another watching close by. Indeed, on the Internet, anyone can be an author, and for much information, there is no clear way to verify its provenance or the author's credentials. Equally concerning, however, is the speed with which information can be spread via the Internet making it remarkably easy for medical misinformation to be disseminated. Concerns such as these are highlighted in an FDA Consumer Reprint:

> The fact that it is easy to publish health and medical information and reach vast audiences without having the information verified by other sources presents potential issues for FDA and other government agencies.[2]

Delegates at the 50th World Health Assembly were particularly concerned that advertising, promotion and sale through the Internet might result in uncontrolled cross-border trade of medical products or fraudulent imitations that may be unevaluated, unapproved, unsafe or ineffective, or used inappropriately:

> This phenomenon ... may present a hazard for the public health as well as a risk for the individual patient, particularly with regard to misleading or fraudulent product information and lack of individual counselling for consumers.[3]

At the first International Health Claim Surf Day held in late 1998, more than 1,200 Internet sites worldwide were identified as containing potentially false or deceptive advertising claims about the treatment, cure or prevention of six major diseases – arthritis, cancer, diabetes, heart disease, HIV/AIDS and multiple sclerosis.[4] The sites were sent email messages informing advertisers that they must have evidence to support their claims and the US Federal Trade Commission (FTC) warned that site designers may be liable for making or disseminating deceptive or false claims. Especially vulnerable, according to the FTC, are patients diagnosed with diseases that have no medical cure, such as AIDS, arthritis, multiple sclerosis, and certain forms of cancer.[5]

Authors elsewhere have also expressed concerns about the ease with which unverified health claims can be made on the Internet,[6] and the ease with which substances with toxic and pharmacological potential can be obtained electronically and across borders.[7] Furthermore, many Web sites now offer commercial or free medical advice in response to unsolicited patient enquiries. Attention has been drawn to the medico-legal and other implications for clinical practice of providing information to patients in such a fashion.[8] According to the Science Panel on Interactive Communication and Health (SciPICH), faulty information or advice can lead to unnecessary or harmful treatment, a delay in proper treatment, or an unwise health decision.[9] The quality of information exchanged electronically via discussion lists and newsgroups has also given rise to concerns that appropriate diagnosis and treatment may elude participants in such discussion fora on a scale that is unprecedented.[10]

Information on the Web

A number of studies have examined the variable quality of information available via the Internet, some of which are summarised in Figure 19.1.

Figure 19.1 Studies assessing the quality of information on the Internet.

Impicciatore P, Pandolfini C, Casella N, Bonati M. Reliability of health information for the public on the World Wide Web: systematic survey of advice on managing fever in children at home. *BMJ* 1997; **314**(7098):1875-1878. Available from: http://www.bmj.com/cgi/content/full/314/7098/1875

Of 41 Web pages that were retrieved using two search engines, only four were found to adhere closely to the main recommendations in published guidelines. The authors suggest 'an urgent need to check public oriented healthcare information on the Internet for accuracy, completeness, and consistency.'

McClung HJ, Murray RD, Heitlinger LA. The Internet as a source for current patient information. *Pediatrics* 1998; **101**(6):e2. Available from: http://www.pediatrics.org/cgi/content/full/101/6/e2

McClung *et al.* assessed the quality of information that a lay person could obtain from Internet sources regarding the treatment of childhood diarrhoea. Of 60 articles published by traditional publishing sources, including major academic medical centres, only

12 (20%) conformed to American Academy of Pediatrics recommendations.

Hersh WR, Gorman PN, Sacherek LS. Applicability and quality of information for answering clinical questions on the Web. *JAMA* 1998; **280**(15):1307-1308.

Hersh *et al.* conducted an observational study assessing the applicability of Web pages to clinical questions and their quality. The authors concluded that the bulk of information on the Web is of low applicability and poor quality for answering clinical questions.

Mailing lists, newsgroups and electronic communication

Culver JD, Gerr F, Frumkin H. Medical information on the Internet: a study of an electronic bulletin board. *Journal of General Internal Medicine* 1997; **12**:466-470.

Culver *et al.* selected a mailing list dedicated to the discussion of painful hand and arm conditions. They discovered that the advice offered frequently had little basis in biomedical science or accepted medical practice and suggested that compliance may in some cases have increased a patient's risk or caused harm.

Desai NS, Dole EJ, Yeatman ST, Troutman WG. Evaluation of drug information in an Internet newsgroup. *Journal of the American Pharmaceutical Association* 1997; NS37:391-394.

In evaluating the quality of information provided in the newsgroup sci.med.pharmacy, the authors found only half of the drug information that was analysed to be correct. Although most was found to be innocuous, a significant proportion (19.4%) was classified as harmful.

Seaboldt JA, Kuiper R. Comparison of information obtained from a Usenet newsgroup and from drug information centres. *American Journal of Health-System Pharmacy* 1997; **54**:1732-1735.

Studying responses from the newsgroup sci.med.pharmacy, the authors found that a significantly smaller proportion of drug information responses were accurate compared with responses from drug information centres.

Eysenbach G, Diepgen TL. Evaluation of cyberdocs. *Lancet* 1998;**352** (9139):1526. Available for subscribers from: http:// www.thelancet.com/newlancet/sub/issues/vol352no9139/ research1526.html

Eysenbach G, Diepgen TL. Responses to unsolicited patient e-mail requests for medical advice on the World Wide Web. *JAMA* 1998;**280** (15):1333-1335.

A request for advice was submitted to a number of cyberdocs. The request suggested a herpes zoster infection in an immunocompromised patient, which would have required immediate treatment with acyclovir. The authors concluded that this method of receiving medical information may not be reliable and may waste valuable time. Furthermore, neither is there a guarantee that communication is actually taking place with a certified doctor, nor is the privacy of emails assured.

In conclusion, a number of concerns have been expressed regarding the quality of health and medical information that may be found on the Internet:

- anyone can publish health and medical information on the Internet;
- authors' credentials may not be easy for users to verify;
- there is the potential for medical misinformation or incomplete information to be easily and widely disseminated;
- the evidence for health claims may be questionable; and
- the information that can be found most easily on the Internet is not generally peer-reviewed or assessed for its applicability to clinical practice.

Evaluating the quality of information on the Internet

Izenberg *et al.* observe:

> Many people – especially young people – tend to believe information presented in print, television, and the Web because these media seem to represent expertise and authority.[11]

Moreover, Robinson *et al.* highlight research which suggests that information from computers may appear more credible than that from television and other media.[12] However, as one *JAMA* article declares: '*caveant lector et viewor* – let the reader and viewer beware'.[13]

The problems highlighted above indicate the importance of discerning use of the Internet. This requires the development of 'cyber literacy skills', an understanding of the potential for anyone to publish information on the Internet, and for information consequently to be biased, inexpert, incomplete or inaccurate.[11] Users are also advised to critically appraise any information that is found.[14] Indeed, some commentators suggest confining access to free sites is 'tantamount to information malpractice'[15] and others recommend that users rely on online versions of traditional sources of medical literature.[16]

The responsibility for evaluating the quality of information frequently lies with the information seeker, be they healthcare practitioners or consumers. It has been suggested that evaluating the actual content, functions and likely impact of health information on clinical processes and patient outcomes would provide the most appropriate and direct measure of its quality.[17, 18] However, measures of this type are usually challenging to assemble[17–19] and indirect indicators of quality are therefore more commonly used.[18] Codes of conduct, benchmarks and evaluation guidelines have been developed to help guide both consumers and practitioners in filtering out the poorer quality information sources. The remainder of this section provides an overview of these guidelines, as well as suggestions for health and medical information users to consider when evaluating Internet-based materials.

Health on the Net Code of Conduct

A voluntary code of conduct is proposed by Health on the Net (HON), a non-profit foundation based in Switzerland. In summary, the following are key requirements for a resource to comply with the HON Code of Conduct:

- Medical/health advice will only be given by medically/health trained and qualified professionals.
- The information provided is designed to support, not replace, the relationship that exists between a patient/site visitor and his/her existing physician.
- Confidentiality of data relating to individual patients and visitors to a medical/health Web site, including their identity, is respected.
- Information will be supported by clear references to source data. The date when a page was last modified will be clearly displayed.
- Claims relating to the benefits/performance of a specific treatment, commercial product or service will be supported by appropriate, balanced evidence.
- The designers of a Web site will seek to provide information in the clearest possible manner and provide contact addresses.

- Support for a Web site will be clearly identified, including the identities of commercial and non-commercial organisations that have contributed funding, services or material for the site.
- If advertising is a source of funding it will be clearly stated.

Sites that comply are encouraged to display the 'HONcode' badge. The HON site suggests that if there is a blatant violation of the principles on a Web site displaying the badge, the owners will be asked to make appropriate modifications or to remove the badge.

> HON Code of conduct: www.hon.ch/HONcode/Conduct.html

JAMA benchmarks

In a 1997 article in *JAMA*, Silberg *et al.* propose a set of benchmarks designed to assist users in assessing the quality of medical information on the Internet.[13] The authors suggest that the same set of quality indicators that helps users of printed medical information should apply in the digital world. However, they also concede that the benchmarks are no guarantee of quality in and of themselves.

The *JAMA* benchmarks, in summary, are as follows:[13]

- Authorship: authors and contributors, their affiliations, and relevant credentials should be provided.
- Attribution: references and sources for all content should be listed clearly, and all relevant copyright information noted.
- Disclosure: Web site 'ownership' should be prominently and fully disclosed, as should any sponsorship, advertising, underwriting, commercial funding arrangements or support, or potential conflicts of interest.
- Currency: dates that content was posted and updated should be indicated.

Hersh *et al.* developed an assessment instrument based on the *JAMA* benchmarks.[16] They discovered that out of 629 Web pages retrieved for 50 predetermined clinical questions:

- only one quality measure (site affiliation) was present in a majority of pages;
- 69% of the pages did not indicate an author;
- more than 80% did not give the author's credentials;
- disclosure of financial or other conflicts of interest was present in only 1%; and
- fewer than 18% of pages gave the date posted or updated.

Evaluation guidelines

As discussed in earlier sections of this book, information gateways such as OMNI attempt to pre-select high quality Internet resources using more comprehensive quality measures. OMNI's evaluation guidelines, for example, focus on three areas of evaluation:

- establishing context (scope, audience, authority and provenance);
- content evaluation (coverage, accuracy of information content, currency/frequency and regularity of updating, uniqueness/comparison with other sources);
- access evaluation (accessibility and usability, charging policy, special requirements, design and layout, user support/documentation).

A collection of evaluation materials produced by the OMNI Advisory Group for Evaluation Criteria is also available. From Spring 2000 OMNI became part of BIOME, a project providing access to high quality resources within the broader area of the life sciences. The BIOME Evaluation Guidelines are designed to meet the needs of the wider audience and are also accessible via the Internet.

> BIOME Evaluation Guidelines: biome.ac.uk/guidelines/eval/
>
> OMNI Advisory Group for Evaluation Criteria: omni.ac.uk/agec/
>
> OMNI Guidelines for resource evaluation: omni.ac.uk/agec/evalguid.html

Evidence-based evaluation

Wyatt suggests that in order to determine the accuracy of information on the Web, it needs to be compared with the best available evidence.[17] Evaluation of this type would aim to meet the more stringent criteria of evidence-based healthcare, complying with those guidelines designed to assess the quality of research published in the health and medical literature. These include the Users' Guides to the Medical Literature available from the Health Information Research Unit (HIRU) at McMaster University. Further information about using the Internet to support evidence-based practice and a discussion of online critical appraisal tools are provided in Chapter 3.

> McMaster Users' Guides: www.cche.net/ebm/userguid/

Conducting your own evaluations: some suggestions

Many regular users of health and medical information on the Internet will gradually develop their own approach to evaluation – this section offers some tips to assist in that process. Short of conducting a full appraisal of the information offered from an Internet-based resource, a number of practical questions can help quickly sift through potentially large numbers of resources to identify those that are likely to be of greatest value. These questions are therefore likely to be most useful when confronted with large numbers of hits returned from generic search engines.

Web sites and pages

How did you discover the resource? Who is providing the resource?

- Bear in mind the source of the information provided. For example, traditional peer reviewed sources (e.g. medical journals) are often easily identifiable and may be distinguished from other sources.
- Links, even from trusted sources, can lead to uncharted territories that will require greater evaluative effort to sift through.
- Information found by conducting a generic search demand the highest degree of scrutiny.

What does the resource itself reveal?

- Is an author's name given, including affiliation and credentials? Are means offered by which to verify the credentials?
- Is a contact email or other address given?
- Does the page give the date it was last updated or originally disseminated via the Web?
- Are references provided to the sources for the information content?

What more can you find out about the resource? Is a link provided to the home page of the resource or the institution providing the resource? Is information provided 'About' the resource?

- If a link to the home page is not provided, you may still be able to identify the parent document or home page: reducing the address to the main domain name may reveal the hosting institution's credentials. For example, although a page about beef and health may superficially appear to satisfy many key quality requirements (http://www.beef.org/library/handbook/nutrition.htm), looking up the main domain name reveals that the host organisation may have vested interests in promoting the value of beef (http://www.beef.org/).

- Alternatively, you may be able to find out more about the origin of a resource by gradually working through the directory levels within the address. For example, reducing the original address: http://www.beef.org/library/handbook/nutrition.htm to: http://www.beef.org/library/handbook/, reveals that the resource is produced for The Beef Promotion and Research Board by the National Cattlemen's Beef Association.

Does the address itself indicate that information is provided in a personal capacity?

- A tilde (~) in the URL may indicate a personal home page. If the resource resides on the server of an Internet service provider (e.g. geocities.com), this again may indicate a personal effort.

Is there any metadata for the source, and is it possible to find additional information about it?

- Click on View/Source in Netscape Navigator or Internet Explorer. This reveals any metadata that may have been assigned - ie additional descriptive information about the resource within the HTML itself.

When was the information created or last modified?

- Viewing information about a Web page may reveal the date that the page was created or last modified - click on View/Info in Netscape Navigator or File/Properties in Internet Explorer.

What do others think of the resource?

- Who links to the resource? If a number of trusted sources provide links to the resource, this may be an indication of broader acceptance
- Many search engines allow you to check who has linked to a resource. For example, using AltaVista, you could identify who links to a report on the use of donepezil in the treatment of mild to moderate senile dementia of the Alzheimer type as follows:

  link:www.epi.bris.ac.uk/rd/publicat/dec/dec69.htm

  Alternatively, *link:www.epi.bris.ac.uk/rd/publicat/dec/dec69.htm - url:www.epi.bris.ac.uk* (using Simple Search AltaVista) or *link:www.epi.bris.ac.uk/rd/publicat/dec/dec69.htm and not url:www.epi.bris.ac.uk* (using Advanced Search AltaVista) will select the links excluding the site hosting the report.

- Does a trusted information provider point to the resource in question?

- Is the resource included in OMNI, Medical Matrix or any other information gateways? Non-inclusion does not imply that a resource is untrustworthy, and if you discover a valuable resource, you might consider submitting a recommendation for future inclusion using the relevant submission features.

> Medical Matrix submission feature: www.medmatrix.org/info/newsites.html
>
> OMNI submission feature: omni.ac.uk/submit-url/

Newsgroups, mailing lists and other communication fora

Discussed earlier in the chapter are some of the quality problems associated with using newsgroups, mailing lists and other communication fora. Many of the same principles of evaluation apply here – e.g. assessing where the information has come from and therefore how reliable it is. Guidelines are available specifically for evaluating this type of information and a summary is provided below of the questions that you might consider.[20]

Where is the information from?

- Is an author's name given, including affiliation and credentials?
- Is it possible to verify their credentials?
- Are references provided to the sources for information content?

Is it possible to establish more information?

- Is there a FAQ file or introductory message for the list or group?
- What information can be gleaned from it? e.g. Is the list/group moderated? (Is there an individual who is responsible for editorial control of the group? If so, are they responsible for ascertaining the accuracy of any information, or simply its relevance?)

What do others think of the resource?

- Again, consider whether the resource is included in OMNI, Medical Matrix or any other information gateway. You might also consider submitting a recommendation for future inclusion using the relevant submission features.

Hernandez-Borges *et al.* have developed a methodology for analysing the likely authority of paediatric mailing lists.[21] The authors conducted a search of the Medline database for the names of those subscribing to the lists and an impact factor was calculated for each of the subscribers. An average impact factor was calculated for each list, as well as an average impact factor per participant and per message. An average number of postings per participant over a given period of time was also calculated.

The authors claim that their methodology offers a technique for assessing the quality of mailing lists because it is:

> Based on the accumulation of defined impact factors generated by published articles of the various members of the discussion groups, a way for any scientific group to gain prestige in a given field of science.

Conducting a quick evaluation: a summary

- Identify the source of a resource;
- Examine the resource itself;
- Examine as much information about a resource as may be available-   e.g. home page, parent document, help files, announcements, FAQ files;
    e.g. view source, view info.
- Examine the URL -
    ~name in the URL may indicate a personal home page.
- Check who links to the resource; and
- Consult other evaluative information.

References

1. On the Internet, no one knows you're a dog [cartoon]. *New Yorker* 1993 Jul 5:61.

2. US Food and Drug Administration. Health information on-line. FDA Consumer Reprint. 1998. Available from: http://www.fda.gov/fdac/features/596_info.html

3. World Health Organization. The World Health Assembly adopts a resolution on the sale of medical products through the Internet. 50th World Health Assembly, press release WHA/6. 1997 May 12. Available from: http://www.health.fgov.be/WHI3/periodical/months/wwhv1n8tekst/180797b3.htm

4. Federal Trade Commission. Remedies targeted in International Health Claim Surf Day: consumer protection, public health, private agencies from 25 countries assess over 1,200 Internet sites [news release]. 1998. Available from: http://www.ftc.gov/opa/1998/9811/intlhlth.htm

5. Federal Trade Commission in cooperation with the US Food and Drug Administration. Fraudulent Health claims: don't be fooled. 1996. Available from: http://www.ftc.gov/bcp/conline/pubs/health/frdheal.htm

6. Bower H. Internet sees growth of unverified health claims. *BMJ* 1996;**313**(7054):381. Available from: http://www.bmj.com/cgi/content/full/313/7054/381.

7. Weisbord SD, Soule JB, Kimmel PL. Poison on line – acute renal failure caused by oil of wormwood purchased through the Internet. *New England Journal of Medicine* 1997;**337**(12):825-827. Available for subscribers from: http://www.nejm.org/content/1997/0337/0012/0825.asp

8. Pies R. Cybermedicine [letter]. *New England Journal of Medicine* 1998; **339**(9):638. Available from: http://www.nejm.org/content/1998/0339/0009/0638.asp

9. SciPICH. Potential problems with IHC applications. Available from: http://www.scipich.org/IHC/problems.htm

10. Culver JD, Gerr F, Frumkin H. Medical information on the Internet: a study of an electronic bulletin board. *Journal of General Internal Medicine* 1997;**12**:466-470.

11. Izenberg N, Lieberman DA. The Web, communication trends, and children's health. Part 5: encouraging positive and safe Internet use. *Clinical Pediatrics* 1998; **37**(7):397-404.

12. Robinson TN, Patrick K, Eng TR, Gustafson D for the Science Panel on Interactive Communication and Health. An evidence-based approach to interactive health communication. *JAMA* 1998; **280**(14):1264-1269.

13. Silberg WM, Lundberg GD, Musacchio RA. Assessing, controlling, and assuring the quality of medical information on the Internet: caveant lector et viewor – let the reader and viewer beware. *JAMA* 1997; **277**(15):1244-1245.

14. Pincock LL. A pharmacist's guide to drug and medical information on the Internet. *Journal of Pharmacy Practice* 1998; **11**(3):144.

15. Snow B. Internet sources of information on alternative medicine. *Database* 1998;**21**(4):65-73. Available from: http://www.onlineinc.com/database/DB1998/snow8.html

16. Hersh WR, Gorman PN, Sacherek LS. Applicability and quality of information for answering clinical questions on the Web. *JAMA* 1998; **280**(15):1307-1308.

17. Wyatt JC. Measuring quality and impact of the World Wide Web [comment]. *BMJ* 1997;**314**(7098):1879-1880. Available from: http://www.bmj.com/cgi/content/full/314/7098/1879

18. Eysenbach G, Diepgen TL. Towards quality management of medical information on the Internet: evaluation, labelling, and filtering of information. *BMJ* 1998; **317**(7171):1496-1500. Available from: http://www.bmj.com/cgi/content/short/317/7171/1496

19. Coiera E. Information epidemics, economics, and immunity on the Internet. *BMJ* 1998; **317**(7171):1469-1470. Available from: http://www.bmj.com/cgi/content/full/317/7171/1469

20. Cooke A. A guide to finding quality information on the Internet. London: Library Association Publishing; 1999.

21. Hernandez-Borges AA, Pareras LG, Jimenez A. Comparative analysis of pediatric mailing lists on the Internet [electronic article]. *Pediatrics* 1997 Aug;**100**(2):e8. Available from: http://www.pediatrics.org/cgi/content/full/100/2/e8

Section 5

Taking control

Previous chapters have shown that the Internet is packed with useful resources, which once located and evaluated, may prove truly useful in the fields of education, research and clinical practice. Having demonstrated that the Internet deserves to command our attention as a source of information, this section will turn away from the question of content and instead consider the tools which are used to access the Internet and the basic skills required to create content for it.

It might be argued that the Internet has succeeded to a great extent because the access tools make the basic processes of connection and navigation from resource to resource almost effortless. This allows the user to concentrate exclusively on the information being presented. Nevertheless, it is worthwhile taking time to become more familiar with these access tools as they frequently offer a range of features that enhance the experience and increase the efficiency of Internet use. Similarly, understanding how Internet resources are built can be invaluable in using them, not least because when they fail to behave as expected, the knowledgeable Internet user will know why and how, in some cases, to get around the problem.

The basic tool for accessing the Internet is the Web browser, and this is the subject of Chapter 20. Many users will probably already be accustomed to using one of the two most common browsers, Internet Explorer or Netscape Navigator. For this reason, the chapter does not seek to contrast them (in any case they offer very similar functionality) but rather to highlight common features which are largely hidden from view and may have escaped the notice of the casual user. This chapter also deals with the topic of security, which gains ever greater significance as the use of e-commerce spreads.

However complete a user's mastery of search engines, Web directories and other search tools after reading Chapters 10–17, there will always be a need to maintain a personal list of frequently used sites. This enables quick access without having to search and avoids the necessity of typing in the same address repeatedly. Chapter 21 describes how Web browsers and other tools may be used to build personal and organisational collections of Web addresses.

A user accessing the Internet through a private Internet service provider is likely to have been given, as part of the access package, a small amount of 'free' Web space for their own use. Chapter 22 aims to equip the reader with enough knowledge to produce a simple Web page, introducing the basic building blocks and describing how a page might be constructed, starting with a blank screen and using any word processor.

Chapter 20

Your browser

The browser is the Internet user's single most important software tool. The software giants Netscape and Microsoft have recently fought an anti-trust case in the USA over whether Microsoft's conduct during the development and marketing of their browser Internet Explorer was good for innovation or anti-competitive.[1] The battle for the hearts and minds of Web users has been pursued in similar cut-throat fashion ever since Netscape first appeared in 1995. As a result the user's choice of browser might represent a political statement, whatever was preloaded on their computer when purchased, or the choice of their IT support unit. Whichever is the case this chapter will help users get the most out of their browsers, from tips for those trying to acquire this essential piece of software for the first time to help with personalising it.

Acquiring Netscape or Internet Explorer

Both Netscape and Microsoft offer free versions of their browser software that can be downloaded from the Web, and similar alternatives to doing so, the need for which will become clear later in this chapter. In both cases there are also premium products sold via the Web and high street stores. Unless there is a particular need for additional features (such as HTML authoring) there is no need to buy a premium product; the free versions will suffice.

Netscape

Netscape comes in two flavours: Communicator and Navigator. Communicator handles email as well as Web pages and is bundled with a range of other software such as plug-ins (see below). Navigator is a stand-alone browser, for viewing Web pages only.

At the Netscape Web site, the user is guided to the appropriate browser by a straightforward series of questions. All the user needs to know is the operating system their computer uses, and a few other details that should be readily available.

Those downloading from the UK should consider using a site outside the US (a range is usually listed) or Netscape's FTP server, as either is likely to result in a quicker download time than Netscape's main site.

Downloading from home over a telephone line can be time-consuming and expensive; the time taken to download Netscape in this way is usually measured in hours rather than minutes. It is possible to avoid this by ordering the software on CD-ROM. This may be done via Netscape's Web site. A small charge is made.

Internet Explorer

Internet Explorer can also be downloaded from the Web. Again the process requires the user to input system details, and state which version is required. Bear in mind those listed as beta versions will be under development and it may be better to choose the most up-to-date finished version (at the time of writing this was version 5.01). Those users downloading a beta version may find that they also need to download updates and fixes later.

Microsoft is less supportive of international download sites than Netscape and at the time of writing there was no approved UK download site.

Other systems

Macintosh, UNIX and PC users should be able to acquire software easily and experience no serious installation problems. The same cannot be said for those using other, less common platforms, such as Amiga, Acorn or Amstrad. For those already online there are plenty of niche-computing Web sites offering support and tips. Otherwise, the easiest way of finding out if your platform is supported is to contact your Internet service provider. For example, Demon supported DOS and Amiga users at the time of writing.[2]

Alternatives to Netscape and Internet Explorer

Although the vast majority of Web users browse with Internet Explorer and Netscape products there are alternatives for the more adventurous. ZDNET maintain a list of links to and reviews of other browsers.

> Internet Explorer: www.microsoft.com/windows/ie/default.htm
>
> Netscape Products: www.netscape.com/download/index.html
>
> ZDNET: www.zdnet.com/products/internetuser/browsers.html

Customising your browser

Both Internet Explorer and Netscape browsers come ready to use and are unlikely to need customisation at first. However, both offer the individual user plenty of scope for making changes later, including:

- integration with other software,
- use of the network,
- display, and
- security.

For the sake of clarity the following remarks concentrate on Netscape Navigator 4.x (i.e. 4.01, 4.03, 4.5 etc.) and Internet Explorer 5. Earlier versions of Netscape browsers and Internet Explorer operate in a broadly similar manner.

In both cases browser configuration is masterminded from a single menu option. Netscape browsers call this option Preferences, and it is located in the Edit menu. Internet Explorer calls it Internet Options and places it in the Tools menu.

Choosing the Netscape Preferences menu option will cause the Preferences window to appear, displaying a list of further options (Appearance, Navigator, Identity, Advanced) to the left and further detail (which changes depending on the option highlighted) to the right.

Choosing the Internet Options menu in Internet Explorer causes the Internet Options window to appear. Further options (General, Security, Content, Connections, Programs and Advanced) are selected by clicking on the appropriate tab at the top of the Internet Options window.

Changing the way Web pages look

Browsers allow the user to influence how certain elements within Web pages appear on the screen. For example, it is possible to alter the font used to display text in Web pages, the background colour and how links are displayed. As many Web pages are designed to appear in a certain way, and to override user settings (see below), altering these options may have less effect than might be expected. However, they may be useful in some instances. For example, increasing the size of the font can be a useful way of enhancing the appearance of sites for visually impaired users.

In Netscape, choosing the Fonts option on the left of the Preferences window displays a collection of drop down menus. The user can select both a variable width font (such as Times New Roman) and a fixed width font (such as Courier). It is advisable to leave the Encoding option set to Western as this is the correct setting for English and most other western languages, but bear in mind that Netscape comes with the ability to deal with other encodings for non-Latin alphabets, such as Cyrillic. The user must, of course, have fonts for these alphabets installed on their computer to be able to make use of this feature.

Choosing the Colors option in Netscape displays boxes containing the colours used at present for text, background, visited links and unvisited links. Click on any of the boxed colours to reveal a color selection palette (see Figure 20.1). Both the Fonts and Colors options allow the user to specify that the browser should use their preferences, overriding instructions from the Web page. However, the success of this feature is sometimes patchy, as Web page designers can get around it by using style sheets and constructing Web pages from images containing text, rather than text itself.

Figure 20.1 Netscape Navigator's colour palette

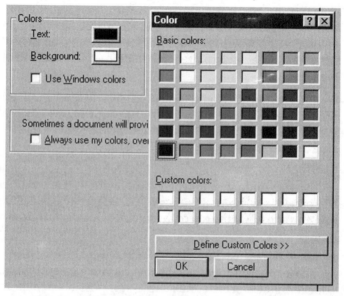

Clicking on the General tab in Internet Explorer reveals (at the bottom of the window) the Colors, Fonts and Accessibility options. These work very similarly to the Netscape features described above, except that the encoding is not present – this is a separate option under the View menu. Also, Internet Explorer 5 has an additional feature – it allows the user to define a 'hover color', which is then applied to any hyperlink passed over by the mouse pointer. The Accessibility option allows users to override completely any formatting applied to text within a Web page, and to set up a style sheet to override the Web page's style sheet, thus giving the user complete control over how text appears. This does not, however, have any effect on text included within images.

Making the browser recall sites

Both browsers have the ability to recall sites previously visited, or to auto-matically go straight to one particular site at the beginning of the session.

Bookmarks and Favorites

A user can ask the browser to make a note of the address of the page displayed at any point. These notes are usually referred to as bookmarks although Internet Explorer calls them Favorites. This is an invaluable feature, and is covered in detail in the next chapter.

Launch page

After installing the browser it is normal to find that whenever a new session starts it automatically visits a site nominated by the vendor. For example, Navigator will always begin with the Netscape Netcenter site when launched. It is possible to pick another site, or if the user prefers, to open a blank browser window, ready for instructions from the user.

In Netscape, the Navigator section gives the user the option to set a home page of their choice; this is the page that will be loaded if the user clicks on the Home button at any point. It is then possible to set Navigator to start with the home page, a blank page or the page visited at the end of the last session.

In Internet Explorer, clicking on the General tab takes the user to the General section where the address of the home page is set. Internet Explorer 5 always starts a new session with the home page, but this can be set to a blank window if required. It is not possible to have both a home page set and to start with a blank window.

History

The history feature allows the browser to recall which sites have been accessed. This is useful as it means the user can click on the Back and Forward buttons to retreat and proceed through a series of pages or sites they have already visited. The history feature also allows the address of recently visited sites to be recalled, not only within a session, but also sites that may have been visited several days ago.

In the Navigator section, Netscape Navigator allows the user to set the number of days for which addresses will be recalled. It is also possible to clear the history (i.e. delete the stored addresses). Back in the main browser window, the Window menu has a History option, which displays all the stored addresses. In addition, clicking on the downward arrow at the right end of the Location bar will display a list of frequently visited domains.

History options are located in the General section of Internet Options in Internet Explorer and are identical in function to those described for Netscape above.

Helper applications and plug-ins

Some resources encountered on the Web may present information that the browser is not able to display. These may be files in formats that are uncommon, or new formats that are unrecognised by the browser.

Generally speaking, as browsers develop, support is built in for more resource and document types. This means that for those using the most up-to-date version of Netscape browsers or Internet Explorer, finding a file the browser cannot process should be a rare experience. If there is no built-in support, the browser calls on other applications to deal with the resource. Programs assisting the browser in this way may be divided into two groups, helper applications and plug-ins.

Helper applications are programs that exist independently from the browser, and may function without its presence. Word processors and spreadsheets are good examples. When a file of a suitable format is encountered, the helper application is called by the browser, and it starts up and runs as it normally would if the browser were not there. Helper applications persist when the browser is shut down, and must be closed separately by the user.

When the browser encounters a file it does not recognise, it will ask the user to choose an application to deal with it, or may offer the option to save the file to the hard disk for viewing later. The user may pick an application they know will be able to display the file, if one exists. Of course it is possible that they will not have access to a suitable application; this depends on how well equipped their computer is.

Plug-ins also work with the browser to extend its capability to display different file types. They differ from helper applications in that they are not designed to run independently from the browser, rather they can be thought of as supplementary software. Plug-ins do not run alone and they do not persist when the browser is closed down (i.e. it is not necessary to close them down separately).

Plug-ins usually exist to deal with a very specific resource type, and they are commonly produced by the same software company that develops the resource itself. Examples include the Adobe Acrobat reader, which allows pages in the proprietary Adobe format, PDF, to be displayed, and the Real Audio player which plays sound files in suitable formats, hardware permitting.

The latest browsers come with many popular plug-ins already installed. In addition, many Web sites making use of unusual formats helpfully tell the user where the appropriate plug-in can be acquired. Netscape also provide a plug-in page that lists hundreds of plug-ins and locations for downloading them. New plug-ins are appearing all the time and this service has a What's New section for recent releases.

Using Netscape, whether a file requires a helper application or a plug-in, the relationship between the file type and the software needed to read it is expressed in the Applications section in Preferences. For example in Figure 20.2 we see that bitmap images will be displayed with Microsoft Paint. Navigator will allow different software to be substituted if preferred; click on the Edit button and use the Browse button to locate the alternative program (in this instance Paint Shop Pro could be substituted if available). New file-software relationships may be set up in a similar way.

On encountering an unknown file type, Internet Explorer 5 launches a standard Windows "Open with" dialogue box, allowing the user to choose an application.

Adobe Acrobat Reader: www.adobe.com/support/downloads/main.html

Netscape Plug-ins: www.netscape.com/plugins/

Real Audio: www.realaudio.com/

Figure 20.2 Picking an application with Netscape Navigator 4.x Preferences

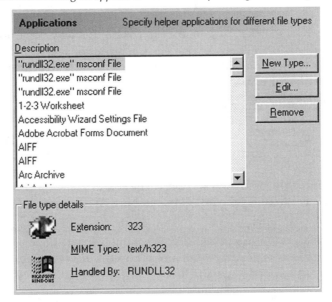

Caching and proxies

Caching is a technique used to speed up access to the Internet. When a page is viewed on the Web, the browser actually downloads one or more files onto the user's hard disk. Caching works by saving a copy of each file downloaded in a folder on the hard disk, called the cache. When the same file is requested again, rather than downloading it a second time from the Web, the copy in the cache is used instead.

Organisations with many network users may take this idea a step further and nominate a computer on the network to store all cached files. For example, consider a business with several Internet users who all use a Web site in the USA frequently. If each employee has a cache on their hard disk, then they will all need to visit the site individually before each of their computers has a cached copy of the files that make up the Web pages on the site. If an organisational cache exists, only one employee need visit the site to set up the cached copy, which may then be used by all, making every subsequent visit to the site faster.

It is also possible for several organisations to arrange to use a joint cache. For example, the academic cache provided jointly by the University of Manchester and Loughborough University serves the whole of the Higher Education community in the UK.[3]

Caching does not always work perfectly, but when it does work the Web will seem much faster. As well as speeding things up, caching files is also a responsible way to use the Web. The fewer files downloaded by a user across the network, the less capacity or bandwidth used and the more there is for everyone else.

Netscape Navigator allows the user to control the way it caches in the Advanced section of Preferences. The Cache options refer to the user's personal cache and the Proxies options to any cache that is further afield (such as an organisational cache).

Using the Cache options, the user can alter the size of their personal cache. There are really two types, memory and disk cache. As their names imply, memory cache is located in the computer's memory (and will therefore be very rapidly accessed and very short term) and disk cache is located on the hard disk (and will be slightly slower to access but will persist, probably for several sessions). The size of each type of cache will be set at a standard level when Navigator is first installed.

More importantly, it is possible to choose how long cached copies of documents are kept. One of the defects of caching is that if a copy of a file is stored in a cache it is no longer updated. The real file on the Web, however, may be updated at any time and the cached copy will then be out-of-date.

To remedy this, it is possible to ask Navigator to check if the cached copy and the real file are still the same. This is a lot simpler than it sounds and is far quicker than downloading the file a second time. Depending on the user's Preferences, Navigator checks every time the cached copy is used, once per session (i.e. at the start) or never. Checking every time is the slowest option (but ensures the cached copy is always up-to-date) and never checking is the quickest (but the cached copy may become out-of-date and inaccurate). Once per session is a compromise between the two.

Cache options are in the General section of Internet Options in Internet Explorer. They are referred to as Temporary Internet Files. Control of the memory cache is not available, but the disk cache may be cleared, and the frequency at which pages are checked set in a similar way to Netscape above. In addition, the user can view a list of cached files, by clicking on the View files button.

Other advanced options

Browsers may also enable the user to control use of some of the more advanced features of the Web, such as scripts, style sheets and cookies. Essentially, the options given are to allow or disallow, and occasionally to be warned about these features when they are encountered.

Scripts

Web pages written exclusively in HTML are essentially static and non-interactive. In order to interact with the user, they must support the processing of incoming data, and this is sometimes achieved by calling an external program or script. However, an increasing number of pages are offering dynamic and interactive features using scripts embedded in the page, commonly Java, Javascript or ActiveX.

Java is a programming language, developed by Sun Microsystems, originally for the consumer electronics industry. Java can be used to write ordinary programs, just like any other programming language. However, it is most commonly used to write applications that sit within Web pages, called applets.

Browsers that support Java can run applets as easily as they can display images. This means that they can download an applet to a user's computer, run it and close it down without intervention, as the Web page that contains the applet is displayed. It is this that allows Webmasters to create more dynamic or interactive pages. The range of things an applet can do is as wide as the range of software the computer can run, depending on the skill of the programmer.

Programmers assert that Javascript is different from Java, but from the point of view of most Web users, they serve a similar purpose.

ActiveX is a product that, like Java, allows Webmasters to add more interactive features to Web pages. It enables programs written in any language to be integrated into a networked environment. ActiveX is capable of doing much more with the user's PC than Java applets or Javascript. For example, it can write data to the user's hard disk. This makes it potentially more useful but also implies a greater risk to the user, and the security implications of using ActiveX have been a major point of discussion.[4]

Netscape Navigator 4.x supports Java and Javascript, which means users can use all the features offered by pages which include these scripts. If preferred, support may be switched off, via the check boxes in the Advanced section of Preferences.

Netscape Navigator 4.x browsers require a plug-in to interpret pages that contain ActiveX.

Internet Explorer 5 allows the user to state whether Java applets, Javascript and Active X should be run automatically, disabled or cause a prompt to be displayed. This is done by setting the appropriate security level via the Security section (described in more detail below).

Cookies

Cookies enable Web sites to achieve a stateful connection with a user's computer. Without cookies, when the user's computer requests data from a Web server, the transaction is usually discrete and self-contained. The same client making another request seconds later will not be recognised by the server as a recent acquaintance, nor will the server make any connection between the requests.

What does this mean practically? One consequence is that servers cannot easily distinguish between a user reloading a page ten times and ten requests from individual users (this may be a disadvantage if the number of hits is important for revenue, for example).

Cookies simply enable the server to connect together requests made by the same user. This is achieved by depositing small chunks of data (called cookies) on the user's hard disk. Cookies are simply strings of characters stored either in a single file or in many files in a specific directory (most commonly in a file called cookies.txt). Once a site can recognise users, it is possible to personalise pages delivered to them, place them at the point in a complex process where they left off previously (such as when shopping or taking an online training course), or simply streamline authentication processes such as logging on with a username and password.

When cookies were first introduced it was not possible to avoid any Web site that wanted to deposit these uninvited guests, they were denounced as an invasion of privacy and thus immediately acquired a reputation. Now most browsers allow cookies to be disabled and they are widely accepted, although some sites still attract disapproval by using them in unusually invasive ways.

It may be helpful to review some myths about cookies:

- Cookies can be used to steal your credit card number: no – there is no way cookies can gather this kind of information, they cannot even pick up an email address from your browser.

- Sites depositing cookies on your computer can snoop around the rest of your files: no – cookies are not programs but text and so cannot open or delete anything on your hard disk.

- Cookies can be used to spy on you: yes and no – this is a very exaggerated version of the much less dramatic truth. Cookies can be used to monitor usage of sites and may thus expose the visitor to a degree of exploitation for commercial gain, e.g. by allowing the Web site to deliver personally targeted adverts.

Using the Advanced section of Netscape Navigator Preferences the user can choose to disable all cookies, accept all cookies or to receive a warning whenever a cookie is offered. Be warned, some sites will refuse to deal with clients who don't accept cookies and some sites deposit cookies liberally, so users choosing the third option may find themselves overwhelmed with warning messages.

Cookies are enabled, disabled or prompted in the Security section of Internet Explorer 5. See below for more details.

Security

E-commerce requires confidence on behalf of the vendor and customer in the privacy and security of dealings taking place via Web sites. Traffic on the Internet, particularly data sent to and fro by Web browsers using HTTP (hypertext transfer protocol), is not secure because:

- it travels via many networks and connections that are outside the control of the sender and the receiver, and

- it is not encrypted (encoded).

Consequently eavesdropping is possible, and the risk attached to using a credit card on the Internet has been compared to that involved in giving it to a waiter or reading the number to someone over the phone.[5]

Some sites offer protection using the secure sockets layer (SSL). The most recent versions of both Netscape browsers and Internet Explorer support SSL. Sites using it have addresses that start:

https://

rather than the more usual:

http://

and so are easily recognised.

Another way to differentiate a secure site from an unsecured site is to check the visual clues and messages given by the browser. In Netscape Navigator (version 3 and earlier) the broken key symbol in the bottom, left-hand corner changes to an unbroken key when a secure site is entered. Later versions of Netscape browsers have a padlock in the same position, which is either open or closed. Internet Explorer also uses a padlock icon to denote a site's level of security (see Figure 20.3).

Figure 20.3 Browser security – visual clues and messages

Internet Explorer

An unsecure site in the
Trusted Sites category

A secure site in the
Internet category

Netscape Navigator

An unsecure site

A secure site

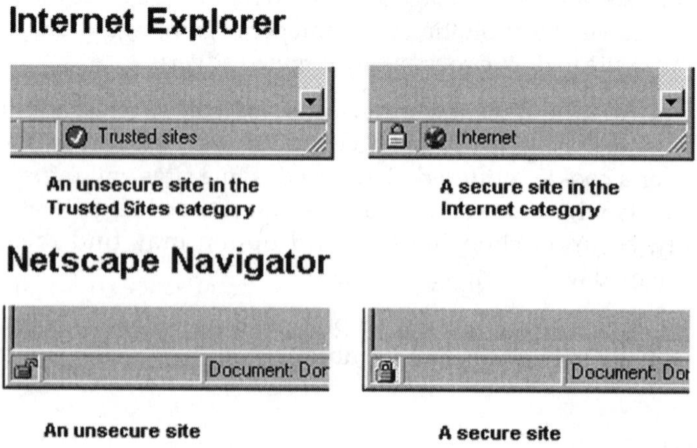

Both Netscape and Internet Explorer browsers can be set up to warn the user when information is being transmitted without security. However, as most users will be happy to submit information such as search queries and messages to discussion fora insecurely, warning messages like these can become irritating very quickly and are often turned off.

Recently the provision of banking and other financial services over the Internet has led to the need for even greater levels of security. This is usually achieved using encryption, i.e. by encoding information before it is sent across the network. Encryption is used by sites using SSL, but companies offering financial services may demand that the user's browser supports a higher level of encryption than the norm, often called '128-bit encryption' or encryption with a '128-bit key'.

Security options are controlled from a Security button on the navigation toolbar in Netscape. Choose the Navigator option on the left to see a series of check boxes and menus for warning, SSL, and to set a password to protect access to Navigator (this might be helpful for users who share a computer with others).

Figure 20.4 Netscape Navigator security options

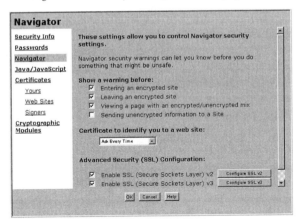

The most recent version of Internet Explorer seeks to tackle the security problem by allowing the user to sort Web sites into categories according to the level of security required when accessing them. Four categories are defined (see Table 20.1), and the user sets the level of security to high, low or medium. A low security setting turns most prompts off and so the user could use this for frequently visited, trusted sites or for frequently visited sites where the type of data transmitted does not demand a high level of security.

Table 20.1: Internet Explorer security categories

Category	Chosen by user?	Sites included
The Internet	No	Uncategorised sites
Local intranet	No	Sites within the user's organisation
Trusted sites	Yes	Sites trusted not to damage the user's computer or data
Restricted sites	Yes	Sites that may potentially damage the user's computer or data

References

1. United States District Court for the District of Columbia. United States of America v. Microsoft Corporation, C.A. 98-1232 – Findings of Fact. Available from: http://usvms.gpo.gov/

2. Demon Internet. FAQs. Available from: http://www.demon.net/info/helpdesk/faq/welcome.shtml

3.   JANET Web Caching Service. The National Janet Web Cache. Available from: http://wwwcache.ja.net/

4.   ZDNet. Active X (developer's page). Available from: http://www.zdnet.com/devhead/filters/activex/

5.   Netscape. Understanding security and privacy. Available from: http://home.netscape.com/security/basics/index.html

Chapter 21

Organising your view of the Internet

Services such as subject gateways (discussed in Chapter 14) help to make sense of the Internet's disorder by dividing resources into categories designed to aid certain groups of users. Although these services are vital, they cannot cater for all the needs of individual users and it is likely that each user will also want to create their own lists of key resources.

Organising one's own view of the Internet does not mean cataloguing huge numbers of resources, but rather having readily to hand those sites that are used most often. Groups of users and entire organisations may also benefit from doing this, and at this level, it can also be a useful way of emphasising sites to promote their usage. Many library services provide a shared list of starting points to help new users take their first steps into the Internet.

This chapter describes how to organise such a view of the Internet, whether on an individual or organisational basis, using standard browsers, and also introduces some Web-based services that may be helpful.

Organisation with browsers: Bookmarks and Favorites

Internet Explorer and Netscape browsers tackle this problem in a similar way. Each browser has the capability to record selected details about an Internet resource: name, address and a short description. Internet Explorer calls these chosen resources 'Favorites', while Netscape browsers (such as Netscape Navigator) prefer the term 'Bookmarks'.

Creating Bookmarks

There are several ways to create a Bookmark, i.e. for the user to add a resource to their collection, using a Netscape browser.

If the resource required is displayed in the main browser window:

- pull down the Bookmark menu and select the option Add Bookmark, or

- right-click within the page with the mouse and choose Add Bookmark from the resulting menu.

If a link to the resource required is displayed in the main browser window:

- right-click the link with the mouse and choose Add Bookmark.

If the resource required is part of a Web resource using frames:

- right-click with the mouse in the appropriate frame and choose Add Bookmark.

To return to a Bookmarked resource at any time, the user pulls down the Bookmark menu and chooses the resource from the list. Note that the name given to the resource is picked up automatically by the browser and may need to be changed (see Editing Bookmarks below).

Creating Favorites

Creating Favorites is essentially the same as creating Bookmarks, but Internet Explorer provides a few extra features.

If the resource required is displayed in the main browser window, to create a Favorite:

- pull down the Favorites menu and select the option Add to Favorites, or
- right-click within the page with the mouse and choose Add to Favorites.

If a link to the resource required is displayed in the main browser window:

- right-click the link with the mouse and choose Add to Favorites.

If the resource required is part of a Web resource using frames:

- right-click with the mouse in the appropriate frame and choose Add to Favorites.

Following any of these instructions will result in the Add Favorite dialogue box being displayed. The user now has the option to choose how much work Internet Explorer will do on their chosen resource. The options are:

- simply to add the resource to the list of Favorites,
- add the resource to the list and set up a mechanism to check it periodically and receive notification by email when it changes, or

- add the resource to the list, set up a mechanism to check it periodically, receive notification when it changes, and download and save a copy of the page (if it is a Web-based resource) for quicker viewing.

To return to a Favorite at any time, the user pulls down the Favorites menu and chooses the resource from the list. Alternatively, clicking on the Favorites button results in the list of Favorites appearing as a frame on the left of the browser Window.

Organising Bookmarks and Favorites

A well-organised collection of Bookmarks or Favorites can be a great time-saver, but all too often lists created using these tools fall into disuse. Most do not stand up to close inspection, being long lists of inadequately labelled resources in no particular order!

However, both browsers allow the user to edit their list of chosen resources. This can be helpful in a number of ways, allowing the user to rename resources (often the name picked up automatically by the browser is not helpful), as well as reorganise and delete items if their list becomes unwieldy. Resources can also be added to the list by hand using the edit feature, although this should be used with caution as it is easy to mistype an address.

Organising Bookmarks

To organise or reorganise a list of bookmarks, open the Bookmark menu in Netscape and choose Edit Bookmarks. A new window will appear containing the Bookmarks arranged as a hierarchical tree. As well as the name of the resource, the browser displays its address, the date when the Bookmark was created and the date when the resource was last visited by the browser.

Organising Bookmarks in Netscape browsers simply involves sorting them into folders. To create a new folder:

- pull down the File menu and choose the option New Folder, and
- enter a name and description for the folder in the dialogue box.

When first created, a folder will always be empty. Bookmarks may now be dragged and dropped into the folder in the Edit Bookmarks window. Folders within folders are permissible.

Bookmarks placed in folders disappear from the Bookmarks menu and now appear in a supplementary menu when the folder name is highlighted (see Figure 21.1).

Figure 21.1 Organising Netscape Navigator bookmarks

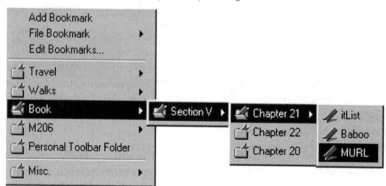

Organising Favorites

Similarly, organising Favorites in Internet Explorer can be approached in the same way as organising files in folders. In fact, the Organize Favorites window is reminiscent of Windows Explorer. To organise Favorites:

- open the Organize Favorites window by pulling down the Favorites menu and choosing this option, and

- create a new folder by clicking on the Create Folder button.

Favorites may be placed in the new folder by dragging and dropping as before. Favorites in folders appear as a supplementary menu when the folder name is highlighted in the Favorites menu.

Shared resource lists

Creating a shared view of the Internet for a group of users or an entire organisation may be achieved by using:

- a shared file on a local network, or

- an external third party.

The first option depends entirely on local resources and expertise, but the second option is available to anyone, through free services on the public Internet.

Several third party services offer to organise lists of chosen sites. They can be used by anyone wishing to create a selection of resources accessible from any computer attached to the Internet, and thus provide a portable set of Bookmarks or Favorites. They are also ideal for sharing a single collection amongst many users.

MURL (standing for My URLs) describes itself as an 'online Bookmark and Favorites manager'. It is a free service, one of many on the Web that is financed by advertising, and may be used by anyone who registers. The service works by recording details about the user's chosen resources on the MURL server instead of on the user's computer. As the list is stored remotely, it may be accessed from any computer attached to the Internet. Resources may be added or deleted from the list and organised into folders, as can Bookmarks or Favorites.

To create a MURL resource list the user must register at the MURL home page by following the Create Account link. All resource lists created using MURL are password protected.

MURL is designed for individuals but can also be used by groups to create a shared set of resources. The main disadvantage is that adding resources is rather cumbersome – the address and title of a new resource must be typed in (and not added via the browser's Add Bookmark or Add Favorite features).

This disadvantage may be overcome to some extent by launching a MURL surfer. Clicking on the Launch MURL Surfer option causes a small window to appear, that contains a text entry box. This window persists when the main browser window moves on to other resources, making it is possible to copy and paste addresses into it while browsing.

ItList and Baboo also supply third party bookmark services.

MURL: murl.com/

itList: www.itlist.com/

Baboo: www.baboo.com/

Chapter 22

Creating your own Web pages

The majority of resources encountered on the Web are written in a language called HTML, or HyperText Markup Language. Writing simple HTML documents is easy and requires no programming expertise. This chapter details the elements common to all HTML documents, describes how to construct a basic Web page, and gives pointers to further reading. It also tells you how to discover whether your HTML is written correctly.

What is HTML?

As its name implies, HTML is a markup language. In simple terms, this means that different sections of the document are labelled with certain qualities or attributes, which influence how those sections are treated by relevant software, such as your browser.

For example, Figure 22.1 shows the beginning of this chapter in HTML. On the left it is displayed as a Web page, that is, interpreted by a Web browser, and on the right it is displayed as a source document, that is, as it would appear if opened and read without the aid of a browser (in this case, using a text editor). These two versions look very different at first sight, but note that all the text in the Web page is also present in the source document. The difference is that the source document has extra characters, and the Web page has text in various fonts. Sections of text in the source document have been marked up in such a way that they will be displayed in a different font by the Web browser.

Figure 22.1 An HTML document and its source

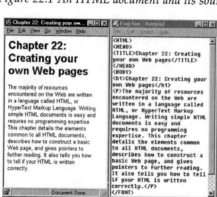

Characters that achieve this are referred to as 'tags' and always appear within angled brackets, i.e. < and >. For example, the heading 'What is HTML?' which appears in the large font in the Web browser is marked with the tag <h1> at the start and the tag </h1> at the end. <h1> is the HTML tag for a level 1 header.

As well as manipulating text, different tags may be used to include and position images, create links to other documents, specify colours, and display dialogue boxes and clickable buttons. Pages that contain all these features have more complex source documents, and are often written with special software, referred to as HTML authoring tools. However, it is possible to write HTML without this software, using a simple word processor or text editor, as we shall see next.

Creating an HTML page with a text editor

If you are completely new to HTML authoring, follow the step-by-step instructions below to create your first Web page. You will need access to a computer with a Web browser and a text editor (if you are using Microsoft Windows try Notebook, or if you are using a Macintosh, Simpletext will suffice).

1. Open a text editor on your computer.

2. Use the <html> tag to specify that this is an HTML document. Most tags appear in pairs, so you will need a start tag <html> and an end tag </html>.

    ```
    <html>
    </html>
    ```

3. Leave a few lines between the start and end tag, as everything else in the document will go here.

4. An HTML document should be split into two segments, one of which contains information about the document, while the other contains the document itself. These segments are denoted by the <head> and <body> tags respectively. Add these tags to your document, remembering that each start tag requires an end tag.

    ```
    <html>
        <head>            </head>
        <body>            </body>
    </html>
    ```

5. Think of a title for your document. The title goes in the head segment, and is labelled with the <title> tag. Information in the head segment is not generally displayed by the browser. To have the title text displayed, it may therefore be necessary to repeat this

information in the body segment. The `<title>` tag may not be used in the body segment, however, so use the `<h1>` tag instead (this instructs the browser to display the text as a level 1 header).

```
<html>
<head>
     <title>HTML is easy!</title>
</head>
<body>
     <h1>HTML is easy!</h1>
</body>
</html>
```

In the examples shown above, elements most recently added are indented for clarity. In practice, indentations, carriage returns and spacing have no effect on the way the document is displayed by the browser. Thus the document above could equally well be written as:

```
<html><head><title>HTML is easy!</title></
head><body><h1>HTML is easy!</h1></body></html>
```

Subheadings may be added with other header tags, <h2>, <h3>, and so on, up to <h6>. The higher the number in the header tag, the smaller the heading. It is good practice to start from <h1> and work upwards but this is not essential.

6.   Paragraphs of text may be added using the `<p>` tag. Each paragraph is enclosed in start and end tags.

```
<html>
<head>
<title>HTML is easy!</title>
</head>
<body>
<h1>HTML is easy!</h1>
     <p>HTML stands for Hypertext Markup
     Language. Most documents on the Web are
     written in HTML.</p>
     <p>HTML is easy to master and can be
     created using a simple text editor or word
     processor.</p>
</body>
</html>
```

Now save your Web page with the file extension .htm (for example mypage.htm). Open your Web browser and use the File/Open option to display your page. Note that the browser decides where your paragraphs should wrap (i.e. where a new line begins). Try resizing the browser window and see what effect this has.

7. Hypertext links from within documents to related information are the hallmark of the Web and these are added with the <a> tag. A hypertext link is more complex than the tags we have seen so far because it requires extra information, namely where the link should lead. Figure 22.2 shows a hypertext link to the OMNI service, with each element explained.

Figure 22.2 A hypertext link explained

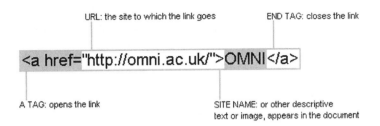

Add the following link to the first paragraph of your Web page.

```
<p>HTML stands for Hypertext Markup Language.
Most documents on the Web are written in HTML.
    There are many guides to writing HTML,
    some available free on the Internet. The
    <a href =
    "http://www.ncsa.uiuc.edu/General/
    Internet/WWW/HTMLPrimer.html">
    HTML Primer</a>
    is one of the most popular.
</p>
```

In the example above we have made a link to a remote document, i.e. a document which resides on a different computer (in this case a computer called www.ncsa.uiuc.edu). It is also possible to refer to local documents, i.e. documents that reside on the same computer. This is achieved by replacing the URL with a filename and path. Try creating a second HTML document and making a link to it. For example, to specify a file named sizes.html in the search subfolder of the temp folder, you would use the address "temp\search\sizes.htm". The link would be expressed as:

```
<a href="temp\search\sizes.htm">sizes</a>
```

8. Images are embedded in documents using the <img> tag. The <img> tag is one of a group of tags, used to include standalone elements, that have no end tag. The location of the tag in your source document

tells the browser where to put the image, but you must also specify where the file containing the image is located. This may be a local or remote file:

Local image: `<img src="filename.gif">`

Remote image: `<img src="http://www.server.somewhere/filename.gif">`

Usually, only a few image types are used in HTML documents, the most common being GIF or JPEG formats. Fortunately, software capable of saving images in suitable formats is readily available – almost any graphics package will do this for you.

After acquiring a suitable image, add the following paragraph to your document:

```
<p>Embedded images brighten up a document.
Associated text can be aligned with the top,
middle or bottom of an image.</p>
<img src="filename.gif" align="top">Text at the
top</img>
<img src="filename.gif" align="middle">Text at
the centre</img>
<img src="filename.gif" align="bottom">Text at
the bottom</img>
```

Take care when incorporating remote images into your documents, you may be in breach of copyright!

More tags

The document you have created uses only a few of the HTML tags available. Other common tags are listed below.

Tags which affect the way text is displayed:

`<font size=n></font>`	adjusts font size, n=1-7
`<i></i>`	displays text in italic
`<b></b>`	displays text in bold
`<em></em>`	emphasises the text (form of emphasis is chosen by the browser)

Tags which structure the document:

` `	a line break
`<hr>`	a horizontal rule
`<centre></centre>`	centred text

Tags which denote lists:

| `<ul></ul>` | a list with bullets, enclose each item in the <li></li> tags |
| `<ol></ol>` | a list with numbers, enclose each item in the <li></li> tags |

There are of course many others.

Although it is possible to create any HTML document using text editors, if you plan to create complex documents it is easier to use an HTML editor. HTML editors range from small pieces of freeware to entire suites of programs designed for managing large Web sites.

Advanced HTML features

Once you have mastered simple HTML, try the following tags to add more features to your documents.

Tables

Tables may be used to display data or to divide a document into sections. See Figure 22.3.

Figure 22.3 An HTML table

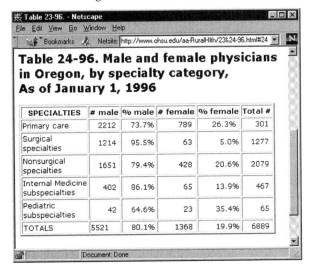

Creating a table is merely a matter of placing discrete pieces of data in specified rows and columns. The `<table>` tag denotes the start of a table in a document, the `<tr>` tag the start of a new row and the `<td>` tag the start of a cell. For example, this is a two row, two column table:

```
<table>
```

```
<tr><td>row1 cell1</td><td>row1 cell2</td></tr>
<tr><td>row2 cell2</td><td>row2 cell2</td></tr>
</table>
```

Frames

Frames allow some sections of a document to remain static while other sections change. For example, frames are often used to create a persistent menu.

In principle, a Web page may be divided up into several frames. However, a simple, two-frame page is very easy to design and illustrates all the principles involved. To do this, you will need to create some new pages. First a menu:

```
<html>
<head><title>Menu</title></head>
<body>
<a href="apples.htm" target="main">Apples</a>
<a href="pears.htm" target="main">Pears</a>
<a href="oranges.htm" target="main">Oranges</a>
</body>
</html>
```

The addition of the instruction `target="main"` to the hypertext link tells the browser where to display the information in the files apples.htm, pears.htm and oranges.htm when those links are selected. Call this file menu.htm.

Now create a file called frames.htm. This file will serve a number of purposes:

- the `<frameset>` tag tells the browser how to divide the screen and which files to display in each division – in this case the screen is divided horizontally into two rows (width ratio 20:80) displaying the files menu.htm and mypage.htm respectively.
- the `<noframes>` tag tells the browser what to display if it cannot display the divided screen.

```
<html>

<head><title>Frames version of my page</title></head>

<frameset rows="20%,80%">
<frame src="menu.htm">
<frame src="mypage.htm" name="main">
</frameset>

<noframes>
```

```
<p>Here I will put information for browsers
that don't display frames. This could be an
apology, or, even better, an alternative method
of accessing the same information without
frames, for example, links to the files <a
href="apples.htm">Apples</a>, <a
href="pears.htm">Pears</a> and <a
href="oranges.htm">Oranges</a>.</p>
</noframes>

</body>
</html>
```

Next create the files apples.htm, pears.htm and oranges.htm. It does not matter what the content of these files is as long as they contain valid HTML. Store all the files in the same directory.

Open the frames.htm file with your browser. The browser window should split horizontally, with the menu.htm file on top. Following any link from the menu causes the relevant file to be displayed in the bottom section while the menu stays in place.

Vertical divisions are also possible (try replacing 'rows' with 'cols' in the example above). Be warned, excessive use of frames will cause your pages to load slowly and may irritate users (especially those using browsers that are unable to display them). Use frames in moderation and always use the <noframes> tag to provide an alternative means of accessing your information.

Colour

Using 'color' attributes it is possible to change the colour of text and background. Colour in HTML is often described by a six digit hexadecimal number, inserted inside a HTML tag such as <body> or <font>. For example:

```
<html>
<head><title>A colourful document</title></
head>
<body bgcolor="#000000">
<p><font size=7 color="#33hh22">This document
has a white background and large purple text</p>
</body>
</html>
```

The future: cascading style sheets

Embedding information about style (font, colour, etc.) in individual pages makes large collections of documents difficult to maintain over time. It is far easier to maintain a consistent style throughout a Web site using a relatively new HTML feature called style sheets.[1] Put simply, style sheets will allow a style to be defined for a series of documents, thus removing the need to specify attributes such as colour and font repeatedly. The newest versions of all major browsers support style sheets.

Making pages interactive: fill out forms

HTML can also be used to create pages that support interaction with users and receive information from them. The simplest way to achieve this is to allow information to be input and sent to an email address, using the `<a>` tag. For example:

```
<p>Please send your comments to <a
href="mailto:j.smith@mail.box">John Smith</
a>.</p>
```

creates a link which, when clicked, allows the user to send an email to the address specified (if the user's browser is correctly configured).

For more complex data manipulation, another set of HTML tags, collectively referred to as forms, may be used. Using form tags, various types of features allowing input of data may be created. An HTML form starts, unsurprisingly, with the `<form>` tag.

```
<form method="post" action="script.pl"></form>
```

Notice the method and action attributes. Data input via an HTML form is passed to a program or script on the Web server for processing, and these specify in what manner the data is passed and which script receives it. The form above would pass data using the 'post' method to a script called script.pl.

Within the `<form>` tag, any of the following elements may appear:

`<input>`	used to specify a simple input element, such as a checkbox, or submit button
`<select>`	creates a picklist (menu) or scrollable list
`<textarea>`	denotes a box for text input

It is beyond the scope of this book to cover all of the intricacies of HTML forms, but there are many introductory guides and even some scripts available online that offer additional information.[2] Embedded scripts can also be used to make pages interactive.

Flavours of HTML

HTML is not static, but has evolved and changed during the lifetime of the Web. The correct uses of the various tags that make up a version of

HTML are expressed in what is known as a Document Type Definition (DTD). The organisation responsible for developing HTML DTDs is the World Wide Web Consortium (sometimes referred to as W3C).

Both Netscape and Microsoft, who produce the popular browsers Netscape Navigator and Internet Explorer respectively, have added support for extra tags in addition to those specified in early versions of HTML in order to expand and cement their market position. This has driven the development of later versions, and means that older browsers may not recognise some tags and even the latest versions of different browsers do not offer exactly the same functionality.

More recent versions of HTML have been developed with the participation of the software companies that produce browsers, editors, etc. W3C's latest recommendation is XHTML™ 1.0.[3]

All HTML documents ideally should include a statement of which version of HTML they use, and this normally appears at the top, before the first `<html>` tag. For example, a document using HTML 4, may begin with the following declaration:

```
<!DOCTYPE HTML PUBLIC "-//W3C//DTD HTML 4.0//
EN" "http://www.w3.org/TR/REC-html40/
strict.dtd">
```

Note that the declaration refers to the W3C pages – a public file describing HTML 4, so that anyone who accesses the document may consult it. The public file also tells the author of the page how to phrase the declaration.

Checking your work

After completing a Web page, there are two steps that can be taken to ensure it is written correctly.

Firstly, display the files using a Web browser. Correctly written pages will display completely and as expected. Unfortunately, this in itself is not enough to test a page, as some browsers are sympathetic to mistakes or deviations from the DTD and will display a document with errors perfectly well.

A second and more rigorous method of testing is to validate the HTML using a special piece of software. There are free validation services available online and one of the best is the W3C service. To validate a document using this service simply enter the Web address of your document in the box provided, click on the 'Submit this URL for validation' button and wait. The validator will return a list of errors that must be corrected if the document is to satisfy the DTD. If there are no errors, you will receive the message 'No errors found'. Once your document is validated, you can add the W3C 'validated' image to your work, so that visitors know your page has been checked and the HTML you have written has been approved.

W3C Validator: validator.w3.org/

Guides to HTML authoring

As with any computing topic, there is a plethora of books designed to help you get to grips with HTML. If you are not ready to purchase a book yet but would like to know a little more, the Webmonkey site, the HTML SourceBook and Tips, Tricks, How To and Beyond offer sensible, well organised introductions.

HTML SourceBook: www.utoronto.ca/webdocs/HTMLdocs/ NewHTML/index.html

Tips, Tricks, How To and Beyond: www.tips-tricks.com/

Webmonkey: hotwired.lycos.com/webmonkey/

References

1.   World Wide Web Consortium. Web Style Sheets. Available from: http://www.w3.org/Style/

2.   Webcom. WWW Fill-out Forms (tutorial). Available from: http://www.webcom.com/~webcom/html/tutor/forms/

3.   World Wide Web Consortium. XHTML™ 1.0: The Extensible Hypertext Markup Language. Available from: http://www.w3.org/TR/xhtml1/

Alphabetical list of links

For clarity, links are listed here without the usual http:// at the beginning. Most browsers allow Web addresses to be input without this preface.

A

A to Z of Evidence-based Healthcare
drsdesk.sghms.ac.uk/Starnet/atoz.htm

ACP Journal Club
www.acponline.org/journals/acpjc/jcmenu.htm

admin-medical
www.mailbase.ac.uk/lists/admin-medical/

Adobe Acrobat Reader
www.adobe.com/support/downloads/main.html

Age Concern Croydon
www.croydon.gov.uk/ageconcern/

AgeLine
research.aarp.org/ageline/

AIDS Knowledge Base
hivinsite.ucsf.edu/akb/1997/

All-in-One
www.allonesearch.com/all1user.html#People

ALLwords Dictionary
www.allwords.com/

AltaVista
www.altavista.com/

AltaVista International
doc.altavista.com/international.shtml

AltaVista Photo & Image Finder
image.altavista.com/

AltaVista Raging Search
www.raging.com/

AltaVista text-only search
www.altavista.com/cgi-bin/query?text

AltaVista Translations
babelfish.altavista.com/

AltaVista UK
www.altavista.co.uk/

Amazon.com
www.amazon.co.uk/ or www.amazon.com/

Amersham Pharmacia Biotec
www.apbiotech.com/

Anderson's Webalog
www.atcg.com/

Anesthesiology
www.anesthesiology.org/

Annual Review of Biochemistry - Planned tables of contents for future volumes
biochem.annualreviews.org/future.shtml

Articles Direct, British Library Document Supply Centre
www.bl.uk/services/bsds/dsc/artdir01.html

arXiv.org e-Print archive
xxx.lanl.gov/
Mirrored in the UK at: uk.arxiv.org/

Ask a Librarian
www.earl.org.uk/ask/index.html

Association of Medical Research Charities
www.amrc.org.uk/

B

Baboo
www.baboo.com/

Bandolier
www.jr2.ox.ac.uk/bandolier/

BBC
news.bbc.co.uk/

Bedside Diagnosis
www.acponline.org/public/bedside/

Beginner's Guide to Molecular Biology
www.iacr.bbsrc.ac.uk/notebook/courses/guide/

Biochemical Journal - online
www.biochemj.org/

BioHunt
www.expasy.ch/BioHunt/

BIOME
biome.ac.uk/

BIOME Evaluation Guidelines
biome.ac.uk/guidelines/eval/

BioMedCentral
www.biomedcentral.com/

Biomedical Research Vacancies
wisdom.wellcome.ac.uk/wisdom/jobshome.html

BioMedNet Jobs Exchange
jobs.bmn.com/

BioMedNet Library
journals.bmn.com/

BioMOO
bioinformatics.weizmann.ac.il/BioMOO/

bionet.jobs
www.bio.net/hypermail/EMPLOYMENT/

bionet.jobs.wanted
www.bio.net/hypermail/EMPLOYMENT-WANTED/

BIOSIS
www.biosis.org/

BioSupplyNet
www.biosupplynet.com/

BioSupplyNet (via Biomednet)
biomednet.com/biosupplynet/

Biotechnology and Biological Sciences Research Council (BBSRC)
www.bbsrc.ac.uk/

Blackwell's Online Bookshop
bookshop.blackwell.co.uk/

BMJ
www.bmj.com/

BMJ Classified
classified.bmj.com/

BMJ Customised @lerts
www.bmj.com/cgi/customalert/

BMJ Search multiple journals
www.bmj.com/searchall/

Books OnLine
www.bol.com/

Brighton Healthcare Trust jobs
www.rsch.org.uk/rsch/jobs1.htm

Bristol Biomed (the Bristol Biomedical Image Archive)
www.brisbio.ac.uk/

British Dental Trade Association
www.bdta.org.uk/

British Library
www.bl.uk/

British Nursing Index
www.bni.org.uk/

British Society for Immunology posts vacant
immunology.org/jobs.htm

Bugs in the news!
falcon.cc.ukans.edu/~jbrown/bugs.html

C

Cambridge Scientific Abstracts
www.csa.com/

Canadian Medical Association (CMA)
www.cma.ca/

Canadian Medical Association Journal (CMAJ)
www.cma.ca/cmaj/

Canadian Task Force for Preventive Services Handbook
www.ctfphc.org/

Cancer Research Campaign
www.crc.org.uk/

CANCERLIT
cancernet.nci.nih.gov/cancerlit.html

CANCERLIT Topic Searches
cancernet.nci.nih.gov/canlit/canlit.htm

CancerNet
cancernet.nci.nih.gov/

CancerNet CancerWeb UK Mirror
www.graylab.ac.uk/cancernet.html

CDC Data and Statistics
www.cdc.gov/scientific.htm

CDC links to international bulletins
www.cdc.gov/mmwr/international/world.html

CDC MMWR Disease Trends: State and Local Health Statistics
www2.cdc.gov/mmwr/distrnds.html

CDC National Center for Health Statistics
www.cdc.gov/nchs/

CDC National Prevention Information Network Educational Materials
Database
www.cdcnpin.org/db/public/ematmain.htm

CDC National Prevention Information Network Funding Database
www.cdcnpin.org/db/public/fundmain.htm

CDC National Prevention Information Network Prevention News Update Database
www.cdcnpin.org/db/public/dnmain.htm

Censorware
censorware.org/

Centers for Disease Control and Prevention (CDC)
www.cdc.gov/

Centre for Evidence Based Child Health
www.ich.ucl.ac.uk/ebm/ebm.htm

Centre for Evidence-Based Medicine
cebm.jr2.ox.ac.uk/

Centre for Evidence Based Mental Health
www.psychiatry.ox.ac.uk/cebmh/

Centre for Information Quality Management (CHiQ)
www.hfht.org/chiq/

Centre for Information Quality Management (CHiQ) Topic Bulletin 2:
Quality assessment of Internet sites
www.hfht.org/chiq/download_pdf.htm

CeReS
www.ceres.uwcm.ac.uk/

CHE.net: Principles: content
www.cche.net/principles/howto_all.asp

cheater.com
www.cheater.com/

CHEST
www.chest.ac.uk/

CIA World Factbook
www.odci.gov/cia/publications/factbook/index.html

CINAHL
www.cinahl.com/

CIRCE
www.gloscc.gov.uk/circe/index.htm

CiteLine Professional free trial and demo
www.citeline.com/screen_2_pro.html

CliniWeb International
www.ohsu.edu/cliniweb/

CliniWeb International Search
www.ohsu.edu/cliniweb/search.html

ClinPSYC
www.apa.org/psycinfo/clinpsyc.html

CMA Infobase
www.cma.ca/cpgs/

CNN Health
www.cnn.com/HEALTH/

Cochrane Collaboration
www.cochrane.org/

Cochrane Reviewers' Handbook
www.cochrane.org/cochrane/hbook.htm

Cochrane Reviewers' Handbook optimal search strategy for RCTs
www.cochrane.dk/cochrane/handbook/
hbookAPPENDIX_5C_OPTIMAL_SEARCH_STRAT.htm

Cochrane Reviews, abstracts
www.cochrane.org/cochrane/revabstr/mainindex.htm

Cochrane Reviews, search the abstracts
www.update-software.com/abstracts/

Cochrane Reviews, current comments and criticisms
www.cochrane.org/cochrane/currcrit.htm

CogPrints
cogprints.soton.ac.uk/

COIN
www.doh.gov.uk/coinh.htm

Communicable Disease Report
www.phls.co.uk/publications/cdrw.htm

Community of Science (COS)
www.cos.com/

Corbis
www.corbis.com/

CORDIS
www.cordis.lu/

CORDIS UK
www.cordis.lu/united_kingdom/

CRISP
www-commons.cit.nih.gov/crisp/

Critical Appraisal Skills Programme
www.phru.org/casp/

critical-appraisal-skills
www.mailbase.ac.uk/lists/critical-appraisal-skills/

Croydon JobMart
www.croydon.gov.uk/jobmart/

CTI-Biology
www.liv.ac.uk/ctibiol.html

D

Daily List
www.national-publishing.co.uk/d_listfr.html

DARE (Database of Abstracts of Reviews of Effectiveness)
nhscrd.york.ac.uk/

Database of CME Events
omni.ac.uk/cme/

Databases: patent full text and bibliographic (US Patent and Trademark Office)
www.uspto.gov/patft/

DataStar datasheets
ds.datastarweb.com/ds/products/datastar/ds.htm

DataStarWeb
www.datastarweb.com/

DDBJ
www.ddbj.nig.ac.jp/

Deja News
www.dejanews.com/

Dentanet recruitment
www.dentanet.org.uk/dentanet/recruit/recruit.html

Department of Health Research and Development Directorate
www.doh.gov.uk/research/

Department of Health Research and Development Directorate - North West
www.doh.gov.uk/nwro/rddnwro.htm

Dermatology Online Atlas (DOIA)
dermis.net/bilddb/index_e.htm

DerWeb
www.derweb.ac.uk/

Dialog
www.dialog.com/

Dialog Authoritative content
www.dialog.com/info/content/

Dialog bluesheets
library.dialog.com/bluesheets/

DialogSelect Open Access - Medicine
openaccess.dialog.com/med/

DIMDI
www.dimdi.de/homeeng.htm

DIMDI Alphabetical list of databases
www.dimdi.de/engl/hoste/dbkurze.html

DIMDI's free grips – WebSearch
gripsdb.dimdi.de/

DISCERN
www.discern.org.uk/

Disease Outbreak News
www.who.int/emc/outbreak_news/

Doctor's Desk
drsdesk.sghms.ac.uk/

Doctors.net
www.doctors.net.uk/

Dogpile
www.dogpile.com/

E

E-Med
www.cshl.org/medline/

EBM search strategies for SilverPlatter Medline
www.mssm.edu/library/ebm/spsea.html

Effective Health Care bulletins
www.york.ac.uk/inst/crd/ehcb.htm

Effectiveness Matters
www.york.ac.uk/inst/crd/em.htm

Electronic Telegraph (*The Daily Telegraph* and *Sunday Telegraph*)
www.telegraph.co.uk/

Electronic Yellow Pages
www.eyp.co.uk/

eLib Programme
www.ukoln.ac.uk/services/elib/

Elsevier Science Contents Direct
www.elsevier.nl/locate/ContentsDirect

Elsevier Science ContentsSearch
www.elsevier.nl/locate/ContentsSearch

EMBASE
www.elsevier.nl/inca/publications/store/5/2/3/3/2/8/

EMBL
www.ebi.ac.uk/embl/

EMBL, Description of
www.ebi.ac.uk/embl/Documentation/NAR/gkc070_gml.html

EMBL Sequence Alerting System
www.bork.embl-heidelberg.de/Alerting/

Emerging Infectious Diseases
www.cdc.gov/ncidod/EID/

Encyclopaedia Britannica
www.britannica.com/

Entrez
www.ncbi.nlm.nih.gov/Entrez/

ERGO
www.cordis.lu/ergo/home.html

ERIC
askeric.org/Eric/

ERIC Digests
www.ed.gov/databases/ERIC_Digests/index/

Esp@cenet
gb.espacenet.com/

EurekAlert!
www.eurekalert.org/

European Bioinformatics Institute (EBI)
www.ebi.ac.uk/

European Molecular Biology Laboratory (EMBL)
www.embl-heidelberg.de/

Eurostat
europa.eu.int/en/comm/eurostat/serven/home.htm

Eurosurveillance
www.eurosurv.org/

Eurosurveillance weekly update service
www.eurosurv.org/update/

Evidence-based filters for Ovid CINAHL
www.urmc.rochester.edu/Miner/Educ/ebnfilt.htm

Evidence-Based Medicine
www.bmjpg.com/data/ebm.htm

Evidence-based Medicine Toolbox
cebm.jr2.ox.ac.uk/docs/toolbox.html

Evidence-Based Mental Health
www.bmjpg.com/template.cfm?name=specjou_mh

Excite
www.excite.com/

Excite UK
www.excite.co.uk/

Experimental Biology Online (EBO)
link.springer.de/link/service/journals/00898/

Expertsearch: evidence-based filters for Ovid Medline
www.urmc.rochester.edu/Miner/Educ/Expertsearch.html

F

FAST Search
www.alltheweb.com/

FDA
www.fda.gov/search.html

FDA 'Dear Healthcare Professional' Letters
www.fda.gov/medwatch/safety.htm

Feet for Life
www.feetforlife.org/findchir.htm

Forum One
www.forumone.com/

FreeMedicalJournals.com
www.freemedicaljournals.com/

FUGU
fugu.hgmp.mrc.ac.uk/

G

GDB
www.gdb.org/

GenBank
www.ncbi.nlm.nih.gov/Genbank/

GeneCards
bioinformatics.weizmann.ac.il/cards/

Google
www.google.com/

Government press releases
www.coi.gov.uk/

Government Statistical Service
www.statistics.gov.uk/

Guidelines for guidelines
www.msd-newzealand.com/guidelines.html

H

HAMSTERS
europium.rpms.mrc.ac.uk/

Hardin MD
www.lib.uiowa.edu/hardin/md/

Health Evidence Bulletins Wales
www.uwcm.ac.uk/uwcm/lb/pep/

Health News
www.health-news.co.uk/

healthfinder
www.healthfinder.gov/

HealthGate Data Corporation
www.healthgate.com/

HealthGate research tools
www.healthgate.com/res/

Heathrow
www.heathrow.co.uk/BAAHome.htm

HEBSWeb
www.hebs.org.uk/

HGMD
www.uwcm.ac.uk/uwcm/mg/hgmd0.html

HGSI
www.ncbi.nlm.nih.gov/HUGO/

HighWire Press: Links to the top 500 science journals
highwire.stanford.edu/top/journals.dtl

HON
www.hon.ch/

HON Browse the MeSH classification
www.hon.ch/MeSH/

HON Code of conduct
www.hon.ch/HONcode/Conduct.html

HONselect
www.hon.ch/HONselect/

HONselect MeSH browsing
www.hon.ch/HONselect/Browse.html

HotBot
www.hotbot.com/

HotMail
www.hotmail.com/

House of Commons Select Committees
www.parliament.uk/commons/selcom/CMSEL.HTM

HTA (Health Technology Assessment Database)
nhscrd.york.ac.uk/

HTML SourceBook
www.utoronto.ca/webdocs/HTMLdocs/NewHTML/

HUM-MOLGEN
www.hum-molgen.de/journals/

Human Genome Mapping Project Resource Centre (HGMP-RC)
www.hgmp.mrc.ac.uk/

I

ICML 2000
www.icml.org/

IHS Library filters
wwwlib.jr2.ox.ac.uk/caspfew/filters/

Images from the History of Medicine
wwwihm.nlm.nih.gov/

Individual.com
www.individual.com/

Information Network for Croydon Health
www.croydon.gov.uk/healthinfo/

Infoseek
www.go.com/

Infoseek United Kingdom
www.infoseek.co.uk/

Infotrieve
www.infotrieve.com/

Infotrieve Article Finder
www.infotrieve.com/

ingentaJournals
www.ingenta.com/

ingentaJournals (via BIDS)
www.bids.ac.uk/

Institute of Health Sciences Library, Oxford University filters
wwwlib.jr2.ox.ac.uk/caspfew/filters/

Inter-Links
www.nova.edu/Inter-Links/listserv.html

Interactive Patient
medicus.marshall.edu/medicus.htm

Internet Drug Index
www.rxlist.com/

Internet Explorer
www.microsoft.com/windows/ie/

Internet Grateful Med
igm.nlm.nih.gov/

Internet Public Library
www.ipl.org/ref/QUE/

Introductory Biocomputing
www.hgmp.mrc.ac.uk/Courses/Intro_3day/index.html

Invitrogen
www.invitrogen.com/catalog.html

ISI Cited Reference Searching: An Introduction
www.isinet.com/training/tutorials/citedreference/

ISI ResearchSoft
www.researchsoft.com/

ISI ResearchSoft EndNote 3 connection files
www.researchsoft.com/en/help/Enconnections.htm

ISI ResearchSoft EndNote Support and Services
www.researchsoft.com/en/help/ENsupport.htm

ISI ResearchSoft ProCite Technical Support
www.researchsoft.com/pc/PCsupport.html

ISI ResearchSoft Reference Manager Technical Support
www.researchsoft.com/rm/RMsupport.html

ISI Web of Science
www.isinet.com/products/citation/wos.html

ISI Web of Science and Index to Scientific and Technical Proceedings
via MIMAS
wos.mimas.ac.uk/

ItList
www.itlist.com/

J

JAMA Medical News Headlines
www.ama-assn.org/public/journals/amnews/amnews.htm

JEFFLINE Evidence-based medicine information
jeffline.tju.edu/Education/courses/informatics/activities
ebm_info.html

JEFFLINE Medline searching strategies
jeffline.tju.edu/Education/courses/informatics/activities/
med_search.html

JEFFLINE Searching basics
jeffline.tju.edu/Education/courses/informatics/activities/basics.html

JISC current content collection: health studies
www.jisc.ac.uk/collections/health.html

Jobs Unlimited
www.jobsunlimited.co.uk/

jobs.ac.uk
www.jobs.ac.uk/

Joint home page of the UK research councils
www.nerc.ac.uk/research-councils/

Journal Club on the Web
www.journalclub.org/

Journal of Biological Chemistry
www.jbc.org/

JournAlert
www.doctors.net.uk/

Journals@Ovid
www.ovid.com/

JournalSeek
genamics.com/journals/

K

Karolinska Institute Library
www.mic.ki.se/Diseases/

Kompass
www.kompass.com/

L

Lab Pages
www.labpages.com/

Lasers for Life
www.merseyworld.com/lasers/

Learning and Technology Support Network
www.ilt.ac.uk/ltsn/index.htm

LectureLinks
omie.med.jhmi.edu/LectureLinks/

Leicester University virology lecture notes
www-micro.msb.le.ac.uk/335/335Notes.html

Library of Congress. Z39.50 Maintenance Agency Home Page
lcweb.loc.gov/z3950/agency/

lis-european-programmes
www.mailbase.ac.uk/lists/lis-european-programmes/

lis-genome
www.mailbase.ac.uk/lists/lis-genome/

Liszt
www.liszt.com/

LocatorPlus
www.nlm.nih.gov/locatorplus/

LookSmart
www.looksmart.com/

Lycos
www.lycos.com

Lycos Pictures & Sound
www.lycos.co.uk/search/options.html#cat

Lycos UK & Ireland
www.lycos.co.uk/

M

Magellan Internet Guide
magellan.excite.com/

Mailbase
www.mailbase.ac.uk/

Mailbase search for people
www.mailbase.ac.uk/search.html

Martindale's Health Science Guide - 2000: the Virtual Medical Centre
www-sci.lib.uci.edu/HSG/Medical.html

McMaster University
hiru.mcmaster.ca/epc/

McMaster Users' Guides
www.cche.net/ebm/userguid/

MD Digests
php2.silverplatter.com/physicians/digest.htm

MED-STUDENT
www.csosl.co.uk/sbmj/ml.html

MedFetch
www.medfetch.com/

MedHunt
www.hon.ch/MedHunt/

MedHunt Advanced Search
www.hon.ch/MedHunt/AdvSearch.html

Medical Matrix
www.medmatrix.org/

Medical Matrix Clinical Searches
www.medmatrix.org/info/search.asp

Medical Matrix guide to Internet guides
www.medmatrix.org/_SPages Medical_Internet_Guides.asp#Directories

Medical Matrix Medline
www.medmatrix.org/_Spages/medline.asp

Medical Matrix Search Hub
www.medmatrix.org/info/searchhub.asp

Medical Matrix submission feature
www.medmatrix.org/info/newsites.html

Medical Research Council (MRC)
www.mrc.ac.uk/

Medical Research Council (MRC) Funded Projects
fundedresearch.cos.com/MRC/

Medical Research Council (MRC) Laboratory for Molecular Cell Biology jobs
www.ucl.ac.uk/LMCB/jobs.html

Medical Student *JAMA*
www.ama-assn.org/sci-pubs/msjama/

Medical World Search
www.mwsearch.com/

medical-education
www.mailbase.ac.uk/lists/medical-education/

Medline Plus, BMA Library
ovid.bma.org.uk/

Medline Workbench
www.cshl.org/medline/

Medline*plus*
www.nlm.nih.gov/medlineplus/

Medscape
www.medscape.com/

Medstudent.net
medstudent.net/

MedWebPlus
www.medwebplus.com/

MedWebPlus News
www.medwebplus.com/subject/News_[Publication_Type].html

MedWebPlus Journals
www.medwebplus.com/subject/Periodicals.html

MedWebPlus Statistics
www.medwebplus.com/subject/Statistics.html

MedWebPlus Vital statistics
www.medwebplus.com/subject/Vital_Statistics.html

MedXtra
medicine.silverplatter.com/

Megasearch
www.thebighub.com/

Merck Manual of Diagnosis and Therapy
www.merck.com/pubs/mmanual/

Merriam Webster WWWebster Thesaurus
www.m-w.com/thesaurus.htm

MetaCrawler
www.metacrawler.com/

MetaCrawler PowerSearch
www.metacrawler.com/index_power.html

Microsoft Network
home.microsoft.com/

Microsoft Network (UK)
msn.co.uk/

Microsoft Network, More Searches
search.msn.com/

MIMAS
www.mimas.ac.uk/

mIRC
www.mirc.co.uk/ or www.mirc.com/

MMDB
www.ncbi.nlm.nih.gov/Structure/

Molecular biology concepts and terminology
www.hgmp.mrc.ac.uk/Courses/UKOLUG/buzzwords.html

Molecular Vision
molvis.org/molvis/

Monster Healthcare
healthcare.monster.co.uk/

Morbidity and Mortality Weekly Report (*MMWR*)
www.cdc.gov/mmwr/

MRCP p@rt 1 question bank
mrcppart1.co.uk/

mRCT
www.controlled-trials.com/

Multilingual Glossary
allserv.rug.ac.be/~rvdstich/eugloss/welcome.html

Multimap
www.multimap.com/

Munich Information Center for Protein Sequences (MIPS) Alert
vms.mips.biochem.mpg.de/mips/programs/alert.html

MURL
murl.com/

Muscular Dystrophy Campaign
www.muscular-dystrophy.org/

MyMedline
www.mymedline.com/medline/

N

National Center for Biotechnology Information (NCBI)
www.ncbi.nlm.nih.gov/

National Database of Telemedicine
www.dis.port.ac.uk/ndtm/

National electronic Library for Health (NeLH)
www.nelh.nhs.uk/

National electronic Library for Mental Health (NeLMH)
www.nhs.uk/mentalhealth/

National Electronic Site Licence Initiative (NESLI)
www.nesli.ac.uk/

National Eye Institute (NEI)
www.nei.nih.gov/

National Guideline Clearinghouse
www.guidelines.gov/

National Institute for Clinical Excellence
www.nice.org.uk/

National Institute for Medical Research
www.nimr.mrc.ac.uk/

National Organization for Rare Diseases, Inc. (NORD)
www.rarediseases.org/

National Research Register (NRR)
www.doh.gov.uk/nrr.htm

NeLH
www.nelh.nhs.uk/

NeLMH
www.nhs.uk/mentalhealth/

NetPrints - Clinical Medicine & Health Research
clinmed.netprints.org/

Netscape Netcenter
home.netscape.com/

Netscape Plug-ins
www.netscape.com/plugins/

Netscape Products
www.netscape.com/download/

Netting the Evidence
www.shef.ac.uk/uni/academic/R-Z/scharr/ir/netting.html

New Zealand Health Technology Assessment Search protocol
nzhta.chmeds.ac.nz/nzhtainfo/protocol.htm

Newjour
gort.ucsd.edu/newjour/NewJourWel.html

Newjour Archive
gort.ucsd.edu/newjour/

News Unlimited (*The Guardian*)
www.newsunlimited.co.uk/

NewsTracker
nt.excite.com/

NHCON - Nursing and Healthcare Resources on the Net
www.shef.ac.uk/~nhcon/

NHS Centre for Reviews and Dissemination
www.york.ac.uk/inst/crd/welcome.htm

NHS CRD Finding studies for systematic reviews: a basic checklist for researchers
www.york.ac.uk/inst/crd/revs.htm

NHS CRD Guidelines for carrying out or commissioning reviews
www.york.ac.uk/inst/crd/report4.htm

NHS CRD Search strategies to identify reviews and meta-analyses in Medline and CINAHL
www.york.ac.uk/inst/crd/search.htm

NHS Direct Online
www.nhsdirect.nhs.uk/

NHS EED
nhscrd.york.ac.uk/

NISS Vacancies Service
www.vacancies.ac.uk/

NLM. Entrez PubMed FAQs:
www.ncbi.nlm.nih.gov/entrez/query/static/faq.html#savesearch

NLM. Entrez PubMed Help:
www.ncbi.nlm.nih.gov/entrez/query/static/help/
pmhelp.html#SavingaSearchStrategy

NLM. Save a search strategy by constructing an IGM URL:
igm.nlm.nih.gov/splash/IGM_url.html

NLM Journal Title Lists
www.nlm.nih.gov/tsd/serials/lsiou.html

NLM Medline
www.nlm.nih.gov/databases/medline.html

NLM MeSH browser
www.nlm.nih.gov/mesh/99Mbrowser.html

Northern Light
www.northernlight.com/

Northern Light usgovsearch:
usgovsearch.northernlight.com/publibaccess/

Nucleic Acids Research (NAR): Molecular Biology Database Collection
www.oup.co.uk/nar/Volume_28/Issue_01/html/gkd115_gml.html

O

Office for National Statistics
www.ons.gov.uk/

Office of Rare Diseases
rarediseases.info.nih.gov/ord/

OMIM
www.ncbi.nlm.nih.gov/omim/

OMNI
omni.ac.uk/

OMNI Index to MeSH headings
omni.ac.uk/umls/

OMNI Advisory Group for Evaluation Criteria
omni.ac.uk/agec/

OMNI Guidelines for resource evaluation
omni.ac.uk/agec/evalguid.html

OMNI Launchpad
omni.ac.uk/other-search/

OMNI Medline Resource Centre
omni.ac.uk/medline/

OMNI submission feature
omni.ac.uk/submit-url/

OMNI Thesaurus
omni.ac.uk/search/thesaurus/

OncoChat
www.oncochat.org/

OncoLink support groups
cancer.med.upenn.edu/psychosocial/support/

OncoLink cancer lists
cancer.med.upenn.edu/forms/listserv.html

Online Medical Dictionary
www.graylab.ac.uk/omd/

Open Directory Project
dmoz.org/

Orthogate
www.orthogate.org/

Orthopaedic Web Links
owl.orthgate.org/

OSLER (Ovid Search: Link to Electronic Resources)
www.cma.ca/osler/

Outcomes Activities Database
www.leeds.ac.uk/nuffield/infoservices/UKCH/oad.html

Ovid Database of the month
www.ovid.com/demo/dotm/

Ovid Online
gateway.ovid.com/

Ovid Online database catalog
www.ovid.com/products/databases/

Ovid Technologies
www.ovid.com/

Ovid tutorial, Duke University Medical Center Library
www.mc.duke.edu/mclibrary/respub/guides/ovidtut/

Oxford University newsgroup FAQ files
www.lib.ox.ac.uk/internet/news/

P

Paediapaedia
www.vh.org/Providers/TeachingFiles/PAP/PAPHome.html

PDB
www.rcsb.org/pdb/

PDB (UK mirror site)
pdb.ccdc.cam.ac.uk/

PDQ
cancernet.nci.nih.gov/pdq.html

plagiarism.org
www.plagiarism.org/

POINT
www.doh.gov.uk/publications/pointh.html

Primer on Molecular Genetics
www.bis.med.jhmi.edu/Dan/DOE/intro.html

Private Health UK
www.privatehealth.co.uk/

ProFusion
www.profusion.com/

ProMED
www.fas.org/promed/

ProMED archives
www.promedmail.org:8080/promed/promed.folder.home

ProQuest Digital Dissertations
wwwlib.umi.com/dissertations/

Protein Science
www.proteinscience.org

PsycINFO
www.apa.org/psycinfo/

PubCrawler
www.gen.tcd.ie/pubcrawler/

PubMed
www.ncbi.nlm.nih.gov/PubMed/

PubMed and Internet Grateful Med training manuals
www.nlm.nih.gov/pubs/web_based.html

PubMed Central
pubmedcentral.nih.gov/

PubMed Clinical queries
www.ncbi.nlm.nih.gov/PubMed/clinical.html

PubMed help
www.ncbi.nlm.nih.gov/entrez/query/static/help/pmhelp/html

PubMed Journal Browser
www.ncbi.nlm.nih.gov/entrez/jrbrowser.cgi

PubMed MEDLINE journals
www.ncbi.nlm.nih.gov/PubMed/fulltext.html

PubMed MeSH browser
www.ncbi.nlm.nih.gov/entrez/meshbrowser.cgi

Q

Quackwatch
www.quackwatch.com/

Quotations Archive
www.aphids.com/quotes/index.shtml

R

Railtrack
www.railtrack.co.uk/

RDInfo
www.leeds.ac.uk/rdinfo/

Real Audio
www.realaudio.com/

REFUND
www.refund.ncl.ac.uk/

Reuters Health
www.reutershealth.com/

Reuters Medical News
www.reutershealth.com/uk/

Roget's Thesaurus 1911 edition
www.thesaurus.com/

Royal College of Anaesthetists
www.rcoa.ac.uk/

Royal College of Pathologists
www.rcpath.org/contents.html

S

ScHARR list of evidence-based health lists
www.shef.ac.uk/~scharr/ir/email.html

ScHARR listing of guidelines
www.shef.ac.uk/~scharr/ir/guidelin.html

ScHARR Seeking the evidence protocol
www.shef.ac.uk/~scharr/ir/proto.html

Schemes
wisdom.wellcome.ac.uk/wisdom/fundhome.html

schoolsucks.com
www.schoolsucks.com/

Science
www.sciencemag.org/

Science.komm Medical journals
www.sciencekomm.at/journals/medicine/med-bio.html

SciPICH
www.scipich.org/

SciPICH Interactive Health Communication checklist
www.scipich.org/IHC/checklist.htm

SciPICH Web site evaluation drill
www.scipich.org/IHC/webdrill.htm

Search.com
savvy.search.com/

Sigma-Aldrich
www.sigma-aldrich.com/

SilverPlatter Information
www.silverplatter.com/

SilverPlatter MedXtra
medicine.silverplatter.com/

Slang Dictionary
www.peevish.u-net.com/slang/

Snap
www.snap.com/

Sociedad Argentina de Pediatría, Filtros Metodológicos para la
búsqueda en Medline
www.sap.org.ar/medline/filtros.htm

SRS
srs.hgmp.mrc.ac.uk/

StatBase
www.statistics.gov.uk/statbase/mainmenu.asp

Stationery Office
www.the-stationery-office.co.uk/

StatSearch
www.statistics.gov.uk/statbase/ss.asp

STN database summary sheets
www.cas.org/ONLINE/DBSS/dbsslist.html

STN Databases
www.fiz-karlsruhe.de/onlin_db.html

STN International
www.fiz-karlsruhe.de/

STN on the Web
stnweb.fiz-karlsruhe.de/

Streetmap
www.streetmap.co.uk/

Student *BMJ*
www.studentbmj.com/

SUMSearch
sumsearch.uthscsa.edu/

Surgical Materials Testing Laboratory
www.smtl.co.uk/

Swetsnet*Navigator*
www.swetsnetnavigator.com/

SWISS-PROT
www.ebi.ac.uk/swissprot/

SWISS-PROT, Description of
www.ebi.ac.uk/swissprot/Information/information.html

Swiss-Shop
www.expasy.ch/swiss-shop/

T

Terrence Higgins Trust
www.tht.org.uk/

The Independent
www.independent.co.uk/

The Institute for Genomic Research (TIGR)
www.tigr.org/

The Lancet
www.thelancet.com/

The Lancet Electronic Research Archive
www.thelancet.com/newlancet/eprint

The Times Internet Edition
www.the-times.co.uk/

Tips, Tricks, How To and Beyond
www.tips-tricks.com/

Tools for guideline development and evaluation
www.nzgg.org.nz/tools.htm

TOXNET Online
toxnet.nlm.nih.gov/

Trauma Moulage
www.trauma.org/resus/moulage/moulage.html

Trawling the Net: ScHARR introduction to free databases of interest to
NHS staff on the Internet
www.shef.ac.uk/~scharr/ir/trawling.html

TRIP (Turning Research into Practice)
www.tripdatabase.com/

U

UK Online User Group Links: bibliographic software
www.ukolug.org.uk/links/biblio.htm

UK Public Transport Information
www.pti.org.uk/

UKMax
www.ukmax.co.uk/

UKOLN Directory of Z39.50 targets in the UK
www.ukoln.ac.uk/dlis/zdir/

UMLS Knowledge Source Server
umlsks.nlm.nih.gov/

UnCover
uncweb.carl.org/

UnCover Reveal and Reveal Alert
uncweb.carl.org/reveal/

Understanding your eye condition
www.rnib.org.uk/info/eyeimpoi/welcome.htm

United Kingdom Research Office (UKRO)
www.ukro.ac.uk/

University College London vacancies
www.ucl.ac.uk/personnel/job.htm

University of Nottingham Division of Microbiology and Infectious
Diseases
www.nottingham.ac.uk/microbiology/

University of Wales College of Medicine, Cardiff home page
www.uwcm.ac.uk/

Update Software
www.update-software.com/

Usenet Information Center
sunsite.unc.edu/usenet-i/hier-s/top.html

V

Vesalius Clinical Folios and Image Archive
www.vesalius.com/

Virtual Drug Store
www.virtualdrugstore.com/

Virtual Hospital
www.vh.org/

Virtual Hospital textbooks
www.vh.org/Providers/Textbooks/MultimediaTextbooks.html

W

W3C Validator
validator.w3.org/

WebMedLit
www.webmedlit.com/

Webmonkey
hotwired.lycos.com/webmonkey/

Weekly Epidemiological Record
www.who.int/wer/

WELDIS
www.westminster.gov.uk/weldis/

Wellcome Trust
www.wellcome.ac.uk/

WHO Statistical Information System
www.who.int/whosis/

World Bank Development Data
www.worldbank.org/data/

World Wide Web Journal of Biology
epress.com/w3jbio/

XY

Yahoo!
www.yahoo.com/

Yahoo! Chat
chat.yahoo.com/

Yahoo! message boards
messages.yahoo.com/index.html

Yahoo! UK & Ireland
www.yahoo.co.uk/

Z

ZDNET browsers
www.zdnet.com/products/internetuser/browsers.html

Index